THE CHILD IN EACH OF US

WORKBOOK

THE CHILD IN EACH OF US

WORKBOOK

A Recovery Workbook for
The Child in Each of Us

DR. RICHARD W. DICKINSON
CAROLE GIFT PAGE & BETH FUNK

VICTOR BOOKS

A DIVISION OF SCRIPTURE PRESS PUBLICATIONS INC.
USA CANADA ENGLAND

Editor: Pamela T. Campbell
Designer: Scott Rattray
Cover Photo: Mike Marshall
Interior Illustration: Terry DeGraff

Recommended Dewey Decimal Classification: 200.19 or 152.92
Suggested Subject Headings: CHRISTIAN LIVING; RECOVERY

ISBN: 1-56476-026-X

CONTENTS

PREFACE

You Go to a Party.
Everyone is a stranger or, at best, a nodding acquaintance. As you gaze at the sea of faces, your heartbeat accelerates and your anxiety level rises. Unwittingly, you erect a defensive wall between yourself and the other guests. As you mingle, you are careful to keep things light and uninvolved. You say only what you think the other guests want to hear, hoping they will accept you.

The inner you—who you are in your soul of souls—remains totally hidden. No one has guessed who you are inside or how you really think and feel. When you go home, you feel empty inside.

You ask yourself, "What went wrong? Why didn't I have a good time? Why did I feel so lonely in the midst of so many people?"

You Argue with Your Mate.
As your voices rise heatedly, you feel yourself erecting a defensive barrier around the fragile, vulnerable person you are inside. You fear that if you reveal the weaknesses and needs of this inner you, your mate will use this information as ammunition against you. So, instead of confiding your needs, you insulate your inner self with an invincible exterior and hurl cruel verbal darts to make your mate suffer as much pain as you feel.

You wonder, "What has gone wrong with my marriage? Why can't we communicate the way I dreamed we would during our courtship? Why don't I feel truly loved and appreciated?"

You Kneel to Pray.
Dutifully you recite familiar prayers for the missionaries, the church, your family, and friends. You ask God to forgive your sins and guide you in your various activities. But as you whisper amen, you feel oddly unsatisfied, as if something vital is missing, as if your prayers have gone no higher than the ceiling.

You cry out, "God, where are You? Do You hear me? Do You care?" Intellectually you know that the Christian life offers joy and fulfillment, but in your heart of hearts God seems remote—an unapproachable Deity, not the intimate, loving Comforter the Bible promises.

You ask, "Does God really accept me as I am?"

Or you may not know God. You look around, searching for a friend to understand. You find no one. You look in a mirror, trying to see inside yourself. You see only turmoil. You look up, crying, "Is there really a God—someone who knows the real me inside?"

Do These Situations Describe You?

In rare moments of insight, you may realize that you wear masks to disguise who you are. You hide behind barriers lest family, friends, and even God Himself see your vulnerabilities and wound you where you are most tender. And because you aren't truly yourself, you rarely receive the response you need from others to affirm and nurture the inner you. Your inner child—that creative, vulnerable, needy part of you—has been forced into molds that distort rather than enhance your true personality.

If you have noticed something lacking in your relationships with your mate, family, and friends—and even with God Himself—then you need to learn how to nurture your own inner child. And as you give God and others access to the true child within, you will become free to give and receive the kind of genuine, affirming love God created you to experience.

The first seven chapters of this journey into your inner child provide a basic understanding of behavior in areas all of us face. Chapters 8 and 9 are designed to help you see how God can make a difference in your life as He works to free your inner child, then nurture it. Chapter 10 offers guidelines for those who desire to help others. It is my prayer that you gain greater insight into yourself and your relationship with others—most of all, your Heavenly Father.

Richard Whitlock Dickinson, Ph.D.
Seal Beach, California
1989

INTRODUCTION

Today many Christians struggle with painful feelings of loneliness, fear, insecurity, and shame. Often this unresolved pain manifests itself in "over-extended" patterns of living. We OVERwork, OVEReat, OVERcommit, OVERspend, OVERspiritualize, and OVERobsess about love and sex. A host of book titles, such as, *We Are Driven, Hiding from Love, How to Balance Time Demands, Help Lord—My Whole Life Hurts,* and *Imperative People* reflect all too well the tenor of our uptight, on-the-edge approach to life. And Christians are not exempt. We must face the reality of our pain-filled past if we are going to proceed through life in a healthy way. That is what this workbook is all about. It is designed to help you find your way back to a place of balance by giving you an opportunity to take an honest look at the painful experiences of your past that have left you emotionally scarred in the present.

What makes this workbook different from the original work of the same title is that you now have an opportunity to *journal* your way through the entire text of *The Child in Each of Us.* Questions have been inserted into the text at key places to help you personalize and record your thoughts, feelings, and experiences along the way.

Journal writing is a time-honored practice that dates back as far as the confessions of St. Augustine and the spiritual diaries of the Quakers. This discipline can serve you well in your individual program of personal growth and healing as you remain open to the Holy Spirit's work in your life. No matter how much hurt you have experienced in the past, you have the choice of opening yourself up to God's love and healing power through the Holy Spirit. As you write down your thoughts and feelings in response to the questions asked throughout the text, the Holy Spirit will gently bring the truth about your past to light and "the truth will set you free" (John 8:32).

HOW EACH CHAPTER IS ORGANIZED

There are four basic elements included in every chapter of this workbook. They are:

■ **The entire text of *The Child in Each of Us.*** This book was first published in 1989 and has helped thousands of readers deal honestly and sensitively with the wounds of their childhood. It is possible that you have at one point or another already read this book. But don't let that stop you from going through it again—*The Child in Each of Us* is a book well worth rereading.

■ **Personal Reflection.** Key questions and reflection exercises have been built into the text to help you filter the truth of the text through the grid of your own experience. Here is where much healing can take place. Application of truth to life leads to transformation. The merits of journaling have already been cited in the paragraphs above. You will greatly benefit from this book by taking time to write down your answers in the space provided. If you are unable to answer a question as you work through the material the first time, move on. The goal is NOT to answer every question. The goal is to get in touch with as much truth as is possible for you. Remember: God does not violate us, invade us, force Himself upon us, or overtake us. As you remain open to Him, the Holy Spirit will gently affirm to you that God can be trusted. He does have your best interests at heart. So trust Him. He will guide you as you read and write your way through this workbook.

■ **Prayerful Reflection.** Prayer is both talking to and hearing from God. At the end of each chapter you will have an opportunity to tell God in writing how you feel about the things you have read. Exercise rigorous honesty with Him. Dare to entrust your deepest fears and secrets to Him. Then listen carefully to hear what He has to say. God will meet you at your place of need.

■ **Personal Renewal.** The final exercise in each chapter is a meditation or memorization activity. One way your life will be transformed is through the "renewing of your mind" (Rom. 12:2). The Bible is the primary source book God has given us for renewing our minds. Hear what the writer of Hebrews tells us about God's Word: "[It] is alive and working and is sharper than a double-edged sword. It cuts all the way into us, where the soul and the spirit are joined, to the center of our joints and bones. And it judges the thoughts and feelings in our hearts" (Heb. 4:12, NCV). Each Scripture in this section reflects a key truth the author writes about in the chapter. Meditate and memorize (wherever possible) the passages listed. God can use His Word to bring tremendous healing to your thoughts and feelings.

HOW TO USE THIS BOOK

The Child in Each of Us is a workbook that presents a series of writing exercises and ideas for personal growth and development. This material is designed for use by individuals as well as groups. No matter what approach you take in using the material, there are some basic guidelines to follow.

Individual Study

Pace yourself through each chapter, taking whatever time you need to complete the Personal Reflection, Prayerful Reflection, and Personal Renewal exercises as you read. You may get through all of the exercises in one sitting, or you may choose to spread your writing out over a longer period of time. Be patient with yourself. Give yourself time to digest the content of each chapter and reflect on its meaning. Share what you are learning with someone you trust.

Do not feel obligated to complete every exercise. However, if you find yourself avoiding a particular exercise or chapter, take a good look at your resistance and then make a special effort to work in that area of the book. This may be precisely the chapter or exercise that can really begin to help you heal.

Write out your answers fully. Don't use just a word or short phrase, but write complete sentences and paragraphs. You will find that the process of writing will help you gain awareness and perspectives that you may not have known you had.

As you work through the material in this book, you may be surprised at the power of the feelings that come up as you write. Give yourself permission to feel your feelings. Denying your feelings will only slow down the healing process; acknowledging them will speed it up and bring about the emotional and spiritual healing you desire.

Group Study
We are broken in the context of relationship; and we are also healed within the scope of relationships. Though there is great value in working the exercises in this book individually, you will find that your healing process is enhanced and accelerated by the mutual support and encouragement that is found in a small group setting.

Appendix One of this workbook gives you complete guidelines for using this material in groups. There is a Personal Journey Summary Sheet provided for each chapter of the book, plus a "Telling My Story" page that should be used the first time the group meets together. The group material has been designed in such a way that it is virtually self-facilitating. If you can read, you can lead. The success of the group is not dependent on one individual. Rather, it is the combined efforts of and group members' mutual commitment to the group process that will bring about an emotionally and spiritually satisfying outcome. Group members will receive maximum benefit from the group process if they have taken time during the week to complete the writing exercises that are in Part 1 of the workbook.

Ideally, a group meeting should last one-and-a-half to two hours. Try to start and end each meeting on time. At your first meeting, communicate clearly the Guidelines for Group Sharing (also found in Appendix One). These guidelines will help provide a safe environment for group members. Safety is essential to the healing process. And confidentiality is essential to feeling safe. You will find additional facilitator helps in Appendix One at the back of this workbook to help you in your group process.

THE VALUE OF SUPPORT

Christ-centered and secular self-help support groups have flourished in the past decade. These groups strive to create a safe and nurturing environment where members can face and learn to effectively deal with the pain in their lives. It helps to know that someone else cares and is willing to share their experience, strength, and hope with us along the way.

Solomon, in the Book of Ecclesiastes, had this to say about the value of supportive relationships: "Two are better than one, because they have a good return for their work: If one falls down, his friend can help him up. But pity the man who falls and has no one to help him up! . . . Though one may be overpowered, two can defend themselves. A cord of three strands is not quickly broken" (Ecc. 4:9-10, 12 NIV). Make a wise choice—employ the power of group dynamics to help you set your inner child free.

PART ONE

Chapter 1
Discovering the Inner Child

I looked at my watch—11 A.M. My new patient had just arrived for his first counseling session. As I entered the waiting room and introduced myself, Jim jumped to his feet and shook my hand with a firm grip. He was a ruggedly handsome man, fortyish, with a square jaw, brown eyes, and a thin, black, neatly trimmed mustache. He was muscular, deeply tanned, a man who obviously took great pride in his physical appearance.

I gestured toward my office. "Come in, Jim. Sit down."

As he settled into the chair across from me, Jim personified success, from his stylish clothes and immaculate haircut right down to his fancy, gold-nugget wristwatch and the large diamond ring on his right pinky.

I met his gaze. "Tell me, Jim, how can I help you?"

He managed an uneven smile. "Well, Doc, it's not me . . . "

Suddenly something in Jim's expression didn't fit his self-assured swagger. His lips were smiling, but not his eyes. They possessed a deep sadness and an inner weariness that matched the hollow tone in his voice.

"It's my wife, Doc," he continued, trying to sound nonchalant. "She's the one who thinks I need a shrink. She says we have, uh, a communication problem."

"Tell me about it, Jim."

He sat forward and rubbed his hands together nervously. "Yeah, well, she says we never talk anymore, and she—she feels like I'm a stranger to her." He gazed imploringly at me. "Can you imagine that—me, a stranger? We've been married twenty-three years, and she says I'm a stranger to her. I just don't understand it!"

For over ten minutes Jim talked on about his wife, avoiding his own problems. I tried gently to redirect him. "Jim, these issues that concern your wife are important, but I have a feeling there are some significant problems going on inside you. Call it a gut-level feeling, but I sense that you're carrying around a very heavy load inside. I'd like to hear about it."

Jim's body sagged. He looked as if someone had pulled the plug and let all the air out of his invincible, self-confident balloon. He stared at the floor, his mask gone, the gloom evident in his face. Tears welled up in his eyes as he announced in a flat, subdued voice, "Would you believe I have every reason to be the happiest man around? No lie. I have a successful computer business that gives me freedom to do what I want. I own a boat. I have a good wife and three super-neat kids. Money isn't an issue. I have all I need."

He paused and swallowed hard, as if he couldn't quite speak over the lump in his throat. At last he said, "But you know, Doc, even though I have everything to live for, I'm not happy. Sounds crazy, huh?" He cracked his knuckles, his voice edged with bitter irony. "To tell you the truth, Doc, most of the time I feel like an actor on a stage, trying to convince myself and everyone around me I've got it made. But I don't. It's a lie. And you know the saddest thing of all?" He sucked in a deep breath. "I can't tell anyone how I really feel, not even my wife."

PERSONAL REFLECTION

■ In what, if any, ways do you relate to Jim's story? Do you feel like you are an actor on stage, trying to make those around you believe you "have it all together" when deep inside you feel like life is just about to fall apart? How long have you felt this way? What are some things you are doing to camouflage your inner pain?

_____

_____

_____

_____

Quietly I asked, "What made you decide to seek help now, Jim?"

He was silent again. Then his words erupted in a broken, staccato pattern. "I—I began to be afraid of what I was thinking. I'd have these crazy thoughts of running my car into a bridge or jumping off the roof of my office building—and lately, Doc, these feelings have been getting stronger." He shifted uneasily in his chair, brushing away unwelcome tears. "Listen, Doc, I'm a Christian, but lately I've begun to doubt whether there even is a God. I feel so alone. In fact, when I pray my words hit the ceiling and bounce right back to the floor. If God is up there, I don't figure He has much use for me."

I met Jim's gaze with a sympathetic nod. "I appreciate your candor, Jim. You've expressed some powerful feelings and that's not easy to do. Would you feel comfortable exploring some of the reasons for those feelings?"

"Reasons? Look at me. Isn't it obvious? I'm a fake. An emotional basket case. I haven't cried like this since I was a kid."

"It's OK, Jim," I assured him. "I want you to feel free to say what's on your mind and in your heart—how you really feel."

He shook his head. "Right now I just feel foolish for blubbering like a kid."

I gave him a moment to compose himself, then asked, "What about your parents, Jim? Like to tell me about them?"

"My parents?" A coldness settled over Jim's features. "Life with Father was a string of broken promises," he said, his voice edged with contempt. "Dad was always saying, 'Something has come up, Son. We'll go to the ball game next week.' Sure, Dad. But next week never came."

"Never?"

"Hardly ever. Dad was a successful businessman, and his life was his work. I respected him, but I hated him too. Even during the rare times we were together, Dad was quick to point out everything I did wrong. It was impossible to please him. The truth is that I was a failure in his eyes." Jim crossed his arms on his chest and stared off into space. "The worst part is that we were never close—no affection, no 'I love you,' no 'I'm proud you are my son.' I waited forever for those words. I waited for nothing, Doc."

Jim straightened his shoulders and rubbed the bridge of his nose. His eyes glistened with tears, but he forced a pained, uneven smile. "Dad died three years ago, Doc, and you know, he never knew how much I really wanted to please him." Jim stared at the floor and said brokenly, "Even my career was my attempt to show Dad I could amount to something. Now I'm not even sure that what I'm doing is what I really want to do. Can you believe that—a grown man of forty still wondering what to do with his life?"

Jim sat lost in his own silent reverie for several moments. I brought him back to the counseling room, asking, "What about your mother, Jim? Think back to when you were a young boy. How do you remember her?"

He uttered a derisive chuckle. "Mom was a different story."

"How so?"

"Well, she and Dad didn't get along well, so she turned to me for emotional support. She wanted to protect me from his aloofness and critical attitude, but she became too protective, too involved in my life. If I had let her, she would have taken over my life, leaving me with no identity of my own."

"Did you ever tell her how you felt about her possessiveness?"

"Sure. But when I accused her of smothering me, she cried and said she loved me and was doing the best she could."

"How did that make you feel?"

The tendons in Jim's jaw tightened. "Lousy. But what could I say— 'You're manipulating me'? Between my guilt and anger, I got so frustrated I just quit talking to her." He sank lower in his chair, his intense anger yielding to dark depression.

I drew in a deep breath. I knew Jim and I had a long way to go.

Over the next several months we spent many counseling hours talking about his life, his relationships with others, and his walk with God. Gradually he came to see that his guilt and anger toward his mother were turned inward against himself, causing him to feel unlovable and worthless. As therapy progressed, Jim was able to talk more openly and with greater insight about his family and their effect on his life. He began to see that he had backed away from his mother emotionally as a way of survival.

His increased awareness was evident in a later session when he talked about his mother and his own feelings of aloneness. "My mother will never know how many times I wanted to come to her for comfort when I felt so alone and hurt by my dad's criticism, but I couldn't. It wasn't safe. Somewhere in all of these inner struggles, I decided I didn't need people. I could be successful on my own. The sad part about all my outward success is that none of my accomplishments can give me what I really need—to be close to someone, to feel loved, to be cared for, to know that I have value to someone without working so hard for it."

I have shared Jim's story with you because I have a hunch that you may identify with how Jim felt. You too may feel alone, unloved, tired of performing. You may feel empty and isolated from those with whom you yearn to be close. You may desire to be excited about life, your relationships with others, and your relationship with God.

PERSONAL
REFLECTION

■ Describe the relationship you had with your mother. Did it resemble the relationship Jim had with his mother? In what ways? How was it different?

_____

_____

_____

_____

_____

_____

_____

_____

■ Now describe the relationship you had with your father. Was your father like Jim's or was he different? In what ways?

_____

_____

_____

_____

_____

_____

Jim's story raises issues that deal directly with the inner child. Who is the inner child? Your inner child is *the real you, your true self, that part of you that feels deeply, needs deeply, loves deeply.* Your inner child consists of *your feelings, your natural talents,* and *your creativity—the unique dimensions of your personality.*

A significant issue in Jim's life was his alienation from his inner child. That child within him was undernourished. While the rest of Jim's abilities developed over the years, the inner child did not. Jim was under the mistaken idea that he could hide that part of himself and it really wouldn't matter. He was wrong. Dead wrong.

This book is about you and your own inner child—that part of you that perhaps you never even knew existed, let alone needed nurturing. Webster defines *nurture* as "the act or process of raising or promoting the development of; training, rearing, fostering."

Ask yourself: "Have I lost my curiosity and wonder about life? Have I become dull in my appreciation of God's magnificent world? Has my childlike fascination disappeared? If so, you have lost touch with the little child inside. But it's not too late.

PERSONAL REFLECTION

■ There is a difference between being *childlike* and being *childish*. Spend a few minutes watching young children. What do you observe about them? Write down your observations. *EXAMPLE: Young children are generally loving. They are accepting of themselves and other people.* Note both the good and bad qualities you observe.

_____

_____

_____

_____

_____

_____

■ When we become alienated from our inner child, we tend to lose the *childlike* (more positive) qualities and oftentimes assume more *childish* (negative or unattractive) characteristics. In what ways are YOU childlike? Have you noticed any childish behaviors in yourself lately? What are they?

_____

_____

_____

_____

_____

We are about to take a journey through the lives of many people, myself included, to show you how to discover, understand, and nourish your inner child. We will explore the inner child as it affects our relationship with God, for I am convinced that only as we allow God to communicate with our inner child can we build a solid relationship with Him.

Now that we've introduced the concept of the inner child, we need to describe it in greater detail so that you will have a clear understanding of what your inner child looks like. Your inner child has three important characteristics.

PORTRAIT OF YOUR INNER CHILD

NATURAL ABILITIES
Our inherent, God-given talents.
To be distinguished from *skills*
which are acquired through
training and education.

FEELINGS
"Any of the subjective
reactions, pleasurable or
unpleasurable, that one
may have to a situation
and usually connotes an
absence of reasoning."
*Webster's New World
Dictionary* (Second
College Edition)

CREATIVITY
The one and only you, what makes you you–
your unique individuality and personality.

❏*Feelings.* According to Webster, the word *feeling* refers to "any of the subjective reactions, pleasurable or unpleasurable, that one may have to a situation and usually connotes an absence of reasoning." The word *emotion* implies "an intense feeling with physical as well as mental manifestations," while the word *passion* refers to "a strong or overpowering emotion, connoting especially sexual love or intense anger."

PERSONAL REFLECTION

■ It is not always easy to attach words to what we feel. Make a list of feeling words, jotting down both painful and joyful feelings that come to mind. How easy is it for you to express your feeings to other people? When you were growing up, were you encouraged to express feelings in your home? Why or why not?

_____

_____

_____

_____

There are several dimensions to our feelings as they relate to the inner child.

√ *Feelings and spontaneity.* When I think of the word *feeling*, my mind immediately focuses on my fourteen-month-old grandson, Andrew—a little towhead with soft blond hair, big blue eyes, and a dimpled grin. Andrew is the embodiment of pure feeling. There is nothing phony or false about him; he is his true self. From moment to moment he may become excited, angry, fearful, happy, or playful. You never have to guess what Andrew is feeling—it's written all over his face.

Andrew reminds me of how far most of us have strayed from spontaneously expressing our real feelings without worrying about what others will think. It's only as we grow older that we lose that spontaneity of feelings so characteristic of the inner child. We often hide our true emotions behind a contrived mask and let ourselves become overresponsible, critical, unhappy, empty adults.

√ *Feelings and curiosity.* The inner child is inevitably curious. When our son, Jeff, was small he was always into things, and one time his curiosity got the best of him. He dug up Jasper, his dearly departed hamster who had been deceased for three weeks, just to see if he had made it to the Promised Land. Needless to say, Jasper was a mere shadow of his former self.

Even at two-and-a-half, Jeff's curiosity was nearly his undoing. One day he climbed up a ladder and seated himself on top of our roof as smug as a little potentate surveying his kingdom. When my wife discovered him on his lofty perch, she began screaming and hyperventilating and nearly succumbed to hysteria.

Of course, Jeff's budding curiosity has its amusing moments too. When we first took him backpacking at two, he shuffled along the trail collecting so many rocks and plants in his pockets that he looked like a walking shrub with his pants at half-mast. But, oh, the look of pure pleasure on his face!

Why is it that we have lost our excitement over simple things?

PERSONAL
REFLECTION

■ Are you able to express your feelings spontaneously and directly? Give an example or two of doing this. If you find this difficult to do, why do you think you struggle with it?

_____

_____

_____

_____

■ When was the last time you got excited over a simple thing? Describe what it was that got you excited. Use as many colorful words as you can to describe why you felt excited.

_____

_____

_____

_____

_____

√ *The need to be touched and held.* There is nothing quite like a mother's touch to bring comfort. To be held when frightened, to be embraced when grieving, to receive a tender touch when feeling alone and rejected comforts the inner child at the point of need.

Only in recent years has human touch been widely recognized as a vital factor in physical, mental, and emotional health. In fact, there are a number of studies that reveal the profound effects of physical and emotional deprivation on infants. Infants deprived of holding and caressing often experience physical retardation in normal growth patterns and, in many cases, even die.[1]

A dramatic case that illustrates our inherent need for touch appeared in the documentary film, *Second Chance,* and was summarized in the popular book, *Born to Win,* by James and Jongeward:[2]

> When Susan's father left her at a large children's hospital, she was 22 months old. However, she weighed only 15 pounds (the weight of a five-month-old baby) and was 28 inches tall (the average height of a ten-month-old). She had practically no motor skills, could not crawl, could not speak or even babble. If people approached her, she withdrew in tears.
>
> After three weeks during which no one had come to see Susan, a social worker contacted the mother. Both mother and father were above average in education, yet the mother complained, "Babies are a poor excuse for human beings." She described Susan as not liking to be held and wanting to be left alone. She said she had given up trying to make contact with Susan and, in regard to taking care of her, admitted, "I don't want to do that anymore."
>
> Examinations showed no physical reason for Susan's extreme mental and physical retardation, and her case was diagnosed as "maternal deprivation syndrome."

A volunteer substitute mother came in to give Susan loving care for six hours a day, five days a week. The hospital staff also gave Susan much attention and she was held, rocked, played with, and fed with an abundance of touching.

Two months later, although she was still markedly retarded, Susan had a highly developed affectional response. She also gained six pounds and had grown two inches. Her motor ability was greatly improved. She could crawl and could walk if holding on. She related to relative strangers without fear. Tender loving care had had a remarkable effect on Susan.

In spite of overwhelming evidence that human touch is crucial to our physical, emotional, and mental well-being, people construct walls around their inner child for self-protection. They feel uncomfortable about letting people close enough to touch them. Because these feelings are so commonplace in human interaction, they warrant extensive investigation in future chapters.

PERSONAL REFLECTION

■ Are you comfortable expressing your feelings through physical touch? Why? What, if any, limitations do you feel in regard to either giving or receiving touch?

_____

_____

_____

_____

_____

■ What kind of touch did you experience in your family as you were growing up? Describe one or two significant touch experiences you had as a child; as a teenager; or as an adult.

_____

_____

_____

_____

_____

√ *Negative feelings of the inner child.* So far we have addressed the more attractive feelings of the inner child, but there is a negative side as well. Imagine a child, age three. You've just taken a cookie away from him because he helped himself without asking. Do you hear him say, "Thank you, Mommy. It's so nice of you to discipline me so I'll develop fine moral character. Please feel free to correct me anytime"? Yes, I admit this isn't your basic three-year-old. What you do hear is yelling and screaming, perhaps accompanied by some foot-stomping, from an angry, red-faced youngster who shrieks, "I want my cookie back—I hate you!"

Temper tantrums are common at this age because the child is naturally self-centered, rebellious, and demanding. Believe it or not, your inner child has these qualities too. Some adults who don't get their own way exhibit infantile behavior by throwing tantrums, and even dishes, furniture, family pets, and one another. Others are too polite to raise their voices or become visibly angry when things don't go their way, but the feelings are there just the same. I'm not suggesting that because we have an inner child we should dump our feelings on others whenever we feel like it. On the contrary, the important issue here is finding ways to place proper controls on the inner child without killing its spirit.

At this point, you may be saying to yourself, "This whole idea of the inner child sounds childish and immature. After all, the Bible says, 'When I became a man, I did away with childish things.' So why should I be concerned about my inner child?" Actually, the negative behavior I've described in this section is only a very small aspect of the inner child. The broader definition of the inner child involves who we really are inside beneath the masks and disguises, the pride and pretenses. Perhaps this is the very child Christ had in mind when He said, "Unless you are converted and become *like* children, you shall not enter the kingdom of heaven" (Matthew 18:3). Christ wants to relate to the real you behind the facade.

Whether those feelings of our inner child are positive or negative, they tell you where you really are at any given moment. You may not always feel comfortable with what you feel, but again, if you are going to establish truly intimate relationships, with others or with God, those relationships must be developed through your inner child.

❑ *Natural Abilities.* A second characteristic of the inner child is *natural abilities*—that is, inherent, God-given talents. I'm not referring to *learned* skills here, although, of course, training can perfect them. In order to distinguish between natural abilities and those skills learned through training and education, a personal illustration may help.

I've always been a rather perceptive, intuitive person. I read people pretty well. I never *learned* to do this; it was just a natural ability. On completion of my master's degree in psychology, I did an internship in a counseling center. I found that my intuitive ability helped me to know what to say and what to do when I worked with clients. If you asked me why I said a certain thing that proved helpful to a client, my response would have been, "It just felt like the right thing to say." When I returned to school to complete my Ph.D. degree in clinical psychology, my intuitive ability did not satisfy my professors. I needed to know theory so that I could explain my instinctive interventions.

As a professional psychologist, I need a theoretical basis for the way I work with people; however, I may lose my effectiveness if I disregard my natural intuitive ability. Over the years I've encountered many people who possess this same intuitive ability to understand and help others, and they minister effectively in their churches without a single course in psychology.

You also have a number of God-given natural abilities that are part of your true self, or your inner child. These abilities may differ from what you have been educated or trained for in life. But you have the capability to achieve a high degree of excellence if you discover and use these natural abilities of your inner child. Moreover, I believe the Bible refers specifically to these inherent abilities in Proverbs 22:6: "Train up a child in the way he should go, even when he is old he will not depart from it." The phrase "the way he should go" refers to a child's natural bent or inherent talents. This is an important passage for parents as they raise their children, but it also helps us as individuals to remember to develop and use our own natural abilities.

PERSONAL
REFLECTION

■ What do you feel are your natural talents? Think of things that come easy to you. Make a list of things that come to mind. Avoid listing skills you have learned by training and education, unless they match your natural talents. Have a friend make the same list about you and then compare the lists.

_____

_____

_____

_____

❑ *Creativity*. A third characteristic of the inner child is *creativity* as evidenced in unique individuality and personality. Do you realize that you are one of a kind? There has never been nor will there ever be someone exactly like you, with the same sum total of your feelings, attitudes, experiences, character traits, hopes, dreams, and goals. Think of it. No carbon copy. No mass-produced duplicate. Just one and only *you*.

One of my patients struggled with his own creativity. A tall, slender young man who has just turned 21. Mark was a gentle, perceptive person with clear, blue eyes that expressed deep compassion. He possessed an appreciation for the hidden nuances in life that many fail to see, and he had an exceptionally dry wit that I thoroughly enjoyed. He was a talented writer who had received much encouragement from teachers and professors during his high school and college years.

But when Mark came to see me, he was obviously frustrated and hurt. "I think my father is disappointed that his only son didn't turn out to be a jock," he confided.

When I encouraged him to tell me more about his father, he said, "Dad was always active in athletics. He dreamed of the day he could shoot baskets or throw a baseball with his son. But I'm lousy at sports and my dad isn't about to brag to his friends, 'This is my son, the writer.' "

"How do you feel about your father's attitude?" I asked.

He managed a brittle little smile. "I guess I use humor to hide my disappointment that I'm not the kind of son my dad wants. It's hard. I feel inadequate, like a failure. These negative feelings overshadow everything I do. Yet being an athlete simply isn't me."

Over the months as I worked with Mark, he began to realize that his father's lack of acceptance was communicating a false message to him—that his unique personality was flawed or inferior. This devastating idea was far from the truth. The issue was not that Mark should work harder to measure up to his father's misdirected goals for him, but that he should be true to his own unique aptitudes and interests. Nine months after Mark began therapy, he was accepted into a master's program in creative writing at a major university. There he received encouragement and affirmation from peers and professors alike. And as he freely explored his talents without guilt or regret, he began to enjoy and appreciate the unique person he was.

Mark's case is not an isolated one. Because we are unique, in a sense each of us stands alone, marches to a different drummer, answers an inner call no one else hears. The very qualities that make us unique and special also tend to separate us from our peer group and sometimes alienate us from our families. Perhaps we don't feel accepted or we are criticized because our way of doing things or looking at things is different from the norm.

One of the great encouragements of the Bible is seen in the diverse natures of the men Jesus called to be His disciples—James and John, the sons of thunder; Peter, the impulsive one; Andrew, the friendly one; Philip, the practical man; Nathanael, the visionary; Matthew, the accountant. And yes, even Judas, the businessman who betrayed Jesus. Each was unique. Jesus never made comparisons. He dealt with His disciples as individuals and loved them as they were. He respected their differences.

When God created us in His own image, He purposely designed us with distinct personalities. No poor imitations or cookie-cutter creations for Him. No reprints, replicas, or reproductions. Each person would be an original, one of a kind, with the inherent worth of an original work of art crafted by the Master Craftsman. Is it any wonder then that He expects us to honor one another as the genuine article—*His* workmanship?

PERSONAL REFLECTION

■ Ephesians 2:10 (NIV) states, "For we are God's *workmanship* created in Christ Jesus to do good works, which God prepared in advance for us to do." The Greek word for *workmanship* sometimes carries with it the meaning of a "work of art." The last part of the verse reminds us of God's sovereign purpose and planning in making us just exactly who we are. There are no duplicates, no mistakes. Describe yourself as God's unique "work of art." Do you ever doubt that God's purposes and planning in making you who you are is somehow not sovereignly being carried out? Why do you think you feel this way?

_____

_____

_____

_____

_____

_____

■ What are some specific ways you can encourage yourself in your God-given uniqueness?

_____

_____

_____

Long before psychology existed or before the world existed, for that matter, individuality thrived in the Trinity. The Father, Son, and Holy Spirit are three distinct personalities with separate functions and unique characteristics, and yet they are one. By their very differences they complement one another in the Godhead.

For me, as a Christian whose profession is psychology, the truth that we are created by God as unique and valuable individuals provides the only basis for healthy self-esteem. However, I wasn't always as aware of this fact as I am today. Seven years of inpatient work in a private psychiatric hospital brought this fact home to me with stunning clarity. During those early years of my career, I found that working daily with very disturbed patients took its toll on me, affecting my outlook on life and on people in general. I developed a hospital mentality that expressed itself in negativism toward my patients—an attitude that they would always be mentally ill, so why should I devote my best efforts to their therapy? After all, wouldn't these same patients be back in the hospital again next week, next month, next year? To my dismay, my patients sensed my pessimistic attitude and began to see themselves as hopeless. They became convinced that they would never get any better. It became a sad and vicious cycle.

Fortunately, the psychiatrist who directed my unit was a godly man who constantly emphasized the integration of the Bible with sound psychological principles. Through my own study and his relentless insistence, I began to see the unique place Christianity has in working with these very sick people. The truth that impacted me the most was that in God's eyes these broken, disturbed people have the same worth and uniqueness as I have. I needed to change my perspective and see myself and them from God's viewpoint, through His loving, caring eyes.

God's perspective provides a distinctive for the Christian mental health professional that the nonbeliever in the field of psychology does not have. The theory of evolution, which claims we evolved from the impersonal to the personal, from nothing to something, offers no firm basis for inherent worth. God, on the other hand, tells us that we have value and worth for *who* we are, not just for what we can accomplish. He not only created us in His image, but also confirmed our great worth to Him through His immeasurable love. It is this love that led Him to pay the ultimate price for us by giving His beloved Son to die on the cross to redeem us from the curse of sin. I am convinced that God desires us to be who we are, the unique persons He created, and to enjoy our individuality as it blossoms and thrives in our personal relationship with Him.

My desire is that you will not only discover your own valuable inner child, but also learn to nurture and care for it so that it will become a healthy part of your adult life and means of deepening your relationship with God and those you love.

PRAYERFUL REFLECTION

■ Write a prayer thanking God for making you just exactly who you are. Use as many descriptive words as you can to communicate what you know about your inner child at this point. Then ask God to help you discover even more of who you are in the weeks ahead.

_____

_____

_____

_____

_____

_____

_____

_____

PERSONAL RENEWAL

■ Keep a journal of the activities and expressions of your inner child this week, particularly the various feelings you experience. Include what prompts your feelings, what the feelings are, and what you do with them. Supplemental journaling pages have been included in Appendix Three of this workbook.

■ Renew your thoughts and feelings this week by memorizing Ephesians 2:10 (NIV). Personalize the verse by substituting the pronoun "I" for the plural "we."

For we are God's workmanship created in Christ Jesus to do good works, which God prepared in advance for us to do.

Chapter 2
Abuses of the Inner Child

Karen was a striking woman, tall and slender, with an olive complexion that gave her an exotic look. Her long, curly brown hair complimented her large brown eyes, and her youthful figure belied the fact that she was the mother of teenage children. Talented and intelligent, she wore the latest fashions and came across as an articulate, self-assured woman who had her life in order.

As a young girl, Karen had suffered both physical and sexual abuse. Under her glamorous, polished facade was an insecure woman who had gone through a string of meaningless affairs, a stormy marriage and divorce, and a recent suicide attempt. But during the early days of her therapy, she remained strangely silent about the details of her childhood experiences.

Then, during one session, the story broke from Karen's lips in strained, halting phrases: "I just stood there looking at my mother's face. It was contorted with rage. I remember the knife in her hand as she lunged toward me. I was frozen with fear. The next thing I remember is the sharp pain. I looked down and saw blood gushing from a jagged wound in my left arm. Blood was spurting everywhere. My mother panicked and ran screaming out the door, leaving me all alone. I began to scream at the sight of my own blood. Dad rushed in and I'll never forget what he said: 'You've cut yourself! We better get a bandage on it.' Can you believe that? His wife goes screaming out the door, his daughter is standing in the kitchen with blood running down her arm all over the floor, and all Dad says is that we need to put a bandage on it!"

It had taken Karen months to gather the courage to pour out her painful story; it took several more months for me to learn all the hidden terrors of her early childhood. Karen confided that her mother had a limited capacity to cope with the pressures of life, let alone motherhood; in venting her rage and frustration, she often struck Karen with her hand or any object that was handy. Unable to understand her mother's anger, Karen began to feel that she herself was somehow bad. These internal "bad" feelings were intensified whenever her mother declared, "Just who do you think you are, you ungrateful brat? You're lucky to have food on the table and a roof over your head! What more do you want?"

"Mom was always threatening to send me to an orphanage," Karen admitted, "and that terrified me. I tried to be the best daughter I could, but it was never enough." She brushed quickly at the tear trickling down her cheek. "All I ever wanted was love and affection, but my longing for closeness turned into a nightmare."

Slowly, painfully, over several sessions, Karen released the unspeakable memories of her father. "Looking back, I can see that my dad was a very unhappy man, and I guess I felt I could make him happy. But I never dreamed it would be the beginning of four years of sexual abuse. Dad played this "special" game with me. He made me promise not to tell anyone. No one else could know, he said, or it wouldn't be special anymore. It started with him putting his hand in places he wasn't supposed to. Eventually he began coming to my bedroom and lying down with me. He wanted me to touch him. I was terrified, but I did what he asked. Finally he tried to put his finger inside me. All I remember is the pain. . . ."

Karen drew in a deep, shuddering breath. "It got so bad I dreaded being alone with him," she said in a soft, wavering voice. "I'd find any excuse to be away from the house. I didn't think it would ever end, but it did. One day Mom came home unexpectedly and found my father in bed with me. We were both undressed. I felt so ashamed. Mom kicked my dad out and eventually divorced him. But I felt like it was all my fault. Even today, when I think of my dad, I still feel dirty inside."

Karen's body stiffened as the agonizing memories washed over her afresh. Her fists tightened. There was a flash of rage that quickly gave way to abject despair. "Why?" she screamed. "Why did my father do those things to me?"

PERSONAL REFLECTION

■ In her book *Door of Hope*, author Jan Frank states that "incest is the biggest hidden problem in the church today." Unfortunately, some victims don't even recall the incidents of abuse. All they know is that their lives are characterized by the symptoms listed on the next page. Check any statements with which you identify.

Symptoms of Sexual Abuse

❑ I frequently feel depressed, angry, fearful and guilty.

❑ I experience a deep lack of trust in my relationships with other people.

❑ I am repeatedly "victimized" (taken advantage of in a variety of ways, including sexual).

❑ I have a difficult time feeling my feelings. I'm emotionally shut down.

❑ I exhibit obsessive/compulsive behaviors (i.e., overwork, over-clean, overexercise, have short-lived sexual affairs, am constantly busy).

❑ I have experienced sexual difficulties.

❑ I consistently struggle with feelings of low self-esteem. I often feel bad or dirty.

If you checked one or more of the symptoms listed above, it is possible that you were sexually abused as a child.

It took more than a year of therapeutic work before Karen could let herself experience the deep pain that her inner child felt. She had learned at an early age to cut off her feelings and use her intellect to protect herself from further pain. Possessing a deep distrust of people, she had developed a superior attitude to keep herself from intimate involvements. Yet by her aloofness and free-wheeling sexual behavior, she unconsciously set herself up to be rejected and to reexperience all the bad inner-child feelings of her past.

While not all assaults on the inner child are as extreme and devastating as in Karen's story, the incidence of both physical and sexual abuse is rising dramatically in the United States. For that reason, we need to consider the shattering effect of abuse, especially sexual abuse, on the inner child. Victims of such abuse usually become damaged adults struggling to survive, while totally cut off emotionally from their inner child. Although their inner child starves for affection, nourishment, and the right to live, these adults paradoxically see their inner selves as bad, unworthy, unlovable, and deserving only of eternal banishment in their own private hell. One of the saddest consequences of father-daughter abuse is the alienation and prejudice the daughter encounters from the very person who should help her.

PERSONAL
REFLECTION

■ Here are some startling statistics about sexual abuse:

❑ Sexual abuse is the fastest growing category of family violence cases reported every year.

❑ Parents who were abused as children are six times more likely to abuse their own children.

❑ Between 60,000 and 100,000 children are sexually abused each year.

❑ Some psychologists believe that 80 percent of sexual abuse victims come from "religious" homes.

❑ One out of three to four girls and one out of five to eight boys experience some form of sexual abuse.

❑ A child can be considered sexually abused without sexual intercourse occurring.

(Based on a study on "Domestic Violence" done by Instructional Aids, Inc., Plano, Texas, 1985.)

■ Facing the reality of childhood sexual abuse is very painful, as is evidenced in Karen's story. Did you relate to Karen's story in any way? How?

_____

_____

_____

_____

_____

Dr. Roland Summit discusses what the abused child experiences internally —the impact on her inner child, and externally—the impact on important people in the child's life, as the child's sexual abuse accommodation syndrome.[1] In order to become familiar with the stages an abuse victim experiences, let's take a look at the five characteristics of the accommodation syndrome.

√ *Secrecy.* When a child first experiences molestation, she will rarely tell anyone about it because she feels guilt and shame, and fears disapproval and punishment from her mother. This feeling is reinforced when the offender says, "If Mom finds out, I'll have to leave. Our family will break up, and I won't be able to see you anymore." Or, "Mom will be mad at you. She won't love you anymore." The very fact that the sexual abuse is kept from Mom defines it as something dangerous and bad. What a heavy burden for a little girl (or boy) to carry alone!

PERSONAL
REFLECTION

■ As a child, do you recall being told by any trusted adult (i.e., mother, father, aunt, uncle, grandparent, older sibling, teacher, baby-sitter, neighbor) to keep something that happened between that person and you a secret? What was the secret? From whom did you keep the secret and for how long?

_____

_____

_____

_____

_____

_____

Feelings of guilt and fear lead to the second characteristic.

√ *Helplessness.* How helpless a little girl feels when she finds herself overpowered and betrayed by her father or other trusted adult males! She is overwhelmed by her feelings of isolation, shame, and guilt, along with her inability to make sense of her father's behavior.

One patient told me she would lie in her bed playing possum when her stepfather came into her room at night. She would do nothing to defend herself. This inability to cry out or to protect herself causes the biggest misunderstanding between the child and those to whom she may turn for help. Unfortunately, people tend to think, "If she really was being abused, surely she could have done something to stop it." This leads to the next "logical" conclusion: "Somehow she must have invited it to happen."

Such judgments on the part of others propel the child into increased feelings of badness and self-condemnation for not taking action to protect herself. Imagine the overwhelming feelings of insecurity and disillusionment the child feels when her private sanctuary, her bedroom, is invaded. It's too much for her to handle. Every abused girl (or boy) needs a caretaker to step in and stop the sexual entrapment; she can rarely stop it herself. Yet she will heap self-blame on herself for not having the power to end it.

PERSONAL REFLECTION

■ A victimized, helpless little child often carries into adulthood those same feelings of helplessness. She will heap self-blame on herself for not having the power to stop something that is happening of an abusive nature. *EXAMPLE: A female who was physically abused as a child marries an alcoholic who hits her and verbally abuses her.* In what ways, if any, do you assume blame for abuse that is happening to you in your adult relationships? Describe a recent situation in which this type of pattern occurred.

_____

_____

_____

_____

_____

_____

_____

√ *Entrapment and accommodation.* At this stage, the sense of helpless victimization the child experiences causes her to exaggerate her own responsibility for the abuse. She begins to despise herself for her own weakness. At the same time she faces a major mental dilemma: "Either my parent is bad or I am bad." The idea of having a "bad" father who refuses to care for his child is too overwhelming for most children. In other words, they cannot consciously accept the reality of having no one to depend on for acceptance or survival if Dad is truly "bad."

The child's only other option is, "I am bad and deserving of punishment and not worth caring for." This "self-scapegoating" is almost universal for victims of any form of parental abuse—a fact that has been evident in my practice as well as in the experience of colleagues. It doesn't make sense to our adult minds, but that's because we don't see life from the child's perspective. The child says to herself, "The reason Dad sexually abused me is because I am bad." This concept forms the basis for the inner child to be self-despising.

PERSONAL REFLECTION

■ When abuse of any kind has occurred in childhood, self-despising messages are set in motion. Many of those messages stay hidden in our subconscious and are carried with us into adulthood and become destructive in our lives. What "self-despising" messages do you continue to tell yourself? *EXAMPLES: If someone I love is unhappy with me, he will leave me. I must never be weak or have needs.* How do these messages affect the way you live and relate to the people in your life?

_____

_____

_____

_____

Along with self-scapegoating, the victim of abuse faces the problem of overresponsibility. The father may lead the child to believe that as long as she continues to let him abuse her sexually, he will not abuse the other children in the family. He may also convince her that the abuse must continue and remain their secret so that Mother won't fall apart, Dad won't have to seek other women, and the home will not be broken. Thus, the child is given the responsibility to keep it together. Roles are tragically reversed: The child must protect rather than be protected. So how does the child survive?

• *Make believe and role reversal.* One way the abused child survives is by developing an imaginary world of companions—a make-believe world of people who care. This can be seen in doll play, in which the little girl becomes the loving mother to her doll—an example of reversing roles. She projects her own needy inner child into the doll and plays the mother who gives protection and love, all the things she herself needs. (Of course, this behavior of itself doesn't necessarily signify an abused child, since most little girls role play with their dolls.) If there are other siblings, especially younger ones, an abused youngster may project her own needy inner child into them and become a dedicated little mother to them, totally absorbing herself in meeting their needs while cutting herself off from her own needs.

• *Multiple personalities.* Another survival technique of the abused child is to develop multiple personalities, each one representing a different part of the child's troubled personality—the helpless person, the bad person, the good person, the beloved person. (You may be familiar with accounts of multiple personalities such as *The Three Faces of Eve* and, more recently, *Sybil.)* While multiple personalities are relatively rare, most cases can be traced back to the trauma of sexual abuse in early childhood.

• *Disconnecting the inner child.* Cutting off feelings, essentially disconnecting the inner child, is a third way of coping with the emotional trauma of abuse. This accounts for the difficulty Karen had in expressing her feelings to me. Even when talking about her father, she could not allow herself to experience the deep emotions his memory provoked.

• *Self-destructive outlets.* What happens when the child cannot create a psychological haven for survival? Her rage and helplessness seek self-destructive outlets. As the child grows older, she may mutilate her body by cutting herself. One patient cut her arms when she felt destructive. Some women will cut their chest or other parts of their body. Adolescents frequently run away from home. Self-hate drives many abused women into promiscuous behavior and ultimately into frequent suicidal attempts.

Surprisingly, an abused girl's greatest rage is usually directed toward her mother. She feels that if Mother had taken care of Dad, the abuse wouldn't have happened. If she becomes convinced that Mom simply doesn't care, she may find it impossible to trust her mother or form a close attachment with her; thus she feels still more dependent on her father. So the destructive cycle continues.

Trust is one of the biggest issues for children and adult women who have been sexually molested. They find it too painful to trust anyone. Even when they seek help, they will severely test their friend or therapist to see if the individual is worthy of being trusted. Sadly, many people, including therapists, lose patience with the victims and thus inadvertently reinforce the abuse syndrome. Proven love, patience, and unconditional acceptance are the ingredients that bring the abused inner child into the open to be nurtured and cared for.

PERSONAL REFLECTION

■ Describe your ability to trust. Do you find yourself trusting people who eventually prove to be untrustworthy? Or do you tend to withhold trust and stay closed to people who try to get to know you intimately?

_____

_____

_____

_____

_____

This brings us to the fourth characteristic: delayed, conflicted, and unconvincing disclosure.

√ *Delayed, conflicted, and unconvincing disclosure.* Most ongoing sexual abuse is never disclosed, at least not outside the family. If there is disclosure, it generally occurs when a family experiences such overwhelming conflict that the abuse can no longer be hidden, or when some person outside the family may have reason to believe that it is taking place. With increased public awareness, more people are becoming educated as to the symptoms of sexual molestation as well as to other forms of abuse and neglect.

Victims who reveal their abuse often face insurmountable obstacles, including the strong possibility of being disbelieved and misunderstood. A teenage girl, who after years of silent rage finally reveals the abuse, is more likely to be misunderstood. People may ask her, "Why complain now? Why didn't you do something when it happened?" Often her story is not believed. Thus, some teens take another approach, that of compliancy, of trying to please everybody by being the good kid, the obedient child who never makes waves.

√ *Retraction of the complaint.* The last characteristic in the accommodation syndrome is retraction of the complaint. Whatever the child says about the incestuous relationship inflicted on her, she at some point is likely to deny it. Why? Because her revelation can create such an uproar in the family that pressure is exerted on her to retract her accusations. She is likely to comply, explaining that she made up the story because she was mad at Dad and didn't mean to cause so much trouble.

People are generally more willing to believe a lie than to take seriously a child's claims of sexual abuse. Her retraction of the accusations confirms adult expectations that children cannot be trusted, and once again the precarious family balance is restored at the expense of the girl. Thus, the child learns to keep her mouth shut; the adults tune out, and people in authority confirm the impression that they don't believe a rebellious child who uses sexual charges to damage the reputations of well-intentioned parents. Where does this leave the child? In her own private hell—a world of self-hate and emotional deprivation.

You may wonder if sexual abuse really occurs in professing Christian families? Regrettably, it does. The church is not protected from sexual abuse. And exposure of the abuse is difficult because traditionally the church is slow to recognize and deal with internal problems of its membership that don't pertain directly to "spiritual" issues. Today, however, a number of evangelical churches are recognizing that deep emotional and behavioral problems exist among their members, and they are developing effective programs to help those who are in need.[2]

PERSONAL
REFLECTION

■ Having read the previous description of sexual abuse, do you suspect having been sexually abused as a child? Write a brief statement telling how you feel about it.

_____

_____

_____

_____

AUTHOR'S NOTE: If you have been the victim of sexual abuse, let me urge you to seek help. There are a number of churches with support groups for abuse victims. Individual therapy from a trained professional who has had experience in counseling abuse victims can also be very helpful. Remember, you cannot heal yourself. You do need outside help.

❏ *Psychological Abuse.* Psychological or emotional abuse may be more widespread than physical or sexual abuse and is certainly much more subtle and difficult to detect. Psychological abuse involves humiliating or degrading a child, or using verbal abuse such as screaming, name-calling, or threats. Other forms of emotional mal-treatment include constant family discord, inconsistent behavior that never lets the child know where he stands, and sending double messages. These mixed signals have a push-pull effect—drawing the child toward the parent, then pushing him away. The child feels frustrated and confused by contradictory messages like these: "Come here, Johnny, talk to me" and "Go away, can't you see I'm busy?" Or, a parent may spank a child in anger and, then, feeling guilty, may smother her with affection.

Psychological abuse is usually endured in silence and rarely ever reported to any kind of authority. Only recently has society become aware of the immense damage that can be inflicted on the personality by verbal, emotional, and psychological assaults.

PERSONAL REFLECTION

■ Based on the author's description of psychological abuse, what abuse took place in your home when you were growing up? Do a quick inventory, citing as many specific instances of psychological abuse as you can recall from your childhood.

_____

_____

_____

_____

_____

_____

_____

_____

Let's look for a moment at a case study that illustrates the profound impact of psychological abuse on the inner child.

Once in awhile you meet someone whose accomplishments make you feel inadequate, a person who immediately demands your respect and even intimidates you a little. Those were my feelings when I first met Ken, a tall, blond thirty-five-year-old psychologist whose penetrating blue eyes seemed to peer right into my soul. He was referred to me by a mutual friend who was concerned that Ken was depressed and was withdrawing from his friends.

I could tell that he felt uneasy about coming to me for therapy. "It's hard for me to admit that I can't handle my problems by myself," he confessed in a deep, resonant voice that easily commanded attention. "After all, I am a psychologist."

Yes, indeed, he was a psychologist, but a very sad and depressed one! In the first few months of our work together, I learned a great deal about Ken's background. He was raised in a church that preached grace but practiced legalism, the implication being that one was saved by the blood of Christ but secured by the do's and don'ts. "Most of my early recollections of the church are surrounded by fear," Ken told me during an early session. "I was scared to death of God. I don't know how many times I responded to the call to come forward for salvation. I was terrified that I wouldn't make it to heaven because of something I did wrong."

At another session, when we talked about Ken's family, he described his relationship with his father. "Dad was a very impatient man who had little tolerance for me because I wasn't the neat, orderly person he was. You might say I was walking chaos. I knew my dad was displeased with me, and I kept thinking, "If I could just be a better son, he would love me more." But it never happened. I couldn't figure my dad out. At work he was always so polite to the customers, but at home he was uptight and extremely critical."

I encouraged Ken to share some specific times when he felt these tensions with his father. "That's easy," he said grimly. "Dad would come to my basketball games, but afterward he would point out everything I did wrong. I remember thinking, *Dad, just once I'd like to feel like I did something right and you were pleased!*

"I recall other times," Ken continued, "when Dad would help me with my math homework. He would explain something and when I didn't understand, he'd lose his patience. Of course, I began to feel stupid and my mind would go blank. Sometimes this went on for hours until I would break down and cry out of pure humiliation. For the longest time I felt like the dumbest person in the world. I think one reason I pursued a Ph.D. was to please my father. Unfortunately, he died six months before I graduated."

"What would have been your fantasy if your dad had been alive to watch you graduate?" I asked.

Ken's expression darkened. "I see myself standing on the platform with my degree in my hand and shouting to my father, 'You see, I'm not stupid! Now will you love me?' "

Tears welled in Ken's eyes as, in a faltering voice, he continued the fantasy. "Then I see myself running to my father and we both embrace, and we're both crying, and he tells me how proud he is of me and how much—how much he loves me!"

Ken's problem was not that he and his father didn't love each other. In truth, they probably had loved each other very much. Ken's brain, or intellect, even told him that this was so. But the little boy inside Ken never felt that he measured up to his dad's expectations. A deep feeling of inadequacy began to develop inside him as a child, an inadequacy that he tried to hide from himself and others. Despite Ken's natural talents and intelligence, much of his adult life was motivated by a desire to prove to Dad, to himself, and to the world at large that he was not a failure. Unfortunately, his "inadequate" inner child never could enjoy the fruits of his hard work. There always had to be more work, more achievement, more recognition—a never-ending pursuit of accomplishment.

Ken's relationship with his mother was a sharp contrast to his relationship with his father. "Mom was just the opposite of Dad," he explained. "Whenever I succeeded in school or sports, Mom went overboard by telling me how great I was. She even sent articles about my athletic feats to all the relatives. I'm sure they were just delighted to read about what I was doing in football or basketball. She was so proud . . . too proud."

During one noteworthy session, Ken told me about his fear of letting women get too close to him. "I've noticed that women have always been attracted to me," he said, "especially women who need to take care of a man—you know, the nurturing type. And the more aloof I am, the more they try to break down my wall."

I asked Ken, "Do you suppose they're responding to something you're communicating even while holding them at arm's length?"

He shrugged. "I don't know what you mean."

"There seems to be a little boy inside you that is very needy and hungry for love, support, and validation. I sense that little kid often in our sessions together, but I feel that if I call attention to him, he'll run away, as if he's afraid to be discovered."

Ken was silent for several minutes. Then, with trembling voice he told me of the great emptiness and sadness he had felt during much of his life, in spite of all his accomplishments. He admitted that he had used his intellect and achievements to intimidate people and thus keep them at a distance. Finally he spoke of his mother. "It seemed like my accomplishments were more important to Mom than to me. She needed me to be successful so that she could brag about her talented son. Maybe that should have pleased me, but it didn't.

Her obsession with my success put as much pressure on me as Dad's critical spirit. I still didn't feel accepted for myself. I still had to perform."

"Did you ever talk to your mother about your feelings?" I asked.

Ken's mouth grew tight; his forehead furrowed with anger. "Of course. Many times. But she never listened to me, or at least she never heard what I was really trying to say. Whenever I confronted her, she would just look hurt and accuse me of being a thoughtless, ungrateful son." Ken sighed heavily. "Then Dad would get mad because I upset Mom, and he'd punish me. I was left feeling angry, guilty, and frustrated. I started believing that they were right—I was an ungrateful, unappreciative son. I felt trapped, guilty for wanting some privacy, a life of my own. There was no way out."

"So what did you do, Ken?" I prompted. "You must have found a way out. How did you handle the hurt and frustration?"

Ken smiled knowingly. "You know how I handled it. We're both psychologists. We know the language. I can tell you intellectually what I did, but I can't deal with it emotionally. You might say I see the problem, but I can't quite touch it."

"OK. So say it, Ken, in any way that's comfortable for you."

He nodded. "I built a wall around myself to keep my mother, my father, and everyone else out. What's that saying—'No man is an island'? Well, I guess I was determined to be an island. I refused to need anybody. I figured building a wall was the only way to protect myself from my dad's criticism and my mother's possessiveness."

"A wall to keep others out, Ken," I reflected. "Or a prison of emotional isolation that trapped you inside?"

Ken looked thoughtful. "I guess it worked both ways."

"And what about your needy, emotionally hungry inner child, Ken? How are you going to nourish it if you never allow anyone on the other side of that wall?"

Ken slowly met my gaze. "I guess that's why I'm here."

Over a period of time Ken was able to understand emotionally what his fear of closeness was costing him. His feeling of being unloved had created an unconscious sense of loss that resulted in persistent depression. Gradually he realized that he had been projecting his own needy inner child into his patients as a vicarious way of nourishing himself. His efforts proved futile until he was willing to address the needs of his inner child directly rather than indirectly. As the weeks passed, Ken began to reveal his needy inner child, first to me and then to others with whom he wanted to be close. The more openly he shared himself, the greater the affirmation he received. His depression lifted as his child within experienced feelings of love and unconditional acceptance.

PERSONAL
REFLECTION

■ In what ways do you relate with Ken's feelings? Write down specific patterns of behavior you have used, or are currently using, to protect your frightened inner child.

_____

_____

_____

_____

_____

■ What has your fear of closeness cost you emotionally?

_____

_____

_____

_____

■ Are you prepared to address the needs of your inner child directly? Why or why not?

_____

_____

_____

_____

_____

❑ *Emotional Abuse in Christian Homes.* It's not unusual to encounter cases of emotional abuse in "fine, upstanding Christian families." Unfortunately, such cases inevitably go unreported. The only outward manifestation of this type of abuse may be seen in the victim's deep sense of inadequacy in a personal relationship with God. Emotionally abused persons may work feverishly at being "good" Christians, but their major motive is guilt. They feel they can never do enough to please God, church, family, or community. Such Christians feel no joy; they hear love words but cannot experience them personally. The pastor's message of Christ's unconditional love never deeply touches these dear brothers and sisters because their inner child is locked up and cannot hear the words.

Emotionally abused Christians may experience immobility, depression, even total despair. When they cannot find peace trying to please God, they may "give up" trying to be good and live their lives seeking after immediate pleasure, which only leads to more despair. This becomes a "deadly trap," for when the Spirit of God dwells in us, we can never be at peace while acting sinfully.

PERSONAL REFLECTION

■ Go back through the two paragraphs you just read and underline or highlight any phrases that describe the way you've operated as a Christian.

■ Now write a brief description of the church you grew up in. If you did not grow up in the church, describe why you think your parents neglected the spiritual aspect of family life in your home.

_____

_____

_____

_____

_____

■ In his book *The Way Out of the Wilderness*, Dr. Earl Henslin describes this type of "spiritual" thinking as *religious shame*. He says that it is "a particularly potent force in the lives of Christians." He goes on to describe religious shame (or legalism) as "a rule-bound spirituality that emphasizes external conformity to a religious standard rather than a fundamental change in the inner person. Under legalism spiritual change is imposed and judged from the outside. What is happening on the inside, in the person's heart and emotions, is basically ignored. Spiritual success is evaluated on the basis of external behavior. If you conform, you are accepted. If your life is sufficiently out of control so that you can't conform, you are viewed as a "bad" person—spiritually as well as emotionally" (Thomas Nelson Publishers, 1992, p. 105). In what ways, if any, has *religious shame* impacted your ability to feel and experience the love of God in your life?

_____

_____

_____

_____

_____

_____

_____

■ If God could speak aloud a word to your inner child right now, what would you like to hear Him say?

_____

_____

_____

_____

_____

_____

_____

Is there hope? Yes! We can experience God's unconditional love when we relate to Him as our loving, nurturing Heavenly Father rather than a harsh and critical inner parent. You may be asking what I mean when I speak of seeing God as a critical inner parent. In order to understand the concept, we must first take a look at your own critical inner parent.

YOUR INNER CRITICAL PARENT

We've talked at length about your *inner* child—that needy, vulnerable, feeling, creative part of you that defines your true self. But what do we mean now by the *inner critical parent?* You may ask, "Are we talking about split personalities or schizophrenic minds?" Not at all. Or you may be thinking that it's getting a little crowded to imagine having both an inner child and an inner parent in one personality. But bear with me, and I think you'll see what I mean.

From our infancy we unconsciously begin to create an invisible parent within our personalities based on our earliest perceptions of our real parents. As children we observe and internalize the way our parents relate to us—what they say, how they behave around us, the way they treat us. A composite image of our parents, however flawed or inaccurate our perceptions may have been, is the model for the inner parent we create for ourselves. This inner parent may have both positive and negative traits; it may be affirming or destructive; but for those who have experienced any sort of emotional abuse, the inner parent is inevitably critical and destructive. In other words, if we received negative or severe treatment from our real parents, then we will have a critical inner parent that continues to treat our inner child with a harsh, critical attitude on into our adult life.

The message our inner parent gives us plays automatically like audio tapes in our mind. Whenever we face a situation similar to a past event that evoked criticism from our parents, the tape begins to roll. For example, suppose you knock over a carton of milk and it spills all over the table and floor. In your head you hear your critical parental tape, "You clumsy idiot, can't you do anything right?" Or you fail a test in school. The tape clicks on, "Face it, Kid. You're stupid. You'll never succeed." Or you don't get the job you applied for. Again, you hear the tape, "What made you think you could get that job? Anyone can tell you're not good enough."

Once these tapes are recorded, they cannot be erased. Think of it this way. If you have a phone-answering machine at home, you record a message to be played when someone calls your number. Whenever the phone rings, on comes the same message you recorded: "Hello. John and Mary are busy right now, but if you'll leave your name and number . . ."

You can call home as many times as you wish and you will always get the same message. It doesn't change unless you record another message over it.

Your critical inner parent tapes are exactly like that. Does this mean doom and gloom for your inner child? No, it doesn't have to. You can place a nurturing inner parent alongside the critical parent, one that gives encouraging rather than discouraging messages. (We'll discuss this further in chapter 9.) The important point to remember is that those inner critical parent messages are filled with error and distortions. You must learn to turn off the bad tapes or ignore them when they begin playing in your head.

PERSONAL
REFLECTION

■ How did your parents relate to you? Write several sentences describing what your parents said to you, how they behaved around you, and the way they treated you.

_____

_____

_____

_____

_____

_____

To help you understand your own inner world better—a world that contains both your inner child and inner parent—I would like to take you on a journey of the imagination. I want you to see life the way you perceived it as the little child you once were. Sit back and relax and allow yourself to experience it as I describe it to you.

First, imagine yourself as a tiny fetus in the womb. You are about nine months old. You've got it made—twenty-four-hour catering service if not a literal "womb with a view." You are at peace—no hunger pangs, no demanding parents, no brothers or sisters to argue with, unless you're a twin, of course. No one bugs you. You can suck your thumb any old time you please. No one can say or do mean things to you; nothing disturbs you, unless Mom likes loud music or eats spicy food and has gas. Basically you're floating in your own little universe of perfect peace—and you're the center of it all!

But get ready for trauma number one: Birth. You don't even have a choice of whether you want to come out. Unfair! The next thing you know, Mom is pushing you out of your comfortable condo. What's worse, since there's no door, you feel like you're being squeezed out the chimney (the natural way) unless, of course, someone takes off the roof (Caesarean) and pulls you out that way.

For the first time you face the cold, harsh world, alone and helpless, totally dependent on your parents for protection, nourishment, love, and care. All you can do at this point is cry, twitch, eat, and fill your diapers, not necessarily in that order.

The world you have just been introduced to is a paradoxical realm of startling noises, odd sights, bright colors, unfamiliar people, darkness, hunger pangs, wet diapers, and the touch of total strangers. You are going to need a lot of help in order to make sense of this new world. You will have to depend on Mom and Dad to teach you, and you hope they do a good job because you won't know any better until you are much older. Actually, you will trust your parents without reservation—what other option do you have?

As you grow you will begin to form a mental picture of yourself through the actions and reactions of your parents and other significant adults in your life. Naturally you will give them plenty of things to react to—spilling your milk, stuffing your rubber ducky down the toilet and flooding the bathroom, wearing your birthday cake all over your face, waking everyone in the middle of the night with your nonstop crying. The list could go on indefinitely.

Unfortunately, Mom and Dad do not have to take a battery of psychological tests to determine whether they are qualified for parenthood. They learn from the University of Experience and their own upbringing. They will treat you the way their parents treated them, and will consider it your fault when they demonstrate impatience, anger, and critical attitudes. After all, you are at the center of your world, so you must be responsible for anything that happens. You are too young to realize that Mom and Dad have their own weighty problems they bring into family life.

As you grow during these impressionable first years, not only do you form a definite impression of yourself and your inner child, but you also begin to construct the image of an inner parent that you will carry around inside you for the rest of your life. The more critical and abusive your experiences with your actual parents, the more critical and abusive your inner parent will be. Conversely, the more caring and loving your experiences with your parents, the more caring, loving, and nurturing your inner parent will be.

PERSONAL REFLECTION

■ Write down what your inner child feels in each of the following situations. Then go back and write down what your inner parent says to you about each situation.

Someone pays you a compliment.

I feel _____

_____

My inner parent says _____

_____

Someone you care about is angry with you.

I feel _____

_____

My inner parent says _____

_____

You like someone you meet for the first time.

I feel _____

_____

My inner parent says _____

_____

_____

Someone you love hurts your feelings.

I feel _____

_____

My inner parent says _____

_____

You hug someone you care about or receive a hug from someone you like.

I feel _____

_____

My inner parent says _____

_____

■ Write down several caring, nurturing messages you want your inner child to hear.

_____

_____

_____

_____

_____

_____

_____

Comprehending how we develop this inner parent is crucial for understanding why we as adults continue to treat ourselves in abusive ways and allow others to abuse us as well. For some of us, our inner parent is very critical, scolding us with such remarks as, "Why can't you ever do things right? Why can't you be more like your brother or sister? You'll never amount to anything. . . . You're stupid, ugly, fat. . . . You are unlovable."

Encountering this kind of inner tyranny and emotional battering, the little child within retreats and hides. When this happens, a significant change takes place in our personality. We'll discuss this change in the next chapter.

PRAYERFUL REFLECTION

■ For inner healing to take place, you must acknowledge and eventually learn to accept the reality of the abuse you experienced in childhood. Accepting such painful realities does not come easily, but it does produce good fruit. Reinhold Niebuhr's "Prayer of Serenity" suggests some practical ways for making peace with our past. After reading through his prayer, write a prayer of your own, asking God to help you take the next step in your journey of healing, whatever that might be.

Prayer of Serenity
God, grant me the serenity
to accept the things I cannot change,
the courage to change the things I can,
and the wisdom to know the difference.
Living one day at a time,
enjoying one moment at a time;
accepting hardship as a pathway to peace;
taking as Jesus did,
this sinful world as it is,
not as I would have it;
trusting that You will make all things right
if I surrender to Your will;
so that I may be reasonably happy in this life
and supremely happy with You forever
in the next.
AMEN.

Loving Heavenly Father,

_____

_____

_____

_____

_____

_____

_____

_____

_____

PERSONAL RENEWAL

■ You can experience God's unconditional love when you relate to Him as your loving, nurturing Heavenly Father, rather than as a harsh and critical inner parent. Psalm 103 is a hymn that speaks of God's love and compassion toward His children. Renew your thoughts and feelings this week by meditating on Psalm 103:8-14 (NIV).

The Lord is compassionate and gracious, slow to anger, abounding in love. He will not always accuse, nor will He harbor His anger forever; He does not treat us as our sins deserve or repay us according to our iniquities. For as high as the heavens are above the earth, so great is His love for those who fear Him; as far as the east is from the west, so far has He removed our transgressions from us. As a father has compassion on his children, so the Lord has compassion on those who fear Him; for He knows how we are formed, He remembers that we are dust.

Chapter 3
The Many Masks We Wear

In 1974, I enrolled in a Ph.D. program in clinical psychology at the Rosemead School of Psychology, and very quickly felt like the old man of the class. While most of my fellow students were in their twenties, I was thirty-six and had been a marriage, family, and child counselor in private practice since 1965, plus a psychology teacher in a local community college for twelve years. Now I was embarking on a four-year, full-time graduate program that would leave me forty at graduation.

Besides wondering how I would relate to classmates so much younger, I was also carrying the bitter emotional baggage of a previous scholastic failure. Several years before, I had enrolled in a doctoral program at a well-known university. At the time I was convinced that a doctoral degree would prove once and for all that I wasn't stupid—an attitude I had battled for much of my life. I was grateful that my graduate record examination was not used as a significant criterion for admission, since my low scores embarrassed me. Fortunately, I had received almost all A's on the coursework required for the doctoral program's preliminary exams and I did reasonably well on the exams themselves, well enough to pass. But when I went for my interview for final acceptance into the doctoral program, I was told I would have to take the graduate record examination over to improve my scores before I would be considered.

I felt stunned and humiliated. They had ignored my good grades and exam scores! Fighting discouragement, I took the GRE again, and guess what. I did worse than before! I was told I could take it again, and keep taking it if I wanted to, but I was afraid I might score so low they would have to assign a guardian to take care of me. I felt like a failure and, worst of all, my fear of being stupid seemed to be confirmed. With my self-esteem at rock bottom, I decided to quit the program and give up my hopes for a Ph.D.

The years following that traumatic experience were marked by emotional ups and downs, deep dissatisfaction with myself, and conflicts in my marriage. During those times of emotional and spiritual turmoil, I learned to wear a number of masks both in my spiritual and personal life, but always beneath the mask lay fear. I was too afraid of God to express my real thoughts and feelings. If I did, He might zap me from on high, and I'd be history. Although I had long ago accepted Christ as my Savior, I had little awareness of His real love for me. In fact, I privately feared that my faith had no substance, that I was just kidding myself that God existed. But, surprisingly, I was to learn more about His love during those darkest days of my life than when I was behaving myself as a "good Christian."

I am not recommending that people find the love and grace of God by rebelling. But for me—a person raised in an extremely conservative church that considered me suspect for asking hard questions—that was the path I took. During this disturbing period in my life, I questioned everything—my faith, who I was as a person, my marriage, my career. I stood at a crossroad, knowing that whatever decisions I made would have a serious impact on my future. Desperate for answers, I read several books by Francis Schaeffer, and God spoke to my needy heart through his writings.

I also became fascinated with the L'Abri Fellowship Center in Switzerland (La-BREE, French for "the shelter"). Started by the Schaeffers, the center ministered to people seeking answers to life's difficult questions, especially practical and intellectual questions about Christianity. I had heard impressive reports about L'Abri from my aunt who had lived there for several years. Even in my confused state of mind, I knew in my gut that this was the place I needed. I wrote to Dr. Schaeffer and told him of my conflicts and my urgent need to find answers. Dr. Schaeffer's reply was an answer from the Lord. He told me to come right away.

Those were the words I needed to hear. I applied for a leave of absence from my teaching job, borrowed some money, packed up my wife and son, and went to Europe. We settled in an obscure little village in the Swiss Alps, making our home for the next three months in a small hillside chalet with a breathtaking view of lofty, jagged mountains and deep green valleys. We knew no one and no one knew us; we were strangers in a foreign land. My wife, Kathy, and I sat in our chalet with no TV, no radio, and a phone that never rang, and stared at each other like total strangers. With no outside distractions, I realized that for the first time my family and I would really become acquainted. But without our usual familiar masks, what would we say to each other?

At this point another of my masks was uncovered. In the States, I was a teacher and therapist, well known in my community; here I was a student like other students, studying four hours a day and working in the community twenty hours a week. Without my credentials, who was I? I didn't know, and I didn't like the uneasy feelings that came with the question.

For a month I struggled with my identity and, as a result of that struggle, I decided to write a paper on the topic of self-image from a biblical perspective. During those days of serious prayer, study, and self-examination, I needed to know why I was a Christian. I had to be certain that my personal relationship with God was genuine and growing. I had the added privilege of spending some time with Dr. Schaeffer, who encouraged me to complete my doctoral degree. I knew he was right.

Almost imperceptibly my life began to change. To my joy and delight, I became intimately acquainted with my wife and son. My relationship with Christ became grounded on a more solid foundation of knowledge and faith. Increasingly, I recognized the validity of intelligent faith that can give a reasoned, articulate defense.

> Sanctify Christ as Lord in your hearts, always being ready to make a defense to every one who asks you to give an account for the hope that is in you, yet with gentleness and reverence (1 Peter 3:15).

When we returned to the States, I had a strong desire to obtain my doctoral degree. I wanted more education in both psychology and the Bible in a program that would also impact me as a person. For the first time I was truly ready and eager to learn.

That's when I applied to Rosemead Graduate School of Professional Psychology (which later became Rosemead School of Psychology under Biola University, La Mirada, California). I was accepted, and for the next four years I encountered a number of stretching experiences, both personally and professionally.

One of those experiences was my own personal therapy, required of all doctoral students in the program. Since I considered myself a strong person, especially verbally, I chose my therapist with care. I knew that if I had a therapist who engaged me only on an intellectual level, I would waste two years of therapy. Even so, I wasn't a very cooperative patient, especially at first. I tried to figure out my therapist and see if I could get him to talk. That failed. He suggested I move to the couch. I refused. The idea of reclining on the couch and pouring out my inner thoughts was too threatening. Only then did I realize how scared I was of self-exposure.

In spite of my resistance, Dr. M. was very patient with me. In the sixth month of therapy, I had a fantasy of a sad little boy sitting alone in a dark concrete room similar to an underground bomb shelter. The boy was sitting against the wall with his head buried in his hands. There was a heavy steel door in the room, but no windows. As my therapist questioned me, I realized I was that boy, and I remember growing fearful and angry that the therapist would try to enter my protective hiding place. Finally I admitted that the child inside of me felt hurt, alone, and scared. The only place I felt safe was in my sterile concrete room.

At this point I began to realize how cut off I was from my inner child and how really unhappy and unprotected I felt much of my life. In his wise and compassionate way, Dr. M. slowly exposed the many ways I was trying to protect my frightened inner child. I didn't like it a bit. As therapy progressed, I could see in my fantasy the big steel door begin to open, just a crack at first. My initial reaction was to push the door shut, but it was only a token effort. Perhaps, subconsciously, I wanted Dr. M. to enter this dark concrete room of mine. I was tired of being alone and needed someone who cared to help me out of that room. I knew I couldn't do it alone.

The insight that stunned me was that I had been convinced even Jesus was not in that room with me. I had no awareness of His presence, no sense of His love, because I was cut off from my feelings. That startling realization helped me to see why my walk with the Lord so often lacked the intimacy I needed. I was a believer, but I walked more with my head than my heart, more out of fear than love, and for a long time I didn't know what was missing. With Dr. M.'s help I came to understand that only love can open steel doors and lead the captive, hungry inner child out into the daylight and to the nourishment that produces growth.

With that awareness came fresh insights into Jesus' appeal to the common people of His day. They recognized the genuine article when they experienced it; they knew Jesus loved them. They could be themselves, open and honest with Him. They knew He accepted them and loved them unconditionally. They didn't care that the Pharisees and so-called religious leaders looked on them with scorn and contempt. After all, the self-righteous wore masks and were wrapped smugly in their good works, but their souls were empty sepulchers. They had never experienced the warmth and wonder of Jesus' love. Actually, Jesus' unconditional love was a precious gift I was just becoming more acquainted with myself.

I've shared my own story with you because I want you to know that what I'm writing about in this book is not a mere academic exercise using random psychological principles. I have been where many of you are now. I've struggled with my inner child and have used masks to protect myself. Sometimes I still do. I've erected emotional barriers, or walls, that have imprisoned me. But God has taught me some important principles—through experience, therapy, and His Word—that have enabled me to free my frightened inner child from that dark concrete room.

PERSONAL REFLECTION

■ Like Dr. Dickinson, you too have a story to tell. What is it? Set aside a block of time. Free yourself as much as possible from all outside distractions. Then spend time writing down your story. Record the most significant events of your life, describing them in as much detail as you can recall. In your story include the feelings you remember experiencing in relation to what happened.

_____

_____

_____

_____

_____

_____

_____

_____

_____

_____

_____

_____

_____

_____

_____

_____

_____

_____

_____

_____

_____

Additional space for writing is available in Appendix Three of this workbook if you need it.

If you are living in a painful, self-imposed prison, I believe God wants to free you. I want to help you put aside the many masks you wear and invite your inner child to step out into the sunlight and experience real feelings, to use your God-given talents joyfully and to love and accept the unique person God created you to be. But before you can let your inner child out, you must first discover where it is hiding.

PERSONAL REFLECTION

■ Can you visualize (see in your mind's eye) your inner child? To the best of your ability, describe what you see of your inner child. Where is your child? What do his/her surroundings look like? Is your inner child hiding, or is he/she out in the open?

_____

_____

_____

_____

_____

_____

I visualized my inner child locked in a concrete room. Many of my patients have imagined similar places. One woman described a dark closet as her place of hiding. Closets come up frequently. Others mention dark rooms, basements, attics, and other solitary places. Why is it that we invariably place the inner child in seclusion? One reason is our fear of our inner parent.

In chapter 2 we learned that we have within our personality an inner parent, made up of our perceptions of what our real parents said to us and how they treated us. However, in the self-centered world of our childhood, we often distorted what we experienced our real parents to be. Remember the illustration in chapter 1 of the little boy whose mother took his cookie away so it wouldn't spoil his dinner? Rather than thanking Mom for her concern about his eating habits, little Bobby cried, screamed, stomped his feet, and said, "I hate you!" His rage over having his desires thwarted caused him to distort and exaggerate his mother's action; rather than seeing the wisdom in his mother's deed, he judged her as cruel and vindictive. An inaccurate perception, yes, but very real to Bobby.

Under normal parenting conditions, your inner parent develops some distortions, but they are not so serious that your inner child is damaged or intimidated. But prolonged and stress-filled situations are another matter. Since the young child is totally self-centered, he perceives that all events in his world relate to or are caused by him. This explains why in a divorce or in cases of abuse, the child often blames himself, thinking, "If only I had been a nicer child, my parent would not have left me or abused me." When emotional, physical, or sexual abuse occurs, the parents are perceived as hurtful and critical and thus the inner parent becomes cruel, sadistic, and condemning. The object of this mean and critical spirit is the inner child.

When there has been a great deal of hurt and pain in early childhood, there comes a point when out of self-preservation we take that sensitive inner child and hide it somewhere safe. It's as if we are saying, "I have been hurt enough. No one is ever going to hurt me again." So we lock our vulnerable inner child in a protected but lonely place; in its place emerges a false child—that is, an adapted, more acceptable self that we present to the world at large. This proper, artificial, and exemplary self hides the true inner child. It is this reworked, remodeled, refinished, white-washed, sanitized version of ourselves that represents the many masks we wear.

PERSONAL REFLECTION

■ If you experienced some form of abuse growing up, then it is likely that you have taken your sensitive inner child and hidden him/her in a safe but lonely place. What childhood abuse are you aware of at this point? Briefly describe that abuse. Do you struggle with deep feelings of loneliness now as an adult? Write a sentence describing those feelings.

_____

_____

_____

_____

_____

_____

_____

_____

■ What adapted, more acceptable self have you learned to present to the world at large because you are afraid the real you might be rejected if exposed? Complete each of the following sentences, jotting down the very first thought that comes to your mind. This exercise will put you a little more in touch with the protective masks you may be wearing.

When someone I care about asks, "How are you?" I say

_____

When I feel frightened, I _____

_____

When I feel embarrassed, I _____

_____

When I feel hurt, I usually _____

_____

When I get angry, I _____

_____

I feel acceptable to others when I _____

_____

In order to be loved, I _____

_____

God is pleased with me when I _____

_____

■ Dr. Dickinson defines a mask as "any type of behavior that hides the inner child who contains our true feelings, natural abilities, and unique individuality." What masks do you think you have worn in the past or may still be wearing today? *EXAMPLE: I wear the mask of humor to keep people from seeing how shy I actually am.*

_____

_____

_____

_____

_____

Now let's take a closer look at some of the masks we wear.

OUTER MASKS, INNER MESSAGES

INDEPENDENCE

COMPLIANCE

"I don't need anyone."

"I'll be whatever you want me to be."

DEPENDENCY

ACHIEVEMENT

"I'll do whatever you want me to do as long as you take care of me."

"I'll work hard. Then you'll like me."

❑ *The Mask of Independence.* This mask can be epitomized in the "I don't need anyone" attitude. Here is the self-made man or woman who considers it a sign of weakness to ask for help or to admit any vulnerability. Such persons would invariably rather struggle alone than reach out to someone for assistance or comfort.

The mask of independence was one of my favorite masks. When Kathy and I were married, we decided to spend our honeymoon in beautiful Carmel, California. However, our honeymoon night found us in a hotel Kathy's dad had arranged for us. "I have great connections," he had told us. "I'll see that you have a fantastic room!"

So, dead tired, we pulled into the hotel parking lot, got out, and headed for the registration desk. Trying my best not to look like a newlywed, I confidently approached the desk clerk and signed in. He looked at me and inquired, "Is the woman behind you a friend?" That woman happened to be my wife of six hours! It seems I had forgotten to include her on the registration form. "No, she's not a friend," I mumbled, embarrassed. "She's my wife."

Duly humiliated, Kathy and I took the elevator to our room. As we stepped out onto our floor and gazed down the dark and dreary corridor, our fantasies of a luxury honeymoon suite plummeted. I wondered momentarily if we were in the condemned section. Our hopes nosedived even further when we entered our cramped room with its drab wallpaper and post-garage-sale furniture. My first thought was that Kathy's dad hated me or that his connection had been with the janitor. It was at least 90 degrees in that sardine-sized room. You guessed it—no air-conditioning! We didn't make love that night; instead, we perspired together!

Carmel made up for that dismal first night; it was beautiful. However, on the second day of our honeymoon I took a walk alone along Carmel's quaint streets, browsing among the various shops, when a very strange thought came to my mind. It was as if I were saying to myself, "If Kathy died, I would live my life just fine." Now that's not the kind of thought you share with your new bride unless, of course, you're looking for the world's shortest marriage. But that paradoxical thought reflected the way I lived much of my life. When I wanted to do something I often did it alone. I rarely shared my feelings with others. In fact, I honestly believed I didn't need anyone; I could depend on myself. My style was to be a loner.

The real truth was that my independent attitude was the mask that insulated me from needing anyone. I believed that needing others was the first step toward hurt and humiliation—something I wasn't about to let happen. My pseudo-independence protected my inner child from vulnerability and pain.

You might be curious as to why I married at all. The truth is that my inner child was faintly trying to express its loneliness behind the steel door of my concrete room. The false child, or my mask of independence, was trying to quiet that faint little voice by convincing me that even though I was married I wasn't really dependent on my wife emotionally or any other way. I was living in a world of self-deception. Obviously I loved Kathy very much and was dependent on her, but I didn't want to admit my dependence. And, of course, I needed loving and nurturing—lots of it—but I wouldn't admit it to myself or anyone else.

For the next many years of our married life, I remained emotionally distant. Once in a while my inner child would briefly appear. It has been only in the last 10 years of our marriage that I have realized how much I need to express my feelings and allow my wife and others to see the little child inside. Age has a sobering effect. It forces us to put our life in perspective and reevaluate what is truly important. I remember thinking, "If I don't do something about my pseudo-independence, I'll be a very lonely old man."

It's my impression that many men wear this mask of pseudo-independence. It can take the form of the super macho male who spends his time with "the guys" in countless sports activities but is never emotionally close to anyone, even his male friends. This same guy is probably very controlling with his wife. He wants dinner on the table when he gets home; he wants her by his side when he watches TV; he even gets angry when she reads a book instead of watching his favorite program. His dependence on her is the best kept secret on the block. His inner child needs attention and nurturance, but because he doesn't recognize this inner child, he cannot be direct and open about his emotional needs.

Usually the wife of the pseudo-independent man is a very nurturing woman who, in spite of his mask, sees his inner child and tries to rescue it. This type of male often takes a tremendous nosedive emotionally if his mate divorces him or dies. At such a time the true dependence and neediness of his inner child becomes evident.

One crusty old gentleman who came to me for counseling had recently lost his wife in an automobile accident. From our conversations I gathered that he had been a harsh, controlling, insensitive husband who showed his wife little affection except when they had sex. He had expected her always to be there for him, waiting on him and meeting his needs; but now she was gone. Her death hit him hard, leaving him with deep regret, guilt, and remorse. It took him a long time to mourn his loss and work through his grief. Slowly he saw how much he needed her emotionally and how little of himself he had given her. Now it was too late. Death and divorce are tough ways to discover the deep needs of your inner child.

Gentlemen, your wife needs to see your true feelings and know where you really "live" emotionally. So do your children. The greatest gift you can give to your loved ones is to share with them your own inner child—that deep, hidden part of you that defines who you are inside, what you need from those you love, and how you really feel. You can never experience genuine intimacy unless you share your true feelings. When you give this part of yourself away, you will receive your family's affections back a hundredfold to nurture your own inner child. The Apostle Paul, writing to the Galatians, underscored this principle of reaping abundantly from what we sow when he said:

> Do not be deceived, God is not mocked; for whatever a man sows, this he will also reap. For the one who sows to his own flesh shall from the flesh reap corruption, but the one who sows to the spirit shall from the Spirit reap eternal life. And let us not lose heart in doing good, for in due time we shall reap if we do not grow weary (Galatians 6:7-9).

Paul's focus in these verses was on the Judaizers who were teaching false doctrine. He was concerned that the Galatian Christians not be taken in by these false teachings. Paul's words offer a principle that is relevant to all aspects of our life. The Judaizers could be likened to the mask or false self we present to others, especially to our loved ones. This false face disguises or distorts the truth about ourselves; when we sow from this fake self, we reap corruption of our personal relationships. If, however, we sow from our true self, the inner self, the inner child, we will reap love, caring, and intimacy from others. Don't lose your motivation to share your true self, for if you persist you will reap your reward.

PERSONAL REFLECTION

■ Is the mask of independence one you wear? Think of two or three times recently when you came across to your spouse, friend, co-worker, or fellow church member with an "I don't need you (or anyone)" attitude. Write a little bit about each situation.

_____

_____

_____

_____

_____

_____

■ How do you get your emotional needs met? What do you most fear about being direct and open with another person about what you need emotionally? Why?

_____

_____

_____

_____

_____

■ Describe what "being close" with another person looks like to you. Is there anyone in your life at present with whom you feel safe being close? Why?

_____

_____

_____

_____

_____

Do you remember the song "Cat's in the Cradle," a bittersweet tale of damaged family relationships? It is about a father who never has time to spend with his child, who always promises *someday* . . . but that day never comes. Dad is always too busy with his own interests to respond to his child. Eventually Dad reaps what he sows. The song concludes when the father is older and wanting to spend time with his son. You guessed it. His son would like to spend time with ol' Dad, but he doesn't have the time—"maybe sometime soon, Dad, maybe sometime soon." Dad knows that line all too well; he coined it.

In case you think the concept of the inner child applies only to 20th-century people, let's look at a sensitive story in which Jesus uncovered the mask of independence and spoke to the inner child of a woman the Jews considered an outcast. We find the incident in John 4. Jesus, on His way to the city of Galilee, was weary from travel. In Samaria He came to Jacob's well and stopped to rest while His disciples went to look for food. It had been a hot and tiring journey, and it would feel good to sit and rest and refresh Himself with a cup of cool water. There was just one problem: the well was 100 feet deep and Jesus had nothing with which to draw the water. It just so happened—in God's providence—that a Samaritan woman approached the well seeking water.

Jewish rabbis did not greet women in public, and certainly not a Samaritan woman with a notorious lifestyle. Talk about a mask of independence. Put yourself in this woman's place. She was a woman who had been married many times and was likely unable to develop any kind of real intimacy with a man. She was considered an outcast by other women and no doubt had developed her mask of independence to protect her vulnerable inner child from any more hurt. When Jesus asked her for water, you can hear the defensiveness in her sarcastic response, "How is it that you being a Jew ask me for a drink, since I am a Samaritan woman?"

No doubt she said to herself, "I'm here to take care of myself. People don't care about me, and I don't care about them. Besides, He probably wants to use me just like the other men I've known."

But Jesus did not think of her as a *Samaritan*. He saw a person with a sad and hurting inner child thirsting for genuine intimacy and lasting love, warmth, and caring. He talked to her about living water that abides forever. Jesus knew that this woman's inner child needed to experience the love of her Creator, the only love that can provide lasting spiritual nourishment.

How did He express that love? By daring to speak with her and defy Jewish custom, by telling her He knew her sordid past without condemning her, and by not allowing her to veer off into an idle discussion of religious differences to escape the truth about Jesus and her need of spiritual rebirth.

Jesus touched this woman's inner child, transformed her life, and subsequently turned an entire city's heart toward God. Just as He spoke directly to the woman at the well—to that hidden, inner place where she really lived—so He wants to minister tenderly to your own needy inner child.

PERSONAL REFLECTION

■ What about this story of Jesus and the Samaritan woman touches you the most? If you had been at the well that day, what do you think Jesus would have said to you? Are you able to let Jesus minister tenderly to your needy inner child? Why?

_____

_____

_____

_____

_____

❏ *The Mask of Compliance.* The mask of compliance conveys the message, "I'll be whatever you want me to be." These people-pleasers refuse to make waves for they hate confrontation; they are quiet, agreeable, and eager for acceptance at almost any cost; they will squelch their own hopes and dreams to become doormats for others. By always giving in to others, they hope to feel good about themselves. Instead, their own individuality shrivels and withers away.

When our inner child is frightened and intimidated by our inner critical parent, compliance is the result. When perfect standards are not met, our inner critical parent may use threats of withdrawal of affection, humiliation, belittling, or other forms of devaluation to keep us in line.

Beth wore the mask of compliance. She sat on my office couch, stiff and proper, her makeup flawless and every hair in place, and her hands folded primly in her lap. She reminded me of a department store mannequin—an observation I naturally refrained from sharing with her. I sensed that her rigid posture and forced smile concealed underlying anxiety and depression.

"What brings you to counseling, Beth?" I inquired.

She sighed and shook her head. "I just don't have any energy. Getting out of bed seems so difficult for me, and when I think about having to go to work, I feel like pulling the covers over my head and never waking up."

Hearing the subtle cry of suicidal thinking, I asked Beth if she had ever considered taking her own life.

"Yes," she admitted, "especially recently. I feel trapped in my home and in my job. At times I feel so desperate I think the only way out is to end my life. But I can't do that. I'd hurt my family and . . . I'd disappoint God. I just wish I could go to sleep and never wake up."

In the sessions that followed, as I got to know Beth and her background, I discovered a very critical inner parent that had totally intimidated Beth's inner child. In defense, she had put on a mask of compliance, hoping that if she did what everybody wanted her to do she would feel good about herself. She was a true people-pleaser, a peace-at-any-price person who felt incredibly bad if someone showed the slightest disappointment in her.

"All my mother would have to do was give me a disapproving look and I would feel awful," Beth confided. "But my brother simply ignored Mom's scoldings. It took the belt to get his attention."

Clearly, Beth was a model child at home and the kind of student teachers pray for. Her parents thought she would make a good nurse; not wishing to disappoint them, she took a major in nursing which led to a job in a large metropolitan hospital.

"Did you like your work?" I asked.

"No," she said quickly. "I knew in college that nursing wasn't for me, but I just couldn't let my parents down."

"Tell me, Beth. When you were a young girl, did you ever have a dream about what you wanted to be?"

Her face brightened. "Oh, yes! I always dreamed of being a ballet dancer. I love ballet and interpretative dance. It's the only time I feel free to be myself." Even as Beth spoke, I could sense her inner child springing to life and growing excited. But she could allow herself to feel good for only a moment before her inner critical parent stepped in and shut off her "foolish talk."

I commented on her rather abrupt change in mood from excitement to sadness. "I get the impression you've heard somewhere that ballet is foolish and a waste of time."

Her reply didn't surprise me. "My parents felt that ballet was frivolous or simply recreational, not something you do for a living."

"How did their attitude make you feel?"

"Angry, I guess. I love ballet. It makes me feel so alive. But I felt I had to go into nursing for my parents' sake."

No wonder Beth was in conflict. A very creative woman possessing natural coordination, rhythm, and a sense of music, she found that ballet expressed her natural talent. But her inner child was so suppressed that she was unable to express these God-given abilities. Convinced that her true feelings and desires were not acceptable, Beth wore the mask of compliance so that Mom and Dad would approve of her.

Like Beth, we all need emotional nourishment. We will get it either by being who we are and finding that others respond warmly to us— or by being who we aren't, by complying in order to receive the emotional stroking we need.

Beth's mask of compliance greatly affected her definition of God. In her mind, He possessed the same traits as her inner critical parent; that is, He was harsh, judgmental, intimidating, and demanded perfection—qualities that produced in Beth an outward compliance to His will, but not true heartfelt obedience. This was obvious during one of our therapy sessions when she told me, "I was always terrified of God. As a child I remember sitting in church fearful that I wasn't going to heaven and fighting the urge to walk down the aisle when the pastor invited people to accept the Lord. I'd accepted Him over and over and yet I still wasn't convinced it had taken. My parents and Sunday School teachers and even the youth pastor assured me that if I had placed my faith and trust in Jesus, I was truly God's child and would spend eternity in heaven. But if that were so, why was I still so scared of God?"

Beth flashed a genuine smile. "It wasn't until I got into therapy that I realized the God I thought I knew was really my own inner critical parent. I could never please that inner parent no matter how hard I tried to comply, and in the same way I felt I could never please

God. I'm just now beginning to see that the God of the Bible loves me and accepts me just the way I am. When I'm able to let that truth sink in, I feel a deep gratitude and an excitement about my life and my relationship with God."

Gradually Beth learned the difference between compliance and true obedience to God. Obedience led her to a more consistent walk with God that came from her heart or, more specifically, from her inner child who felt loved and valued for who she was. Disobedience caused her to experience a loss of that loved and valued feeling because a barrier called sin blocked her fellowship with her loving Heavenly Father. Because of her love for God, which again sprang from her inner child, she desired to restore that intimate relationship with Him, so she confessed her sins and asked for His forgiveness. As she experienced the cleansing power of His forgiveness, she felt her relationship with God growing stronger, more satisfying, more intimate.

Beth came to see that her compliance, on the other hand, resulted from her fear of rejection, disapproval, and humiliation of her inner child. It caused her to see God as a harsh and critical Father whom she began to resent, and thus she fell into what I call the repent-and-repeat syndrome. She consistently kept doing things she felt God didn't want her to do; she would feel guilty and repented before God did a number on her; but almost immediately she found herself repeating the misdeed.

Such a cycle can go on for years. What is really happening here? Actually, when we act out of compliance, we are not truly repentant for our behavior; our heart is not sorrowful because we have offended our beloved Savior. Rather, our hidden motive is anger with God that stirs within us the desire to rebel. Yet we are afraid of His retaliation, so we quickly repent before a bolt of lightning hits us. Only the love of God ministering to the inner child can remove fear and anger and stop the repeat-and-repent cycle.

PERSONAL
REFLECTION

■ In what ways do you relate to the description Dr. Dickinson gives of the person who wears the mask of compliance?

_____

_____

_____

_____

_____

■ Are you a people-pleaser? Make a list of people you are trying to please at present. How successful are you at keeping them happy?

_____

_____

_____

_____

_____

■ Who from your past is the person you were never able to keep happy? What is it you want from that person so much so that you are willing to "sacrifice" your very self to have it?

_____

_____

_____

_____

_____

■ Has your need for acceptance and approval impacted your ability to relate to God in an open, vulnerable way? How?

_____

_____

_____

_____

■ In what ways do you identify with this statement: "True obedience comes from the heart—a heart that feels loved and valued for who he/she is"? Are you convinced at a heartfelt level that God loves and values you for who you are? Why or why not?

_____

_____

_____

_____

_____

_____

■ Try to think of as many truths from Scripture as you can that reinforce the reality that God loves you and places great value on you as His child. Write down everything that comes to mind.

_____

_____

_____

_____

_____

❑ *The Mask of Dependency.* A person who wears the mask of dependency virtually promises, "I'll do whatever you want me to do as long as you take care of me." Ultimately he is willing to surrender his rights, his freedom, his very personhood, in exchange for security and protection. He will go to almost any length to avoid the challenges and responsibilities of the adult world, desiring instead to be taken care of, even at the expense of his own development as an individual.

One of my patients who wore the mask of dependency was Cindy, a petite blonde whose conservative dress somehow matched her short, straight hair and limpid blue eyes. Her husband, Bill, had sought out marital therapy because of Cindy's lack of communication and low sexual interest. During their first session, Cindy sat quietly next to her husband while he did all the talking. Whenever I attempted to direct a question to Cindy, she looked at Bill as if to get his approval, then tentatively began to speak. But Bill inevitably interrupted and completed her thoughts.

As our session came to a close, I remarked to Bill that he seemed to do a lot of talking for his wife. He quickly defended himself by insisting that Cindy never had much to say anyway and that if he didn't speak, no one would say anything.

But I had my own opinion about Cindy's reluctance to speak. It's been my experience that when you genuinely show an interest in people and what they have to say, they talk. So I invited Cindy to attend the next session alone. She agreed. And what a contrast! At first, however, Cindy entered the office hesitantly and stood in the middle of the room until I invited her to sit down. She seemed nervous and had a lost-puppy-dog look, as if she didn't know what to do without her master/husband.

I began the hour by saying, "Cindy, I learned a lot about your husband in our first session, but I'm really curious about you. I sensed from your facial expressions that you were feeling some things you never expressed in words."

That was all the encouragement Cindy needed. For the next 45 minutes, she talked about herself and her relationship with Bill. She had come from an unhappy home where her father dominated and terrorized the rest of the family. Her mother was too weak to stand up to him, so there was no one to offset his controlling influence. At 18, Cindy met Bill at a school dance and immediately felt an attraction to him. Within a year she ran away from home and married him. At first she thought Bill was the exact opposite of her father, but gradually she realized the two men were very much alike. She found herself becoming dependent on Bill just as she had been on her dad.

Bill was strong, always knew what to do, and was an authority on any subject. Cindy accepted the fact that as long as she was the dependent little girl, he would take care of her, tell her what to think and do, select her clothes, and generally run her life for her. She could have a form of love and security in exchange for being a nonperson. But Cindy's inner child was so subdued and overpowered that there was no vitality or enjoyment in her existence. Even as I talked with her that day, I sensed that her inner child wanted out but that fear kept her trapped.

Marital therapy proved very difficult for both Cindy and Bill. During the early phases of treatment, counseling only increased the conflicts between them. This is actually a common situation because, as one person begins to change, it puts pressure on the other person to change. Change generates anxiety and uncertainty. As Cindy opened up and began talking about her thoughts and feelings, and as she recognized her own talents and abilities, Bill's sense of security was shaken. The more she allowed her inner child to be expressed, the more he realized that his control over her was diminishing.

Bill was at a point where he could either let Cindy express herself and rebuild their relationship on a more mature foundation, or use intimidation to force her back into the mold of the submissive wife he married. At first Bill did what any of us might do—he tried to return to the old way of relating. But with much support and understanding, he relinquished his need to control Cindy and found that as she grew as a person and became less dependent, the relationship grew stronger. At times he stepped in and tried to dominate, but as the months passed he felt more comfortable in talking out his feelings with Cindy than in hiding his fears and insecurity behind his domination.

The transition was hard for Cindy too. She had to grow up and let go of her overdependency. She could no longer use this trait to avoid the anxieties of being a fallible human being in a complex world filled with conflict, pressures, and daily crises. She had paid a dear price for her dependence on Bill—the freedom to enjoy her inner child and the vitality of being an independent person in her own right.

With a mixture of tears, anger, frustration, and dedication to their marriage, Cindy and Bill began to establish a relationship that allowed both partners to be themselves. They created an atmosphere in which the child within each of them was free to be openly and directly expressed. Cindy conversed more with Bill because he showed greater respect for her thoughts, feelings, and ideas. Her sexual desire increased because she felt that Bill appreciated her for who she was and thus she felt more love for him.

PERSONAL REFLECTION

■ Do you wear the mask of dependency? If so, what "price" have you been willing to pay to wear this mask? Are you ready to give up your need for security and protection and become an independent person? Why or why not?

_____

_____

_____

_____

_____

_____

■ What do you most fear about giving up your mask of dependency?

_____

_____

_____

_____

Does the mask of dependency influence our relationship with God? The answer is a resounding yes! In Cindy's case she related to

God much like she did to her father and husband—by feeling fearful and intimidated. She wanted God to take care of her in an infantile way so that she would not have to face the challenges of being a growing adult in a world that required making decisions, resolving conflicts, being vulnerable, and taking risks. You might find yourself asking at this point, "But doesn't God promise to take care of us?" Yes, He does. Perhaps the psalmist said it best:

> Even though I walk through the valley of the shadow of death, I will fear no evil; for Thou art with me; Thy rod and Thy staff, they comfort me (Psalm 23:4).

Did you notice that he says "through the valley" rather than over, under, or around the valley? The comfort God gives us comes in our own shadow of death, whether it be illness, a profound loss, emotional problems, financial struggles, or difficult relationships with our mate, children, friends, or relatives. Wearing the mask of dependency is our attempt to protect our frightened inner child from the normal dangers of living by "hiding our heads" and asking God to keep the bad things from happening to us. Only when we honestly bring before our Heavenly Father our inner child's fears, anxieties, disappointments, and frustrations, can we feel nourished and strengthened and able to grow through the trials of life.

PERSONAL REFLECTION

■ In what ways, if any, do you identify with Cindy's view of God? What fears, anxieties, disappointments and frustrations do you want to bring to God today? List them.

My Fears _____

_____

_____

_____

_____

My Anxieties _____

_____

_____

_____

My Disappointments _____

_____

_____

_____

My Frustrations _____

_____

_____

_____

❑ *The Mask of Achievement.* Those who wear the mask of achievement say by their actions, "I'll work hard. Then you will like me." But such workaholics are usually so busy trying to accomplish impossible goals that they inevitably send themselves down a path of self-destruction. Those they love and want most to impress are usually left strewn by the wayside, ignored and deserted.

Tim was the prototype of the workaholic, your basic Type A personality. Talk about money, status, influence, and power—he had it all. Just trying to find time to schedule our first therapy session was a challenge in itself. During that session, he seemed like a time bomb about to explode into a thousand pieces. He sat stiffly on the edge of his seat, ready to spring up at any moment. His facial muscles were taut and he spoke in a staccato, frequently stopping in mid-sentence as if several thoughts were coming at once. He glanced frequently at his watch.

Within a few sessions it was evident that Tim was the kind of guy who could take an enjoyable activity and turn it into a demanding, high-pressure experience. When he talked about his newly discovered interest in racquetball, he complained, "I can't find anybody who will play with me. My friends tell me I'm too intense, and they don't like it when I get angry after missing a shot or losing a game."

Tim's intensity was obvious in everything he did. His family felt it, as did friends and business associates. They didn't want to get too close to him for fear he would humiliate them with his heated words and short temper.

Tim's spiritual life was negatively affected by his obsessive need to be an overachiever. He found it difficult to trust God. It was much easier to take the spiritual ball and run with it according to his own game plan. Tim professed faith in God and genuinely believed with his head. But his inner child, locked inside by fear and anger and smothered by the mask of achievement, prevented him from emotionally experiencing the love of God in his life. He couldn't believe that God or anyone else could truly love that scared, inadequate person inside him. So, in his rush for success, he buried his inner child in a tower of achievements along a spiraling road to self-destruction.

Let's look more closely at Tim's symptoms. His achievement-oriented behavior had all the classic indicators of the workaholic.

√ *First, there was his need to accomplish more than other people.* I realized that Tim's need to achieve was the result of poor self-esteem which he tried to mask with overcompensation. It was as if he were saying, "How can I possibly be inadequate? See how much I've accomplished!" The problem was that Tim's high achievement goals were motivated by his inner critical parent who continually told him he was inadequate. Tim kept trying to prove his inner parent wrong by setting unreachable goals. Because he could never attain all of them, he could never escape a gnawing sense of inadequacy.

√ *A second indicator was Tim's tendency to be overly dominant in relationships with others, from his family to his business associates.* You could see it in whatever he set out to do; from a simple game of Ping-Pong to closing a business deal, he was ruthless. He never let people get the best of him because, if they did, his inner child would experience nagging feelings of inadequacy.

√ *A third indicator was Tim's underlying anger, even in trivial incidents.* He had a short fuse while he waited at a traffic light, when service was slow, or when he lost a game of handball. Tim's hidden hostility expressed itself in his vocabulary, for he used words that were devaluing to others, like, "That's stupid . . . ridiculous. He's idiotic . . . dumb."

√ *A fourth symptom of Tim's workaholism was his need to do everything in a hurry.* To see how many things he could accomplish in a day, he would write faster, talk faster, read faster, eat faster, and drive faster. Along with his compulsion to hurry, he always tried to do two or more things at once. He would shave in the morning while reading an article in a business magazine, or talk on the phone while jotting notes to himself about another corporate deal. While driving to work he made appointments on his car phone and listened in vain to tapes on how to relax. Fast-food restaurants were designed for people like Tim: Talk to the box, grab a burger, inhale it on the run, and give one mighty belch without losing a beat.

√ *The last of Tim's classic symptoms was his steady drive toward self-destruction.* The quality of his work suffered because he could not keep up his frantic pace. He caught colds easily and they hung on for weeks; he felt a loss of energy which prompted him to work harder, and that only made matters worse. By the time he made his appointment with me, he was depressed and complained of chest pains. His career was in jeopardy. Emotionally and physically, Tim was on the verge of collapse.

I strongly urged Tim to consult his family physician about his chest pains. He argued that he didn't have time to wait in a doctor's office, but finally went anyway. He wasn't happy to learn that his pains were stress-related. He would have to make major changes in his lifestyle or pay the consequences, physically and emotionally.

Therapy offered Tim his first real chance to let someone else see his inner child. Always before he had been so busy trying to reach impossible goals that the people who knew him never glimpsed his inner needs and vulnerabilities. Slowly Tim began to trust me and reveal the person he was inside. For a time he made real progress. Unfortunately, Tim received a promotion that required a great deal of traveling, so he dropped out of therapy. It will be all too easy for Tim to fall back into his destructive lifestyle, unless he seriously reorganizes his life in such a way that he allows his inner child its rightful place. The last time I saw Tim he was still running on fast-forward.

PERSONAL REFLECTION

■ Would those people who know you best describe you as a "workaholic" or an "overachiever"? Why not find out? Ask one or two of your closest friends if they would use either of those terms to describe you. Ask them why. Jot down what they tell you in the space provided below.

_____

_____

_____

_____

_____

■ Which symptoms of workaholism describe you? Check all that apply. Be honest.

Symptoms of Workaholism
❏ The need to accomplish more than other people.
❏ Sets unrealistic or unreachable goals.
❏ A tendency to be overly dominant in relationships with others.
❏ Underlying anger, often giving the appearance of being a person

with a "short fuse."
❑ The need to do everything in a hurry.
❑ A steady drive toward self-destruction.

■ Which of these symptoms is costing you the most at present? Describe exactly what it's costing you.

_____

_____

_____

_____

_____

_____

■ Have you ever thought this: "I find it hard to believe that God or anyone else could truly love me." What about yourself do you see as being unlovable? Be as specific as you can.

_____

_____

_____

_____

_____

_____

_____

The four masks we've considered are only a few of the many people can wear to hide who they really are inside. Think about yourself and those you love. Can you discover other masks you hide behind? Remember, a mask is any type of behavior that hides your true feelings, natural abilities, and unique individuality. Behind all masks is a wounded, angry, and needy inner child. The tragic result of wearing a mask is that while you think you are protecting yourself, you are actually preventing yourself from experiencing true intimacy with others and with God.

PERSONAL
REFLECTION

WOUNDED, ANGRY,

NEEDY INNER CHILD

■ What other masks do YOU wear to protect your wounded, angry, needy inner child? Name them by writing words for them across the mask above.

■ What is the most important insight you've gained as the result of working the material in this chapter?

_____

_____

_____

_____

_____

_____

_____

PRAYERFUL REFLECTION

■ To get in touch with your inner child you need to surrender your protective masks to God. Try to identify in one or two words the mask you wear most often. Then when you are ready, write a prayer of surrender to God, asking Him to help you take whatever steps are necessary for you to get more in touch with your inner child.

Lord Jesus,

_____

_____

_____

_____

_____

_____

_____

_____

PERSONAL RENEWAL

■ Nothing about who you are or what you've done surprises God. He made you and planned out every day of your life. There's no need to wear any mask for His sake. Think about that this week as you spend time reading and reflecting on Psalm 139:1-10, 13-18 (NCV).

Lord, You have examined me and know all about me. You know when I get up. You know my thoughts before I think them. You know where I go and where I lie down. You know everything I do. Lord, even before I say a word, You already know it. You are all around me—in front and in back—and have put Your hand on me. Your knowledge is amazing to me; it is more than I can understand. Where can I go to get away from Your Spirit? Where can I run from You? If I go up to the heavens, You are there. If I lie down in the grave, You are there. If I rise with the sun in the east and settle in the west beyond the sea, even there You would guide me. With Your right hand You would hold me. . . .You made my whole being; You formed me in my mother's body. I praise You because You made me in an amazing and wonderful way. What You have done is won- derful. I know this very well. You saw my bones being formed as I took shape in my mother's body. When I was put together there,

You saw my body as it was formed. All the days planned for me were written in Your book before I was one day old. God, Your thoughts are precious to me. They are so many! If I could count them, they would be more than all the grains of sand. When I wake up, I am still with You.

Chapter 4
Why We Feel So Alone with Others

In a room filled with people, have you ever felt utterly alone? Have you found yourself sitting across the table from someone you cared about, nervously trying to keep a conversation going for fear you might run out of something to say? Have you walked alone in a shopping mall or along the beach watching others share moments of intimacy and sensed a deep emptiness and longing for the closeness of another human being?

PERSONAL REFLECTION

■ Do you relate to any of the scenarios described in the paragraph above? Describe the loneliest experience you've ever had with one other person or with a group of people. Why do you think you felt so alone?

_____

_____

_____

_____

_____

_____

Social psychologist, Philip Zimbardo, tells of a handsome, successful young television director who sought help because he was unable to relate to a woman after the fifth date. For the first five dates he was exciting and entertaining because he had rehearsed conversation to impress his date. But he struck out when he ran out of scenarios and had to be himself.

Sadly, he's not alone. Many people have never learned to be intimate, to form a close relationship with another person, to make disclosures about their past, their fears, their frustrations, and future plans—in short, to reveal the private self behind the public mask. Disclosure presupposes trust which in turn is nourished by sharing; this trust gives substance and meaning to intimate contacts.[1]

PERSONAL REFLECTION

■ How easy is it for you to form a close relationship with another person? On the continuum below, circle the number that best describes your ability to be close to another person.

1	2	3	4	5
IMPOSSIBLE	NEARLY IMPOSSIBLE	BECOMING MORE POSSIBLE	POSSIBLE	VERY POSSIBLE

■ Describe the most intimate relationship you have at present.

_____

_____

_____

_____

_____

_____

■ True intimacy comes in learning to make disclosures about our past, our fears, our frustrations, and our future plans. What keeps you from freely and candidly disclosing who you are to other people?

_____

_____

_____

_____

_____

■ Can you think of a time when you tried to self-disclose to another person and felt like you failed? Describe what happened. Do you recall having tried and succeeded in self-disclosing to another person? Also describe that experience.

_____

_____

_____

_____

_____

_____

Many writers have suggested that loneliness is the major emotional problem of the 80s and 90s. From my experience as a psychologist and educator, I'm inclined to agree. It seems that people today are more intimately acquainted with their computers, television sets, electronic games, hobbies, and favorite pastimes than with the people in their lives.

The church is not immune to this problem. There are many lonely people in Bible-believing churches; they hear outstanding teaching, yet feel isolated and alone in the congregation. The Apostle Paul, writing to the Corinthians about spiritual gifts and the church declared:

> that there should be no division in the body, but that the members should have the same care for one another. And if one member suffers, all the members suffer with it; if one member is honored, all the members rejoice with it (1 Corinthians 12:25-26).

Would anybody in your church know if you were suffering? Would you feel safe in sharing you needs, hurts, and concerns? The closest we usually come to sharing is in "unspoken prayer requests." Now, really, how can you get excited about unspoken requests? You don't know how to pray for such vague generalities, nor do you feel any personal relatedness to the needy people involved because they remain virtual strangers. Could "unspoken requests" be a symptom of the lack of intimacy among Bible-believing Christians? If God ever slumbers—which He doesn't, it must be during prayer meetings. I believe our lack of intimacy in the social and personal arenas of our lives spills over into our fellowship with other Christians. This is indeed sad.

PERSONAL REFLECTION

■ Have you ever felt isolated and alone in your fellowship with others in your church? Give an example.

_____

_____

■ Do you feel safe sharing your needs, hurts, and concerns with others in the church? Why?

_____

_____

■ What would make it easier for you to share your personal concerns with the people in your church?

_____

_____

For much of my adult life I have taught Sunday School classes, and I have felt a deep need to create an atmosphere of safety in my classes to encourage personal sharing. Only then can we as members become part of one another's lives, thus living out Jesus' commandment to love one another by sharing one another's burdens. After all, how can I share your burden if I don't know what it is and you don't feel safe to confide it?

I remember teaching a class of couples in the 40- to 60-age range. When I began, the prayertime was short and very impersonal. The president would stand up and ask for requests. Someone would suggest we remember the government, the sewer problems, Aunt Matilda's hemorrhoids, and a host of nonpersonal issues. I'm not suggesting that Aunt Matilda's problem was not a concern to her, but I didn't know dear Matilda; she wasn't a member of my class; I couldn't get involved in her life. But I did want to connect with the people right in that room.

I recall wondering how many of my class members were in emotional pain. Some of them were having marital problems; some were lonely and afraid; others were deeply concerned about their grown children, but nobody was talking about their personal lives and concerns.

At the time I was in great need of prayer support myself. I was in graduate school completing my doctorate and working full-time; I was also trying to be a husband and father while maintaining a private practice. Many times I felt overwhelmed with the responsibilities.

I realized that the members of my class were not used to sharing personal concerns. They had the mind-set that personal matters were private and best kept to oneself. I began to change this attitude in class, slowly and patiently, by exposing my needs to them. I have learned that you model the behavior you want from others, especially with people who are not used to sharing their private lives.

There were a number of times when I felt painfully exposed because I sensed that the class members were uncomfortable with my needs. But I believed in the atmosphere of intimacy I was trying to establish, so I continued to risk rejection. Slowly, sometimes falteringly, people began to share their burdens. They opened their broken hearts and confided their hurts and hopes and disappointments. Within the year, our class atmosphere had changed from a cool impersonality to a genuine warmth and compassion. It was gratifying to see people honestly expressing their concern and then talking to one another after class to see how their prayer requests were being answered. Their encouragement and prayer support for me personally gave me strength to continue my endeavors. There were times when the entire Sunday School hour was taken up with requests and real intercessory prayer. On many occasions I was moved to tears by the earnestness and sincerity of class members as they prayed for one another.

I follow this same format with the class I am now teaching. It is my conviction that the church should be a refuge for all of us, but perhaps especially for those who have been damaged early in life by abuse or a lack of love. However, if we continue to wear our masks in the church environment, we will continue to be alone. This is not what God intends for us. For many, a loving and caring church can be the first place where it is safe to unmask and grow toward intimacy. But this doesn't just happen. There are principles and practices that bring about intimacy and relatedness. Let's look at some ways that intimacy develops in both our personal and church life.

PERSONAL
REFLECTION

■ What "masks" do you think the people in your church wear? What "church masks" have you worn? Describe what an "intimate church" looks and feels like to you.

_____

_____

_____

_____

_____

_____

To Know You Is to Love You—somebody reading this title may be saying, "You're crazy. If you really knew what I'm like, you would probably tell me to get lost." That type of statement is typical of the inner critical parent we often project onto others. In other words, if I don't like myself (my inner child), nobody else will like it either. As you recall, a mask provides both a protection for the injured inner child and a means of gaining approval from others. However, the approval one receives while wearing his mask does not feed and nourish the inner child; rather it only reinforces the continuance of the mask and perpetuates aloneness. The inner child is fed only when a person lets others see it directly, as it really is, but this involves the risk of inner exposure.

PERSONAL
REFLECTION

◙ Have you ever thought this: "If you really knew me, you wouldn't like me"? What "hidden" truth(s) about yourself, if revealed, do you think would cause another person to reject you? Write down anything about yourself you are afraid to disclose to another person. *NOTE: Exposing our hidden parts by writing them down or sharing them with safe people can bring healing in our lives. Therefore, the more honest you can be in answering this question, the more opportunity you have ultimately of finding healing at the inner child level.*

_____

_____

_____

_____

_____

_____

_____

_____

_____

_____

When I was in high school and college, one of my masks was athletics. I achieved a certain degree of success in both water polo and basketball. I desperately needed this recognition and approval, but it was never enough. I always had to be better than others to maintain my validation. At the same time there was a deep sense of inadequacy that kept me from using my full potential. I never thought I was good enough. This struggle between my inner child and critical parent would at times paralyze me. My identity was shaped around my being an acclaimed athlete instead of the person I really was inside.

A mask I wore later on was related to my identity as a psychology teacher and then as a psychologist. My first teaching job was in a community college. Fresh out of graduate school, I found myself teaching both younger and older college students and adults. Talk about anxiety! Afraid that someone would discover how little I knew, I prepared copious notes to keep from running out of material. That way there would be no time for questions I couldn't answer. Inside, I continued to feel like a fraud. I figured I didn't belong in this profession because I wasn't smart enough. No matter what I did I was plagued by this inner sense of inadequacy, but I could never let anybody know how I felt.

Considering my negative feelings, you may wonder how I advanced. God used my natural talents and intelligence in spite of my deep sense of inadequacy. But instead of enjoying and appreciating the talents God had given me, I constantly belittled myself and focused on my uncertainties. It was only through my own therapy and the love of significant people in my life that I began to believe that the child inside of me was worth knowing and loving. This process could not have happened apart from my willingness to expose my inner child and to challenge the destructive messages of my inner critical parent. This brings us to the importance of knowledge, for without knowledge there can be no intimacy. What kind of knowledge? The knowledge that comes from self-disclosure.

PERSONAL REFLECTION

■ Do you believe that the inner child in you is worth knowing and loving? Affirm your own value by writing a brief paragraph expressing why you are worth knowing and loving. Be honestly affirming of yourself.

_____

_____

_____

_____

_____

_____

_____

In self-disclosure, you share the thoughts and the feelings you are experiencing within you right this minute. Let me give you two examples of disclosure.

At this very minute I am *thinking* about how far behind I am in writing this book. There's so much I have to do this week that I don't think I can get it all done. It will be hard to sit down at my computer to work on this chapter, especially after my relaxing weekend. I'd rather be on my boat watching the sun set, savoring the cool ocean breeze, and smelling the salty air.

Now let me give you a second disclosure. Right now I am *feeling* anxious. I need to get moving on this book and it seems to be going so slowly. It frustrates me that I personally resist some of the very material I am writing about. I'm not very open to my feelings right now. I wonder if I'm avoiding something inside me that I don't want to deal with. I feel sad right now too. My wife and I had such a close, relaxing weekend, but tomorrow it's back to work—ten patients to see, some very difficult. Not enough time for my needs. Weekend too short . . . not ready to go to work . . . need more emotional nourishment for my needy child inside.

As you read and compare these two disclosures, which of them gives you a more intimate glimpse into me as a person? Which gives you the better insight into my inner self—my inner child? Which allows you to know me better? The second one, you say? You're right. What made the difference? If you look carefully, the first disclosure said nothing about how I was feeling inside. It told you more about what I was thinking. The second disclosure revealed four feelings—anxiety, frustration, sadness, and a wistful longing (for that relaxing weekend!), plus recognition of my neediness. In my definition of self-disclosure I emphasize feelings over thoughts because feelings tell us the present state of our inner child, and it is through the inner child that we develop intimacy with others and they with us.

PERSONAL REFLECTION

■ Now it's your turn to try this thinking–feeling exercise. Jot down the thoughts and feelings you are experiencing within you at this minute. If expressing feelings is unfamiliar to you, or uncomfortable for you, you may struggle with this writing exercise. But give it a try! Do the best you can for now. Meaningful self-disclosure takes time and practice.

_____

_____

_____

_____

_____

_____

_____

Another aspect of self-disclosure is the part your past plays. Did you know that you can cleverly hide your present feelings and avoid intimacy by focusing on your past hurts and painful experiences?

What I want to underscore here is that preoccupation with the past—even the very recent past—can obscure present feelings. I encounter this problem frequently with my patients. Often they will give me a blow-by-blow account of the week or try to pick up where we left off in the previous session. If I let that happen, they may walk out of the session without addressing what they are feeling at the moment. When I sense this happening, I usually say something like, "Mary, right now I notice my mind wandering. That usually means I'm hearing your words but your feelings are somewhere else." Most of the time I'm right, and Mary is free to discuss the uncomfortable feelings she is hiding.

You may wonder if the past has any value in intimate self-disclosure. Yes, so long as it helps to clarify what you are presently feeling. Let me illustrate. Suppose you develop a close relationship with someone, and the two of you consider yourselves very much in love. Then one day, without warning or explanation, this person stops calling and avoids all contact with you. You feel very hurt, angry, and confused, wondering whether you said something wrong or misjudged the relationship. Then you finally decide to confront this person about his or her feelings and gradually the truth comes out: "Yes, I love you very much, but several years ago I was deeply hurt in a relationship. The one I loved left me for someone else. I vowed I'd never be hurt again. It was my fear of being hurt that made me break off my relationship with you."

With such a frank disclosure, the two of you can begin to address your heartfelt needs and rebuild the relationship on much firmer ground. This is an example of how the past helps to clarify present feelings. However, revelation of all your past hurts and traumatic experiences, without some connection to your current feelings, is not part of intimate self-disclosure.

Think of the number of times important people in your life ask you how you are and you say "Fine!" when things aren't fine. In our close friendships we constantly feel various emotions. But all too often I hear spouses say they never know what is going on inside their mates. Women especially say this about their husbands. We males have grown up with the notion that men should be tough—the strong, silent type—and that to show feelings is a sign of weakness.

I rarely saw my dad show warm, tender feelings. I saw his anger and impatience, but seldom his tears. Recently my mother gave me a letter I wrote my father some years ago in which I told him I was 40 years old before I ever heard him say he loved me or needed me. Of course, I knew he loved me by the way he provided for me and by his interest in my various activities. But it took 40 years for me to hear the words, "Son, I love you." For much of my childhood I felt I was a real disappointment to Dad. I desperately needed to *hear the words* that he cared for me. As I grew older I understood why it was so hard for Dad to show his emotions, for his father had also been a stern, private man who had never shown his son his inner feelings. I often wonder what our relationship might have been like if we had felt free to communicate what we felt inside.

PERSONAL REFLECTION

■ Do a quick *feelings inventory.* Are you obscuring any present feelings because you are preoccupied with the past—even the very recent past? What feelings have you felt in the past 24 hours? Jot those feelings down and the situations that caused those feelings to surface.

_____

_____

_____

_____

_____

_____

A lack of intimate self-disclosure affects not only our relationship with family and friends, but more important, it affects our relationship with God. When we have a difficult time sharing our feelings with others, we are likely to encounter the same problem in our prayer life. In my own prayertime, I find that I tend to pray for all the "right" things. But talk to God about my feelings? That's difficult. Does He really want to know? Doesn't He already know? Yes, He does, but it's important that we tell Him, for we are the ones who benefit. Our ability to tell Him how we feel reveals the kind of relationship we have with Him. He is our gracious, loving Heavenly Father. He wants us to come to Him with our inner child and pour out our hearts to Him.

> Let us therefore draw near with confidence to the throne of grace, that we may receive mercy and may find grace to help in time of need (Hebrews 4:16).

What an invitation! God's grace and mercy are exactly what we need when we feel sad, alone, scared, angry, frustrated, or anxious. Imagine the closeness and privilege of such a father–child relationship when God Himself invites us to confide in Him with confidence and intimacy in our times of need.

PERSONAL REFLECTION

■ How easy is it for you to come to God in prayer and pour out your heart to Him? Describe a time when you did this. How did you feel after you prayed in this way? If you find it difficult to approach God in an intimate, self-disclosing way, what do you think keeps you from being able to do this?

_____

_____

_____

_____

_____

There are three basic principles of self-disclosure that bring about intimacy in our relationships with God and other people.

√ *First, the more we disclose, the more we are liked.* You may be saying, "I'm not going to put myself in a vulnerable situation where someone can take a clear shot at me. I need my masks. No one's going to attack *my* inner child. I couldn't handle it. I'll take loneliness over rejection."

Such a defensive way of thinking often reflects the painful experiences of the past. But when we self-disclose—that is, reveal our inner selves to others—they usually respond with empathy and caring.

Professional people, especially pastors, psychologists, and mental health workers, often have great difficulty in being open with colleagues. Part of the problem is that we don't want to look incompetent to our peers. Our assumption is that others do everything right; they never make mistakes or act in a manner unbecoming to their professions.

At our counseling center we set aside times for our staff to talk about personal or professional problems and feelings. On one occasion I was struggling with my feelings toward a patient I had counseled for some time. I cared for this person and was fearful that some of my feelings might be sexually oriented. I felt guilty and wondered how I could be of any help to her when I was baffled by my own conflicting emotions. I was reluctant to share my dilemma with my colleagues, but I knew if I didn't, my own effectiveness as a therapist would be hindered. With fear and anxiety I confessed what I was feeling, knowing I risked rejection or disfavor from my peers.

Surprisingly, that time of sharing proved beneficial for my associates and me. I discovered that what I labeled as sexual feelings were, in fact, feelings of protectiveness. I wanted to protect my patient from pain and abuse and comfort her inner child so she wouldn't hurt anymore. I might not have gained this insight if I hadn't talked the problem over with my colleagues and received their feedback. Afterward, several of them told me they felt closer to me because I had risked sharing my feelings with them. I showed I trusted them and valued their input.

In a variety of situations I have seen my own self-disclosure bring closeness and compassion to hurting people in my Sunday School class during prayertime, in homes where couples risk sharing their hurts with each other, and in families where parents disclose to their children some of the mistakes they've made. Occasionally someone may feel uncomfortable with my disclosures, but for the most part the responses are positive and the risk of exposure well worth taking.

PERSONAL
REFLECTION

■ Are you able to relate in a positive way to the personal example Dr. Dickinson shares here? Briefly describe a time when you self-disclosed, risking rejection, and found that the person or group you disclosed to responded with empathy and caring.

_____

_____

_____

_____

_____

READER'S NOTE: Risking rejection through self-disclosure is never easy. If you struggle with this, then the first step for you may be to find one person or a small group (such as an anonymous Twelve-step group) with whom you feel safe. Jot down the name of at least one person you trust. You should perceive this person as someone who can be objective and is unquestionably able to maintain confidences.

√ *Here is the second principle of self-disclosure: The more we self-disclose, the more others will self-disclose.* When we communicate with one another, we subtly set up ground rules that let the other person know just how much personal disclosure is allowed. Terry and her husband, Cliff, came to see me because, as Terry put it, "We just don't communicate with each other. Instead of talking things out, all we do is fight." Terry was a bright, articulate woman; yet in her husband's presence she was timid and cautious, choosing her words carefully so as not to set her husband off on an angry tirade. Cliff was a hard-working, no-nonsense man, proud of the contracting business he had built from the ground up. To Cliff, life was either black or white; gray didn't exist. His parents had never talked about feelings, just about hard work and responsibility. Cliff didn't know how to disclose his feelings to Terry and became defensive when she attempted to share with him on a personal level. It was as if Cliff considered her disclosures a personal attack on him. His underlying message to her was, "Don't tell me how you feel. Just accept things the way they are." So it wasn't long before Terry shut down in the sharing-of-feelings department and began to feel isolated and angry with Cliff.

In working with Cliff, I often felt myself walking a fine line between helping him understand his feelings and stirring up his frustrations over his lack of understanding. It helped Cliff when I shared some of my personal difficulties in identifying certain emotions. Cliff responded by gradually sharing some of his feelings that had been buried for years. My disclosures gave him permission to let his inner child speak about feelings. Again, by modeling intimate disclosure we invite others to share on the same level.

PERSONAL REFLECTION

■ In what ways do you identify with the communication pattern going on between Cliff and Terry? Write down anything you've observed in your communication patterns with other people, especially those you think you're closest to.

_____

_____

_____

_____

_____

_____

■ Is there anyone in your life at present who indirectly communicates to you the message, "Don't tell me how you feel. Just accept things as they are"? Describe how you feel when this happens.

_____

_____

_____

_____

√ *The third principle of self-disclosure is this: The more we self-disclose, the more authentic we become. Authentic means* "the genuine article, the real thing, believable and trustworthy." Ever watch a children's choir sing in a church service? Talk about authentic. One kid was picking his nose, a little girl pulled up her dress to adjust her socks, a boy was staring out into space—no doubt in la-la land—a girl was waving and smiling at her parents. Small children can't help but be authentic. They haven't learned yet to wear masks. They tell you directly what they think and feel. We could learn some valuable lessons from them.

As you allow your inner child to be more visible in your daily life, you will develop relationships characterized by the ability to talk about what you feel and think. You will be able to recognize your special talents and rejoice in them. You will be thankful for the unique person God has created you to be. And you will desire to be no other than who you are. This is the way you nurture your inner child. As you desire to become what you are, your language becomes the language of intimate self-disclosure. Others grow in awareness of who you are and what you are like. You slowly drop the mask that hides your true self, your inner child.

Can you imagine a marriage where you don't have to put on a mask for your mate or children, where you can be loved for who you are, even when things get tough? Can you visualize a church that encourages Christians to be authentic, whose motto is, "We encourage real people to worship here"? Can you envision your relationship with God free from superficiality, pretense, and placation, and filled instead with His acceptance, closeness, and love? This is what God desires your relationship with Him to be. In fact, Jesus was constantly confronting the hypocrisy of religious people and comforting the sinners. Authentic people enjoyed His presence because He was authentic with them. Intimate self-disclosure produces authenticity in your personal relationships. It's the only way to know you are loved for who you really are.

PERSONAL REFLECTION

■ How comfortable are you telling another person *directly* what you think and feel? Cite one or two examples when you self-disclosed in this way.

_____

_____

_____

_____

■ Communicating uneasy feelings, such as anger or fear, in a direct way is difficult for most people. Why do you think learning to express "hard" feelings can still produce intimacy? Have you ever felt closer to a person after they shared feelings of fear or anger with you? Explain.

_____

_____

_____

_____

_____

■ How *real* are you? What, if anything, keeps you from being
authentic with other people?

_____

_____

_____

So far we have looked at ways to develop intimate relationships
with others in order to avoid loneliness. We've learned that self-
disclosure of present feelings is an integral part of intimacy. There
are, however, two other important aspects of our relationships we
need to consider besides self-disclosure and intimacy. They are
feedback and *self-awareness*. Perhaps the best way to illustrate the
relationship of feedback and self-awareness with self-disclosure and
intimacy is by using the diagram (below) adapted from the Johari
Window.[2]

JOHARI WINDOW

	Known to Self	Unknown to Self
Known to Others	**PUBLIC AREA** Information that is known to me and others	**BLIND AREA** Information blind to me, but known to others
Unknown to Others	**HIDDEN AREA** What I know about me, but others don't know	**UNKNOWN AREA** Information about me unknown to any of us

As we carefully examine the four areas in the chart on page 98, I trust you will gain valuable insights to help you grow in intimacy with others and with God.

√ *The public area.* Let's take a look at the first square, *public area,* which consists of information about myself that is known both to me and to others. Suppose you and I meet in a social gathering. I know nothing about you, and you know nothing about me. For both of us, the public square is very tiny. There is no intimacy because there is no knowledge available between us. Intimacy is based on knowledge, whether we are talking about a relationship with God or with each other. Intimacy is not pure feeling. I may see someone who is very attractive and may feel drawn to that person, but I know nothing about the individual. All I have is a feeling or response, and that is not enough for genuine intimacy.

PUBLIC AREA	BLIND AREA
HIDDEN AREA	UNKNOWN AREA

√ *The hidden area.* For us to develop an intimate relationship, I need to share my thoughts and feelings with you and you share yours with me. We have to expand the size of area number one. This means that the hidden area must decrease. We must both reveal our thoughts and feelings to each other. Your job is not to guess what I'm feeling and thinking, and I'm not to guess what you're thinking and feeling. We need to tell each other directly.

Take a moment to think about this. Who in your life right now knows what you really think and feel? Or do the important people in your life find you a complete mystery? Do they say such things as "I never know what you're thinking," or "I think I know you but I'm never sure"? Do you refuse to talk about yourself, then expect others to read your thoughts and guess what you're feeling? If this describes you, then you know what feeling alone is all about. You can be in the same room with your family or friends and at the same time feel isolated because your inner child is not allowed to be a part of your life—or a part of their lives. Sharing your thoughts and feelings builds intimate relationships.

Do you ever consider that intimacy with God is based on the same principle? If God did not share Himself with us, we could never have an intimate relationship with Him. "Wait a minute," you say. "God doesn't just appear in a room with us and start disclosing Himself, does He?" He doesn't have to, because He has given us His self-disclosure in the Bible. Speaking to the religious leaders of His day, Jesus said:

> You search the Scriptures, because you think that in them you have eternal life; and it is these that bear witness of Me; and you are unwilling to come to Me, that you may have life (John 5:39-40).

What He was saying is that mere knowledge of the Scriptures (the Bible) is not enough to insure a personal relationship with God; rather, Scripture reveals who Jesus is—very God in human form. That knowledge of who Christ is and what He has done on our behalf opens the door for us to *accept Him personally* and gain entrance into eternal life in heaven. Left to ourselves, how could we ever know the God of the universe in a personal way? Certainly we could learn something of His greatness from all that He has created; but for us to know Him personally, He must reveal Himself—self-disclose—in a language we can understand.

He has done just that in His holy Word. There is a hidden part of God that He has decided to share with us, what the Apostle Paul calls the mystery of the Gospel (Ephesians 1:9; 6:19). The information God has given us about Himself from His hidden area now belongs to the public area. By His self-disclosure we have the privilege and opportunity to know God and His Son, Jesus Christ, in a loving, intimate way.

Let's continue on our journey from loneliness toward intimacy, using the diagram of the Johari Window. So far we have seen that intimacy is based on knowledge regarding thoughts and feelings. This knowledge comes from the hidden area representing what I know about myself and am willing to share. As I reveal myself, my public area increases and my hidden area decreases.

An important part of disclosure involved feedback. Feedback, letting other people know how you see them and experience them, is essential for healthy relationships. Its purpose is to build and enhance relationships by giving you more accurate information about yourself and others you value.

When Fred and Betty came to me for marital therapy, Fred was an uptight businessman. He had started his own company in his garage and built it into a very profitable business. He was demanding, rigid, and had little tolerance for errors. He was hard on himself, on his employees, and on his family as well. Betty was your typical peace-at-any-price person whose main job was to put out Fred's fires. Her greatest goal in life was not to upset Fred, something she did regularly anyway. Whenever she spoke to Fred in our sessions together, she sounded as if she were tiptoeing through a mine field. What Fred didn't realize was that Betty was fed up with his behavior and had one foot out the door of their marriage.

It was clear from the beginning that Fred had no idea how Betty felt, and Betty knew little about what Fred was thinking or feeling. I couldn't approach Fred with "the key to good relationships is talking about your thoughts and feelings" routine without blowing us all out of the water. So I decided to have each of them take a session and talk about their family backgrounds uninterrupted. This started the ball

PUBLIC AREA	BLIND AREA
HIDDEN AREA	UNKNOWN AREA

rolling. As Fred told about his painful background, some of his feelings began to show. Briefly his inner child peeked out—not for long, mind you, but it was a start.

Over a period of time Fred began to lower his protective mask, and Betty was able to give him some feedback about herself and their relationship. Fred was shocked to learn Betty's feelings about their marriage, since he had assumed everything was fine. Eventually, Betty was able to help Fred see how controlling and unreasonable he was. She was surprised to learn that he was more sensitive and vulnerable than she had realized. Not only were Fred and Betty able to disclose more of themselves, thus enlarging the public area, but in their disclosures they were able to provide valuable feedback which gave them both a more accurate perception of the other.

√ *The blind area.* One of the more important benefits of feedback is that it helps us see our blind areas, those facets of ourselves that we would rather not know about. The blind area is a secret closet in which we store all the things we don't want to own about ourselves. It represents the many things our inner child tries to hide from our inner critical parent. In the illustration of Fred and Betty, Fred was blind to just how dominating he was and how negatively his controlling behavior affected Betty and their children. Without his openness to Betty's feedback, their marriage may not have lasted. It wasn't easy for Fred to admit that he was dominating and insensitive, but his willingness to look honestly at himself helped him to correct the problem.

All of us need caring feedback. Years ago, my son, Jeff, helped me to see a part of myself that wasn't very attractive. One Halloween he brought home a large brown bag brimming with candy. While he was at school the next day, I went to his room and helped myself to some of the choicest pieces. After all, candy would just ruin his health and rot his teeth; so as a responsible parent, I'd spare him that grave misfortune.

Well, that afternoon Jeff came home and headed immediately for that big brown bag of candy. How was I to know that he had memorized every piece in that bag and that the pieces I had chosen were his favorites? Jeff was mad—real mad. I had eaten his candy; but even worse, I had walked into his room and helped myself to what was his without asking his permission. I had violated his rights as a member of the household. As he stood there glaring at me, I tried to defend my irresponsible behavior with, "You listen to me, Son. I'm your parent, I own this house, and I have a right to enter your room. Besides, you have more candy in that bag than you could eat in a year!"

My arguments didn't fly because I knew Jeff was right. I was insensitive about his possessions. His feedback made me face my selfishness and lack of respect for his property. Because he confronted my blind area, I learned a very important lesson about myself. To this day I have never failed to ask permission to use anything of his, and I know he appreciates my respect for his things.

Feedback directed to my blind area with loving concern provides me with greater self-awareness. I saw myself in a more accurate light as a result of my son's feedback. And Fred was more aware of his real self as a result of Betty's feedback.

Can you imagine living in a house with no mirrors? Naturally, you women are deft enough at applying makeup that it wouldn't be Halloween revisited. Nor would your hairdo resemble the Nevada nuclear test site. Yet, without feedback (a mirror), would you be able to know how you really looked? You would be blind to yourself. You would be totally unaware of the person others saw when they looked at you. In a similar way, intimate friendships require self-disclosure and feedback.

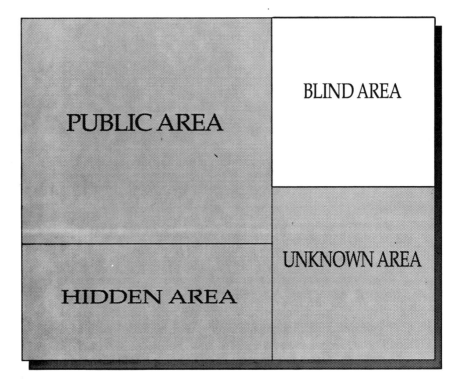

PERSONAL
REFLECTION

■ Think of the person you feel closest to in your life right now. Draw the Johari Window that describes your relationship with that person. How large is your public area? Your hidden area? Your blind area? Refer back to the diagrams on pages 98–101 for examples of how to do this exercise.

■ Have the person you are closest to draw his or her Johari Window of your relationship in the box below. How large is his or her public area? His or her hidden area? His or her blind area?

■ Is there a difference between the two Johari Windows you drew? What do you think accounts for the differences?

_____

_____

_____

_____

■ List four or five reasons why it is hard for you to reveal information about yourself that is from your hidden area.

_____

_____

_____

_____

■ How open to feedback are you? Can you think of a time when a friend or family member, out of loving concern, gave you some honest feedback? What did he or she say? How did you respond?

_____

_____

_____

_____

Can you begin to see how these principles apply to your relationship with God? In His Word, God tells us how much He loves us, cares for us, and provides for us. He also shows us our blind areas . . . through feedback. The writer to the Hebrews talks about the power of God's Word to reveal truth:

For the word of God is living and active and sharper than any two-edged sword, and piercing as far as the division of soul and spirit, of both joints and marrow, and able to judge the thoughts and intentions of the heart. And there is no creature hidden from His sight, but all things are open and laid bare to the eyes of Him with whom we have to do (Hebrews 4:12-13).

What an unsettling passage. In one sense we feel ourselves exposed before God. All that we are and think and feel is laid open to Him. Yet, if we are His people, notice the comfort we have in our Lord Jesus Christ:

Since then we have a great high priest who has passed through the heavens, Jesus the Son of God, let us hold fast our confession. For we do not have a high priest who cannot sympathize with our weaknesses, but one who has been tempted in all things as we are, yet without sin. Let us therefore draw near with confidence to the throne of grace, that we may receive mercy and may find grace to help in time of need (Hebrews 4:14-16).

God wants us to see ourselves in the mirror of His Word. At times He reveals the sin in our lives so that we may do what is necessary to correct it and restore our fellowship with Him. But in His Word He also tells us of our great worth and value to Him; not because we have value in ourselves, but because He has given us our value as individuals created in His image. If we were to remove God from the scene, our worth as human beings would be based on what we could produce, which means some of us would be more valuable than others. But in God's eyes, we are all of value.

How then do we develop intimacy with God? We come to know who God is through His Word, the Bible. As we read the Scriptures, we gain knowledge of God and his Son, Jesus Christ; we become aware of the ultimate price Jesus paid for us through His death and resurrection. Then, as an act of our will, we accept Christ as our personal Lord, Savior, and Friend. Our response to God's love is to share our thoughts and feelings with Him in prayer. This decreases our hidden area and strengthens our closeness with God. And as we read the Bible and pray, we develop a larger public area of knowledge about God. His Word gives us feedback that helps us overcome our blindness. As a result, we see ourselves more like He sees us. As this process continues in an ongoing relationship, intimacy builds.

Like light in a dark place, intimacy displaces loneliness. But intimacy cannot occur without the involvement of your inner child. To reveal your inner child, you must gradually surrender all your protective masks.

PERSONAL
REFLECTION

■ To have an intimate relationship with God you must disclose your true self to God and He to you. This week, make a list of specific things you share with God in prayer.

_____

_____

_____

_____

■ As you read His Word, note those things you feel God is disclosing to you about Himself. Write down what you learn.

_____

_____

_____

_____

■ Also jot down anything God reveals to you about yourself this week as you read the Bible.

_____

_____

_____

_____

■ At the end of the week, write a paragraph describing any changes you've had in your feelings of intimacy with God. What do you think made the difference?

_____

_____

_____

_____

_____

_____

PRAYERFUL REFLECTION

■ Often it is during times of painful self-revelation—when God exposes the inner weaknesses of our lives—that He makes clear to us His true character. For all we are *not*—God is. *EXAMPLE: Suppose your inner child identifies his or her unconscious fear of abandonment or rejection. At that point of need, God longs to comfort your inner child with this truth about Himself: "I will never leave you nor forsake you" (Joshua 1:5). What emotional comfort that truth about God brings to a terrified inner child.* Can you think of a time when God made Himself very personal to you during a time of pain? Describe that experience in the form of a prayer of thanksgiving. Express to God how you feel about the truth He revealed to you about Himself at that time.

_____

_____

_____

_____

_____

_____

PERSONAL RENEWAL

■ The writer of Hebrews talks about the power of God's Word in revealing truth. Let your thoughts and feelings be renewed through the power of God's Word this week as you meditate on Hebrews 4:12-16 (NIV).

For the word of God is living and active. Sharper than any double-edged-sword, it penetrates even to dividing soul and spirit, joints and marrow; it judges the thoughts and attitudes of the heart. Nothing in all creation is hidden from God's sight. Everything is uncovered and laid bare before the eyes of Him to whom we must give account. Therefore, since, we have a great high priest who has gone through the heavens, Jesus the Son of God, let us hold firmly to the faith we profess. For we do not have a high priest who is unable to sympathize with our weaknesses, but we have one who has been tempted in every way, just as we are—yet was without sin. Let us then approach the throne of grace with confidence, so that we may receive mercy and find grace to help us in our time of need.

Chapter 5
Why Marriages Often Fail

I scanned the directory of names listed alphabetically: Dr. Ben Jones, M.D., Cardiology . . . Dr. Harold Krager, M.D., Proctology. . . . There it was—Dr. Mary Lane, Ph.D., Marriage, Family, and Child Counseling. My stomach knotted as I turned and headed for the elevator. The little numbered lights flickered on the elevator panel as we passed the second floor, the third, and stopped finally at the fourth. This was it. Reluctantly I stepped out and walked toward the door marked SOUTH COAST COUNSELING CENTER. I was hoping that the waiting room would be empty. No such luck. Two other people sat on opposite ends of a long couch, obviously trying to avoid each other.

The waiting room was nicely decorated, with a homey atmosphere that helped to ease my discomfort. My eyes settled on a huge fish tank filled with brightly colored tropical fish. I sat down and stared long and hard at those fish, wondering if any of them had marital problems. I figured that staring at fish in a tank beat striking up a conversation with the two couch people who sat glaring at each other, no doubt entertaining thoughts of homicide. Besides, what do you say to people waiting to see a therapist? "How are you? How are things going? What's happening, Buddy?"

At last my wife, Kathy, showed up. She had been given the wrong directions by—guess who? That's right—me. So I was flustered and made a mistake. Why not? After all, this was our first appointment for marriage counseling.

Yes, this psychologist needed marriage counseling. It's much easier to help other people solve their marital problems than to solve your own.

Outwardly, my wife and I had a very good marriage. We were respected in the Christian community and frequently spoke together at couples' conferences. We were each successful in our own right. Kathy taught Bible Study Fellowship for nine years and did an outstanding job. She was a successful real estate agent and taught a women's Bible study at church. I had a thriving practice as a psychologist and had taught psychology courses at a local community college for 25 years, plus adult Sunday School classes for as many years as well. So how could we possibly have marital problems?

Well, we did. After 30 years of marriage we had problems. Not big ones, but a number of small ones that were adding up to one big one. The little problems got us because it was easy to ignore them and hope they would go away by themselves. But they didn't.

It all came to a head one evening when Kathy expressed her frustration with my lack of attention toward her. We were so busy in our separate worlds that it became easy to ignore each other's needs. For me, being busy was a convenient way to avoid my own growing discontent with Kathy. We have very different personalities, and sometimes when we try to talk, we feel that the other doesn't understand. On this particular night our mutual lack of understanding was so evident I realized my psychological training was of no help. I was too emotionally involved to see things clearly. I needed help. We both needed someone on the outside who could help us talk to each other with understanding.

So now we sat in Dr. Lane's waiting room, masking our pain and nervousness with silence. Finally the inner office door opened and an attractive middle-aged woman with gray hair emerged. She turned warm brown eyes on us and offered an infectious smile. "Hello. You're the Dickinsons? I'm Dr. Lane. Please come into my office."

Dr. Lane's friendly manner eased my anxiety. As the session progressed, I found talking to her easier than I had anticipated. And what transpired in the following weeks significantly changed the course of our marriage toward more open and compassionate communication. We discovered significant issues at the root of our discontent that revolved around the inner child in both of us. Essentially, Kathy and I were neglecting the feelings, natural abilities, and unique individuality of each other's inner child. The lack of emotional nourishment in our marriage was causing us to build barriers to protect ourselves from the hurt we were experiencing. Counseling enabled us to change our relationship, lower the barriers, and revitalize our marriage.

PERSONAL REFLECTION

■ How do you respond when your spouse or best friend seems to misunderstand you?

_____

_____

_____

■ When was the last time you sat down with your spouse or best friend and shared some of your inner feelings? If it has been a while, write down some of the barriers you feel have prevented you from doing this.

_____

_____

_____

_____

If you are married or involved in a close relationship with someone, you can't neglect the feelings of the inner child. During our second counseling session with Dr. Lane, after exchanging some social pleasantries, she asked Kathy, "What animal would you say best describes you in your relationship to Dick?"

Kathy thought for a moment, then said, "A cat."

Then Dr. Lane asked, "Kathy, what animal would you say best describes Dick?"

Again my wife thought for a moment, then replied, "A hamster."

Anger sprang up inside me. I thought, "How degrading! Hamsters are ugly little creatures. Besides, in the clutches of a cat they have a very limited future." I remembered when Jeff was small and had a pet hamster named Jasper. Frequently, Jeff would take him for a boat ride in his plastic wading pool. Unfortunately, the plastic boat was unstable and the boat often sank, much to the dismay of both Jeff and Jasper. Emergency procedures were often in order: Jeff would rescue the poor drenched creature from the clutches of death, then take him into the bathroom and blow-dry him with the hair dryer on high heat. Jasper would sit in a catatonic stupor, no doubt preferring death.

As I sat in Dr. Lane's office, I knew Kathy didn't share my negative reaction to the animal she had picked for me. Still, I felt humiliated.

Then Dr. Lane turned to me and asked what animal I would choose to describe myself.

"A teddy bear," I shot back. To me, teddy bears are big and strong, yet huggable and lovable.

"What about Kathy? How would you describe her?"

My first thought was not of an animal but a china doll to be placed on a shelf and admired. China dolls were fragile and required careful handling lest they break.

"If I had to choose an animal, I'd say I see Kathy as a cat," I said at last.

"Why?"

"Because cats need attention, they need to be admired, and they are somewhat aloof and untouchable." But the more I thought about the animal exercise, the more questions filled my mind. If I saw myself as a huggable, lovable teddy bear, then why wasn't that more evident in my relationship with Kathy? If Kathy saw me as a hamster, an animal that needed to be taken care of, why did I feel so degraded?

Dr. Lane used the animal technique to open some areas of our lives that were blocking intimacy. I realized that bears were not only huggable and lovable, but they were also very protective and good providers. I had always been a good provider in our marriage; this was very important to me, but I began to see that the warmth and tenderness were lacking. Yet in recent years I often felt lonely and hungry for closeness and affection. Was the problem Kathy's inability to meet those needs—or was the problem in me?

Gradually I came to realize that my experience was not that much different from the experiences of men I've counseled. My suspicion is that many men in mid-life crisis, who suddenly dissolve a long-standing marriage, feel deprived of closeness and affection in their marriage and attempt to find it elsewhere. In other words, their inner child is undernourished and their tendency is to blame the wife without looking carefully at the origin of the problem. In my case, I had great difficulty asking for what I needed; I expected Kathy to know my emotional needs intuitively. It seemed that this 6' 7" teddy bear was in hibernation.

When Dr. Lane suggested to Kathy that she plan a weekend doing something just to please me, Kathy's first response was fear that I would not be pleased with her efforts. As she shared that fear, I thought, "Am I that critical that she would be afraid to do something special just for me?" My second reaction was discomfort at the idea of her doing something just for me. As I thought about my uneasiness, I realized this reaction was true of all my relationships. I was much more willing to do for others than to let others do for me. In fact, I discouraged them. I could feed the emotional needs of others, but my inner child went hungry.

The truth stunned me: I was a psychologist in a perpetual state of hunger, helping others but unable to let others help me. I knew if I let the problem remain unsolved, I'd be like so many mental health professionals who experience burnout. I realized I could give only so much of myself with little in return before becoming empty, disillusioned, and cynical. I knew too that emotional burnout can occur in a marriage or close personal relationship when the inner child of one or both partners remains unnourished. That's what was happening in our marriage!

I agreed to let Kathy plan a weekend just for me. She kept it a secret until the day we were to leave. We drove to a luxurious hotel and checked into a quaint room overlooking a garden patio. The European decor reminded us both of our stay in Austria. We had a romantic dinner with candlelight and roses and spent a quiet, intimate evening together. Once Kathy resolved her earlier fears of displeasing me, I think she had as much fun as I had basking in her attention.

Kathy and I found that one of the great benefits of marriage counseling was being able to express our inner feelings and needs, knowing that we were being heard and understood by the other. As I explored my difficulty in receiving attention and my resistance to telling Kathy what I needed, she found it easier to respond to my needs. The fact that I needed something from her helped her to feel that she was important to me.

For me, the need to be appreciated for the way I provided for Kathy was very important. One of the ways I expressed my love and caring for her was to give her those things that would make our life more comfortable. Often men who are reluctant to verbalize their feelings express their love by providing materially for their mate and family. Of course, women need more than material possessions to feel emotionally close to their husbands. On the other hand, it is easy to take husbands for granted and complain about their lack of verbal communication. Perhaps the first step in nourishing your husband's inner child is to compliment him for the way he provides for you.

PERSONAL REFLECTION

■ In the previous seven paragraphs, Dr. Dickinson highlights some thought and behavior patterns that were keeping him and his wife from experiencing an intimate connection in their marriage. *EXAMPLE: I had great difficulty asking for what I needed.* Underline and list below the things he mentions in those paragraphs.

_____

_____

_____

_____

_____

■ Which of the items you listed above have created problems for you in your relationship with your spouse or in a close personal relationship? What steps do you feel you need to take to restore the intimacy in that relationship?

_____

_____

_____

_____

I also discovered within myself the need to expose my fears, weaknesses, and limitations to my wife without feeling degraded or humiliated as a man and a provider. Because I am 6' 7" tall and weigh 225 pounds, people seldom see me as a fearful person with weaknesses and limitations. I'm very athletic and work hard to keep in shape. In fact, I've been told I look like I could go bear hunting with a switch. But people misread me too, because of my reluctance to tell them what is going on inside. I feel pressured to live up to the expectations I've set for myself, an image that doesn't include weaknesses.

Early in our marriage Kathy depended on me a great deal for emotional support. Since I didn't feel strong or confident in my abilities to provide for her emotionally or materially, I kept my inner anxieties to myself for fear she would lose respect for me. In our counseling sessions I was able to share more of my inner fears and concerns with her, and the counselor was able to help Kathy understand my feelings and not be threatened by them. Gradually the teddy bear came out of hibernation.

PERSONAL REFLECTION

■ Admitting our fears, weaknesses, and limitations to the person we feel closest to is often difficult. It leaves us in a very vulnerable place. Sometimes we cannot even admit these things to ourselves, but that is where we must begin. Write down any personal fears, weaknesses, and limitations you are in touch with at this point. What keeps you from sharing them with the people you are most intimate with?

_____

_____

_____

_____

Another way we began to nourish each other's inner child was our manner of greeting after a long day at work. Typically I would come home late, say "Hi," sit down and grab a bite to eat, watch a little TV, then go to bed. Now we make an effort to greet each other at the door with a kiss and a warm embrace; it's our way of acknowledging our love.

Wives, I suggest you take time to study your husbands. What are their strengths? Do you take them for granted? What do you expect him to be as a man, father, and husband? Do you take time to do things for him that he really enjoys? Do you ever surprise him by planning something different and unexpected? Do you greet him in a way that tells him he is special to you? Do you listen for the subtle clues that reveal his inner emotions? Do you encourage him to talk about his day, his feelings, and concerns but without nagging him? Are you a good listener? These are only a few of the ways you can nourish his inner child and strengthen the emotional bond between you.

PERSONAL REFLECTION

■ FOR WOMEN ONLY. What are your husband's or your closest male friend's strengths? Write them down. Do you take his strengths for granted? In what way? When was the last time you expressed value for any of his strengths?

_____

_____

_____

_____

■ What do you do to make your husband or closest male friend feel that he is important to you? Do you take time to do things that he really enjoys? Do you talk about his day, his feelings, and concerns without nagging him? Are you a good listener?

_____

_____

_____

_____

■ What more can you do to nourish your husband's or boyfriend's inner child and strengthen the emotional bond between you?

_____

_____

_____

_____

I have taken more time to talk about men and their needs because they traditionally have not been encouraged to share their feelings with others, nor have they seen this kind of behavior modeled by male relatives. Women generally tend to be more open with their feelings and are more comfortable in sharing.

However, my advice to wives applies to their husbands as well. What I need from Kathy is often what she needs from me. I'm not talking about artificial pampering but about encouraging genuineness in one another. Kathy needs me to listen to her concerns and feelings. To interrupt her or appear inattentive while she is talking gives her the distinct impression that what she has to _say_ isn't important, which makes her feel that _she_ is not important. Kathy needs to be needed by me. While our personalities are very different, there is enough commonality that if I take time to help her understand my needs, she is willing to respond to them. She doesn't want to be a mother to me, but she does want to be a companion.

Husbands, do you take the time to listen to your wives and try to understand their feelings? To test your listening ability, try restating your wife's expressed thoughts and feelings back to her in your own words. Do you respect her point of view, even though you may not agree? Does she feel comfortable revealing her vulnerabilities to you? Do you take time to make her feel special by remembering special occasions? Do you go out to dinner, have a date night alone, get away for an occasional weekend? These are ways you can nourish your wife's inner child and strengthen your emotional bond.

PERSONAL REFLECTION

■ FOR MEN ONLY. What are your wife's or your closest female friend's strengths? How often and in what ways do you let her know you value her strengths? Give an example of a time when you did this. How did she respond?

_____

_____

_____

_____

■ How would you describe your ability to listen to your wife or your closest female friend? What things that you do while she is talking might communicate to her a lack of interest? What more could you do to be an attentive listener for her?

_____

_____

_____

_____

■ Do you respect your wife's or your closest female friend's point of view, even though you may not necessarily agree with her? How do you let her know it's okay for her to disagree with you?

_____

_____

_____

_____

■ How comfortable would you say your wife or closest female friend feels in revealing her vulnerabilities to you? What would you say are her most vulnerable areas? When was the last time she let you in to that vulnerable part of herself? How did you feel when she did that?

_____

_____

_____

_____

Before we leave this important subject, I want to touch on what I consider counterfeit means of stroking the inner child, and that is through sex. A number of couples I've counseled have substituted sexual relations for emotional intimacy in an attempt to meet the inner child's need for affection and closeness.

After Lucy and Steve had been separated for five months, they made an appointment to see me for counseling, shortly after deciding to make a go of their marriage. Steve, who had left Lucy for another woman, found that the single life wasn't what he expected. But Lucy was still deeply hurt and felt distrustful of Steve. "I thought we had a good marriage," she confided. "Steve and I always had a good sexual relationship. In fact, six months before he left, his sexual appetite increased. It seemed like he wanted me all the time."

"How did you feel about that?" I asked.

"I felt flattered that he wanted me so much."

I questioned Steve about his sudden increase of libido just before leaving Lucy. When I asked about his satisfaction with their sex life, he made a significant statement: "Even though I wanted sex more often, I found that it never seemed to satisfy me. Sometimes I felt compelled to have sex; something inside was driving me."

I gathered from Steve's remarks that he, like so many men, equated a sexual relationship with affection, closeness, and intimacy. When sex is substituted for intimacy and affection, it almost always leads to dissatisfaction and ultimately leaves a person vulnerable to outside sexual relationships. The sad fact about extramarital relationships is that what you think you will find—closeness, intimacy, and affection—continues to elude you. Using sex as a way to nourish your inner child simply won't work.

This is the hard lesson Steve learned; fortunately for him, Lucy wanted him back. Often a betrayed spouse is not so forgiving and the wandering partner winds up with nothing. Keep in mind that emotional nourishment for the inner child comes by sharing one's feelings, needs, and vulnerabilities, by listening carefully, and by striving to meet each other's needs with mutual love and respect.

One added note. I believe men need holding and touching in a nonsexual way as much as women do. In our culture, it is rare for fathers to feel comfortable holding or touching their sons. Our need for touching gets translated into sexual desire, which sets up the inability to distinguish between the two. In our society it's much more acceptable for a man to desire sex than to ask to be held. Probably for this reason men usually don't understand the need in women to be held and touched nonsexually.

One of the more startling insights I have discovered about myself is my need for my wife's touch; I'm more able now to simply ask her to hold me. Such moments of closeness provide real emotional food for my hungry inner child—and, I believe, for hers as well. With our needs for closeness, affection, and intimacy met more directly, our sexual relationship becomes more satisfying because it is not being substituted for nonsexual needs.

PERSONAL
REFLECTION

■ Have you substituted sex for intimacy and affection thinking it would make you feel close to your partner? What eventually happened in the relationship? From your perspective, what is the most destructive part of subtituting sex for genuine intimacy and affection?

_____

_____

_____

_____

■ Do you understand your own need for nonsexual holding and touching? Describe how it feels when someone you love holds or touches you in a way that is nonsexual. How much holding and touching goes on in your relationship with your spouse or the person of the opposite sex you are in a close relationship with?

_____

_____

_____

_____

In my relationship with my wife I discovered that I was failing to recognize and value her unique inherent abilities. Inherent abilities are God-given and form an important part of the inner child and one's unique identity as a person. Such neglect is often a major cause for marital disharmony.

In the early years of our married life, Kathy worked so that I could finish my senior year of college and then earn my master's degree in psychology. Looking back on our relationship, I see that her identity was derived more by being my wife than by being a person in her own right. After I completed my master's degree, Kathy stopped working and spent most of her time taking care of our home and our son, Jeff, with some limited involvement in women's clubs. As Jeff reached his teen years, Kathy became very active in Bible Study Fellowship, first as a discussion leader and then as a teaching leader for nine years.

During those years things began to change in our relationship. It was subtle at first. Kathy would share with me the many good things happening to the women in her class. As these women took God seriously, their lives began to change and their marriages were positively impacted. I should have been happy for my wife, pleased that she was so effective and that God was dong great things through her. I should have been glad that Kathy was such a talented teacher and that the women loved her so much. Yes, those would have been the right and proper responses, but they weren't the feelings I was experiencing. Instead, I felt jealous, envious, and threatened—so threatened that I even tried to invalidate the changes Kathy saw in these women's marriages by insisting the improvements were superficial and wouldn't last. After all, I was a licensed marriage counselor and I didn't see such significant changes in the people I counseled. I simply couldn't handle the fact that my wife was developing a successful ministry of her own that had nothing to do with me.

Up until that point in our relationship, I had been number one. I was the professional with the degrees. I was the speaker at the conferences. I was the professor of psychology and the Sunday School teacher. Kathy was Mrs. Me. It slowly began to dawn on me that I really didn't know Kathy very well, especially her inherent natural aptitudes for excellence. It took her involvement outside the marriage for her to develop her talents and for me to finally see them. At last it struck me that Kathy could never be happy or fulfilled living her life through me; she had to be free to be the person God made her to be.

What a sad commentary this was for me—a psychologist who sincerely enjoyed seeing people grow and use their God-given talents! I was able to help my patients, but I was a hindrance to the person most important to me, my wife. Yet if you asked me if I was all for my wife's personal growth, I would have uttered a resounding, "Yes, of course I am!" My words said yes, but my behavior said no!

Tensions really mounted when my wife left Bible Study Fellowship and started a career in real estate. It's one thing to have a wife who's successful at something that doesn't pay a salary; it's quite another thing when she starts earning a substantial amount of money. During her first year in real estate she sold $3 million worth of property; her second year, $4 million; and her third year, $5 million. When her income nuzzled up to mine, it tested my security as a man and a provider. You see, I was raised in a home where my father worked and my mother stayed home, waited on the children, and took care of the house. Working full-time, Kathy found it difficult to keep up with her traditional role of cooking and cleaning and pampering hubby. Household chores went undone, the laundry piled up, and the cupboards were bare. Meanwhile, my irritation grew.

You might suggest that I could have stepped in and helped Kathy out—gone shopping, cooked a meal, straightened the house, run an errand or two. You're right. I could have, but I didn't—not at first. Why not? Because I figured cooking, cleaning, and pampering was Kathy's job, her way of showing she loved me. After all, that's how it was in my parents' home; that's what marriage was.

The shock came when I realized I was behaving as if Kathy's value lay in what she could do for me rather than in who she was as a person. I had to ask myself, "Who is this person I married? Do I really know her? Do I really love her for herself? Do I have the slightest idea of her natural, God-given aptitudes for excellence?" I had to admit I didn't.

PERSONAL REFLECTION

■ Do you know what YOUR natural, God-given aptitudes for excellence are? What things are you able to do easily and well without getting worn out or tired of doing them? Jot down what you know up to this point.

_____

_____

_____

_____

■ What natural, God-given aptitudes have you observed in your spouse or your closest friend? In what ways have you expressed value for his or her natural abilities?

_____

_____

_____

_____

How do we come to understand and appreciate one another's natural, God-given aptitudes? To help me answer these questions, I'd like to introduce you to an organization that assesses their clients' natural aptitudes, the IDAK Group, Inc. in Portland, Oregon, which specializes in mid-life career redirection. The name IDAK comes from two words—ID for "identity" and AK, the Hebrew word for "unique," or "unique identity." I deeply appreciate IDAK granting me permission to duplicate their talent names and respective definitions for use in this book. John Bradley, IDAK's president, has spent many years developing identifying natural talents and has designed an assessment process for identifying inherent abilities. This assessment process is especially designed for career evaluation.

Every person—you, your mate, your children, and friends—has a number of natural aptitudes for excellence that contribute to a unique identity. I'm using the terms _natural talent_ and _inherent aptitude_ interchangeably. However, we need to distinguish between aptitudes or talents and skills.

NATURAL APTITUDES vs. SKILLS

Present at Birth

Learned by Training
and Education

The major distinction between these two terms is that natural aptitudes are present at birth while skills are learned by training and education. You may possess a high school or college diploma, a master's degree, or even a doctorate. What does it tell you? That you have achieved a certain level of competency or a particular number of skills in your chosen discipline. Your degree doesn't necessarily mean that you are operating in your area of natural talent. You can't build a lifetime of satisfaction on skills alone. It requires too much effort for the moderate benefits you receive, and by age 35 these people often become dissatisfied and gradually decline in work performance. This is one reason why so many people experience job burnout.

Natural talent cannot be taught. It comes naturally. Often the person possessing the talent takes it for granted because it requires so little effort. "Doesn't everybody do this?" he wonders.

You might be asking, "What does all this have to do with marital problems?" If your mate does not recognize and encourage your natural talents, you are likely to feel frustrated and dissatisfied. If you don't feel appreciated in your marriage, you are more likely to turn elsewhere for recognition, either throwing yourself into your work or getting involved in an outside relationship.

What kinds of talents do we need to recognize in our mates? Let's take a look at three talent categories.

√ *Relational talents.** Have you ever heard a dialogue like this?

Sue: Tom, what's the matter? You just sit there and say nothing. You let me do all the talking.

Tom: I have nothing to say.

Sue: That's the problem. You never have anything to say.

Tom: That's not true. I talk if I have something important to say. Otherwise, I'm content to just sit and listen.

Sue: But people think you're so unfriendly. They don't know you like I do. I'm afraid they'll get the wrong impression.

Tom: You worry too much about what people think. It bugs me—you're trying to get me to be more social when I'm happy the way I am.

Sue: You just don't try to be friendly. You won't put yourself out.

Tom: So I don't need to talk as much as you do. Besides, I feel uncomfortable around lots of people, especially strangers. You enjoy meeting new people. I don't.

I often hear this sort of dialogue in my counseling room. So often couples fail to realize that one's ability to relate effectively with others is more a function of natural aptitude than a deliberate attempt to irritate one's mate. There are three relational aptitudes:

• *Multirelational.** The multirelational person enjoys meeting new people and mixes easily in large groups of strangers. He opens a conversation with ease and quickly gets to know those around him. He's never at a loss for words and has scores of friends wherever he goes. He's a natural in a crowd; it's a talent he was born with. The only problem? Even after your 10th meeting, you probably won't know him any better than you did after your second encounter. Repeated contacts generally won't deepen the relationship.

• *Singular-relational.** Contrast the multirelational with the singular-relational—a person like Tom in the dialogue above who prefers to do things with only one or two people or by himself. He is perfectly content working alone for long periods of time and usually prefers the solitude. His friendships are long-lasting but few in number. The singular-relational person often is accused of being shy or feeling inferior, but this is not necessarily the case. He simply enjoys his private times and is content unless a multirelational person keeps bugging him.

My wife is a multirelational person and I am singular-relational. We have talked at length about our different relational aptitudes. Kathy's agenda during the early years of our marriage was to change me so that I would be more outgoing. It didn't work. This doesn't mean I shouldn't work to develop more social skills; it means that multirelational will never be my preferred way of relating to others. Since Kathy and I have recognized our opposite relational talent, we've found greater harmony in our marriage; we appreciate our differences rather than viewing them as personal attacks.

• *Familiar group-relational.** This person feels uncomfortable meeting new people, but as he develops familiarity with the same group, his comfort increases and his relationships deepen. With a history of group participation, he or she is probably a member of a fraternity or sorority, athletic team, or special-interest group. He joins groups more for the friendships than for the activities.

PERSONAL REFLECTION

■ What do you think your natural relational talent is? Check the sentence below which best describes how you see yourself.

❑ I enjoy meeting new people and mix easily in large groups of strangers.

❑ I prefer doing things with only one or two people or by myself.

❑ I feel uncomfortable meeting new people, but as I develop familiarity with the same group, my comfort increases and my relationships deepen.

■ How does your relational talent differ from that of your mate or your best friend? What kind of conflict, if any, has your relational talent produced? How can you resolve the conflict?

We not only have relational talents, we also have communication talents. Let's look at some examples.

√ *Communicational talents.** About 10 years ago Kathy and I started speaking at conferences as a couple. Initially it was very difficult for me to share such weekend speaking engagements with Kathy. I was used to doing the speaking, and I knew exactly how I wanted to do things. But whenever I tried to "help Kathy out," she would get angry and we would have an argument. Our problem was that we had different talents.

• Kathy has more of a *teaching talent**; that is, she has the natural ability to clearly express a concept, theory, Bible passage, or principle so that others understand. We all have had teachers who make their subject matter so wonderfully clear; we also have had teachers who make their subject matter utterly confusing. In the teaching profession, we rarely consider whether people have a natural talent to teach. If they have a degree, know the subject matter, and possess a teaching credential, they're teachers.

• I am more of a public speaker with some teaching talent. I am animated and can be very persuasive. A person with a *public speaking talent** is one who communicates particular ideas or opinions in such a way as to motivate others to action. I, of course, thought Kathy should be more persuasive, tell funny stories, and be more energetic and animated, but that's not Kathy. I finally learned to let her do what she does best. Now we're both effective, doing what we're talented to do.

• Another communicational talent is the use of *colors and patterns** as a way of expressing yourself. Many women are excellent with colors, whether they pertain to the home or to clothing. One woman told me that people who enter her house always remark that her home is an expression of her personality. Many husbands who fail to recognize this communicational talent in their wives become critical and restrictive in the way they let their wives care for or decorate the home. The frustration these wives feel is immense. It's like putting tape over the mouth of a person whose communicational talent is speaking.

• *Painting** is another form of communication. I have a patient who tells me more about what goes on inside her through her art work than through our conversations.

• *Writing** is communicational talent—the ability to express your feelings and ideas through the written word.

• Still others are *singing,* playing a musical instrument,* and acting.** A singer with inherent musical talent moves you with his song so that you feel the words and the music; someone else with musical skills may be technically proficient and still not communicate in a way that touches you deeply. An actor is a communicator too, for he can take on another personality and make that character become real before your eyes.

Have you ever taken the time to look at your friends, your children, or your mate and asked yourself, "What is the most effective way they communicate?" Do you know what your own communicational talent is? How many conflicts have you experienced in your marriage or in other relationships because you expected others in your life to communicate the same way you do? You might be talented in the use of words, but your mate or child may be more expressive in the areas of creativity or performing.

How easy it is to downplay or dismiss communicational talents that are different from our own. Remember, the little child in all of us has a unique way of expressing itself because God has given each of us inherent aptitudes for excellence in the area of communication. Do you know what your own aptitude for excellence is?

PERSONAL REFLECTION

■ What is the most effective way you communicate? You may have more than one communicational talent. For now, check the statement below that describes how you *most effectively* communicate.

❑ I am able to clearly express a concept/idea so that others understand it *(teaching talent*).*

❑ I am able to communicate particular ideas or opinions in such a way that others are motivated to take action *(speaking talent*)*.

❑ I am able to express myself using colors and patterns *(designer talent*)*.

❑ I am able to express myself through painting *(artist-painter talent*)*.

❑ I am able to write down my ideas and feelings in a way that clearly expresses who I am *(writing talent*)*.

❑ I am able to express myself musically in such a way that others are emotionally moved by it *(music talent*)*.

❑ I am able to take on another personality and make that character come alive before an audience *(acting talent*)*.

■ Describe how others respond when you use your communicational talent when you are with them? Have other people affirmed you in the use of your talents? Cite an example.

_____

_____

_____

_____

■ How do your communicational talents differ from those of your spouse or best friend? Is that person able to accept and appreciate your God-given communication ability? What, if any, conflict have you experienced because you are different in this talent area?

_____

_____

_____

_____

■ One arena of life in which communicational talents can come into conflict is in the work setting. What tensions have you experienced because you and your boss or coworkers have different communicational talents?

_____

_____

√ *Functional talents.** Functional talents fall into at least two categories—those related to *organization* and *supervisory* talents.

• *Organizational talents.** There are two organizational talents. One is the *organization of priorities and time.** The person possessing this talent naturally lists his tasks to be accomplished in the order of their importance and then promptly gets them done. Time is important to this person, whether it involves arriving at an appointment on time or meeting a deadline.

The second is the *organization of space.** I am presently working on this manuscript in what is called a bonus room, alias my study. One whole wall is lined with bookshelves crammed with books. Fortunately, my desk is large, all the better to pile more stuff on top of it. On a scale of 1 to 10, 1 being messy and 10 being neat, my room would rate about 4. I'm comfortable here surrounded by my things, with the cat sitting contentedly by my chair.

But my wife is uncomfortable in this room. She says, "How can you stand all this clutter?"

I say, "What clutter? Everything is where I can find it. If I put it away, I won't be able to find it."

So my wife throws her hands up in exasperation and sends the cleaning lady in to clean my room. When she is done, I'm confused. Everything has been rearranged. I can't find anything. The problem here is that Kathy has a strong organizational talent while I have a strong creative talent. Our differences in this area of organization have caused many arguments and at times put a strain on our marriage. I get angry when Kathy tries to fit me into her organized structure. Kathy gets upset with me when I don't keep things neat and in their place.

When it comes to common living space, I believe I need to exercise my learned neatness skill and keep things put away. But when it comes to my own areas, such as my study, then it is important to me to be able to do what is most comfortable and natural. It took Kathy and me a long time to realize that we differed in our inherent aptitudes for organization and creativity and that it is not simply a matter of one of us trying to be difficult.

If you are strong on organization of space, you have a place for everything. Keep in mind that this talent is not the same as neatness, for neatness is a learned skill. Space organization is a talent that comes naturally and is likely evident in childhood. The world would be a disaster without the organizers.

Creative people are often poor organizers. Their minds are on other more important matters, such as creating something new or new ways of doing things. When a creative person works with an organized person, you have a potentially stressful situation, whether it's in a marriage or on the job. The organized person has a set procedure for doing things and is all-efficient. The creative person likes to experiment, try new things, explore new ideas. That's when things get lively. As opposing ideas clash, the organized person feels attacked and the creative person feels frustrated. But when both parties learn to accept their God-ordained differences and work together, then a relationship can move from conflict to harmony and everyone benefits!

I have learned to appreciate Kathy's organizational talent, especially since she enjoys doing the detail work that drives me up the wall. You might say I come up with the ideas and she executes them. It's become a great "marriage of unlike talents." I must admit, however, that our organizational and creative dispositions stirred great conflict in the early days of our marriage. I would come home from work and on the spur of the moment decide to take off for the weekend. But my excitement would be shortlived when Kathy responded, "I can't."

"Why not?" I would ask irritably.

"I've got too many things to do."

"Forget them. Do them when we get back."

But Kathy didn't work that way, so I seethed inside, wondering why she always took the fun out of spontaneity. Little did I realize that organized persons cannot have fun just dropping everything; they worry about unfinished tasks while they're away. Kathy needed to know our plans ahead of time so she could tie up loose ends and make preparations to go. Then she could feel free to enjoy her weekend away. Once I realized that she wasn't deliberately trying to ruin my weekend, I didn't mind giving her advance notice so she could get organized.

PERSONAL REFLECTION

■ Are you a person who is more concerned about keeping to a schedule or keeping things in order? Check the statement below that best describes how you see yourself.

❑ I am able to quickly list the tasks that need to be accomplished in order of importance and promptly get them done. One of my pet peeves is people who are late for appointments.

❑ I have a good sense of how things fit into a given space and can organize that space easily. I naturally have a place for everything and have everything in its place.

■ It often happens that people who are naturally gifted at organizing priorities and time are attracted to people who are more gifted at organizing space. Has this been your experience? How have you resolved the tension points that seem to come with being different in this way?

_____

_____

_____

_____

_____

• *Supervisory ability.** What happens when you are married to a woman who has the talent to run a business or corporation? I've encountered a number of women in my practice who were gifted with supervisory talent but were held back by their own low estimation of their ability or by husbands who kept tight control over their activities. There are three specific God-given aptitude types for supervision:

√ *The developer/initiator.** This person envisions new goals for a group of people, a department, a company, or organization. He or she motivates others to accept these new goals and initially supervises their implementation. However, once the program is up and running, the developer/initiator needs to move on to other challenges.

√ *The planner.** This person can project his or her thinking into the future to determine the sequence of events, resources needed, potential problems, and hidden costs as they relate to a group project.

√ *The manager.** This person has a natural talent for coordinating the efforts and activities of others in achieving a common goal. The manager encourages each individual in the program to make a maximum contribution, and provides optimum use of all available resources. Know anybody like this? I do.

Rae, a tall, striking woman with long blond hair and blue eyes, made the initial appointment with me. She was frustrated with her marriage and was seriously considering leaving Tim. She had married him right out of high school and was soon pregnant with the first of their three children. Rae, a devoted wife and mother, centered her life around her family, using her natural talents to fix up her house and make things for her children and friends. But as much as she loved her family, she felt an underlying sense of frustration with her life.

Rae's husband, Tim, was content to come home after work, eat dinner and watch TV until he fell asleep in his favorite chair and finally drag himself off to bed. He wanted Rae to sit with him at night and watch TV, but Rae much preferred to read. Because she required more mental stimulation than Tim did, her frustration with her marriage grew.

As time passed and their children entered their teen years, Rae found she had more free time. She wanted to work outside the home, but Tim wanted her to be available when he telephoned and to have dinner on the table when he arrived home from work. Still, Rae found time to use some of her supervisory talents at church. She was frequently chosen to lead committees and always had creative ideas to offer. A natural developer/initiator, she was able to motivate people. When she talked about her work with others, her face lit up and her voice reflected her enthusiasm. The more others noticed her talent, the more opportunities she had to work outside the home. She found her church work and her position as acting chairwoman of the Christian Women's Club more exciting than her homelife with Tim. This prompted more guilt and more dissatisfaction.

The final blow came when a friend in the women's club offered Rae a job. The woman owned a business designed to guide women in proper clothing selection, hairstyles, exercise, and nutrition. It was the kind of opportunity Rae had always dreamed of. But when she excitedly told Tim of her good fortune, he became angry and upset. Wasn't her life with him fulfilling enough? Why did she have to go outside the home to find excitement?

What Tim didn't realize was that Rae's God-given talents needed some form of expression outside the home. The more threatened he felt, the more he clamped down on her, which only increased the tension between them. Rae loved Tim and wanted to be a good wife, but she also needed to utilize her natural aptitudes and become more fully the person God created her to be.

Counseling helped Tim see this truth for himself. Both Rae and Tim began to understand the need to share their feelings in order to dispel their private fears and anxieties. As Tim released his obsessive controls on Rae and gave her freedom to express her talents, she found her love for Tim growing and she urged him to develop his own unique abilities.

PERSONAL REFLECTION

■ Which supervisory talent* best describes you? Check one.
   ❑ I am able to envision new goals, can motivate others to accept these new goals, and want to initially supervise their implementation (developer-initiator*).
   ❑ I can project my thinking into the future to determine a sequence of events, resources needed, potential problems, and hidden costs (planner*).
   ❑ I am able to naturally coordinate the efforts and activities of others to achieve a common goal (manager*).

■ How are you currently using your natural supervisory talent? Are those around you encouraging your use of that talent or have you experienced some conflict because you've used it? Give an example. Where else might you be able to use your supervisory talent so that you feel more fulfilled?

_____

_____

_____

_____

Recognizing and encouraging the development of one another's God-given natural aptitudes for excellence is essential in the context of marriage, friendship, in the workplace, and with our children. Our talents are a vital part of our inner child. All of us need to be nourished not only with love and affection, but also with encouragement to develop our natural talents. The home should be the primary place for this nourishment to take place.

PERSONAL REFLECTION

■ What have you done to encourage your spouse, best friend, or children to develop their natural talents? What more can you do to foster growth in the areas where they are naturally talented?

_____

_____

_____

_____

■ What does your spouse, best friend, and/or boss do to encourage you to grow in your God-given talents? Do any of these people hold you back from developing your natural talents to their fullest? Who does and in what ways are they doing it?

_____

_____

_____

_____

PRAYERFUL REFLECTION

■ In their book *The Blessing*, authors Gary Smalley and John Trent emphasize the importance of blessing other people, especially those who are part of one's household. Write a prayer of blessing for your spouse, best friend, and/or children. State what you believe are each person's God-given natural talents. Then prayerfully entrust that person to God and express the potential you see for his or her future. Pray daily that God will bring about the blessing you've written down for that person. Pray too that God will bless others through that person.

_____

_____

_____

_____

_____

PERSONAL RENEWAL

■ In Psalm 8, we see that the greatness of God assures us of our worth. The all-powerful Creator cares for His most valuable creation—people! Be assured of your uniqueness and worth this week as you renew your thoughts and feelings in Psalm 8 (NIV).

O Lord, our Lord, how majestic is Your name in all the earth! You have set Your glory above the heavens. From the lips of children and infants You have ordained praise because of Your enemies, to silence the foe and the avenger. When I consider Your heavens, the work of Your fingers, the moon and stars, which You have set in place, what is man that You are mindful of him, the son of man that You care for him? You made him a little lower than the heavenly beings and crowned him with glory and honor. You made him ruler over the works of Your hands; You put everything under his feet: all flocks and herds, and the beasts of the field, the birds of the air, and the fish of the sea, all that swim the paths of the seas. O Lord, our Lord, how majestic is Your name in all the earth.

* The talent name and corresponding definition have been developed and copyrighted by the IDAK Group, Inc., Portland, Oregon and is used by permission. Other talents named in this chapter and their corresponding definitions have also been developed and copyrighted by IDAK and used by permission. Reproduction of these talent category names and respective categories and definitions is prohibited unless permission is granted in writing from the IDAK Group, Inc.

Chapter 6
Creating Children in Our Own Image

For a long moment I stared out the window of our Swiss chalet at the glistening, snow-covered Alps, but I couldn't hide my irritation as I glared back at my son, Jeff. His eyes were wide with despair and tears had begun to roll down his cheeks. The look on his face expressed it all: "I must be the dumbest kid in the world."

We had remained at this same difficult impasse for three weeks. I was upset with Jeff because he didn't catch on to the math problems I was teaching him during our sojourn at L'Abri. I was convinced my explanations were so clear that he could understand them if he would only try. But the more I tried to get through to Jeff, the louder my voice grew and the more impatient I became. And the more Jeff locked me out!

As I looked at his frightened face, it hit me. I was doing the same thing to Jeff that my father had done to me when I was a child struggling with math! I remembered how humiliated I felt and how stupid I thought I was because I didn't understand what my father was trying to teach me. My dad's voice would become shrill and his face red with frustration as I sat immobilized. I'm sure Dad thought his instructions were clear, but they weren't. As a child, I blamed my own stupidity, not my father's poor teaching.

Now I was doing the very same thing to my own son. What saddened me most of all was my total lack of empathy for what Jeff was feeling. If anyone in the world was in a position to understand his turmoil, I was. Instead, I remained callous to Jeff's feelings and our stressful relationship until it finally dawned on me what I was doing: *I was creating Jeff in my own image.* That is, I was repeating the painful experience from my childhood, except this time I was in the role of the stern, overbearing father and Jeff was the frightened, humiliated boy.

This process of creating our children in our own image repeats itself over and over again in all our lives. It is happening right now to you in your own family, and you are probably not even aware that it's going on. Why does it happen? And why are we so blind to its insidious occurrence in our own lives? The answer to these questions is found in the degree of awareness, or *lack* of awareness, we have of our own inner child and the inner child of others. Our natural tendency is to shut off our inner child so that we can avoid the pain of hurtful memories.

PERSONAL REFLECTION

■ FOR PARENTS ONLY. Complete the following statements:

Something I've done to my child that my father did to me is

_____

One thing I've said to my child that my mother said to me is

_____

Something my parents did that I swore I'd never do as a parent is

_____

_____

■ FOR NON-PARENTS ONLY. Finish each of these sentences:

One thing I do now as an adult that my mother did when I was a child is _____

_____

A behavior of my father's that I find myself doing as an adult is

_____

Something my parent(s) did to me as a child that I never want to repeat if I ever become a parent is _____

_____

During those months at L'Abri in Switzerland, as I taught Jeff math to keep his schoolwork current, something else was happening within me. Old, unconscious memories of encounters with my father were activated—painful recollections that stirred up feelings of humiliation, stupidity, and rejection. Faced with a situation that stirred up long-buried pain, I could do one of two things: I could allow my inner child to relive the memories and thus experience the pain; or I could avoid the painful feelings and thus keep them out of my awareness.

I already had a legitimate defense for avoidance: I was Jeff's parent. But in this case, I was playing the part of the parent to avoid those nagging, humiliating feelings of the little child within me. You may be thinking, "Well, you are Jeff's parent, so how is that being defensive?" The problem is that *I was parenting without compassion or empathy.* I was not putting myself in my son's shoes. To have empathy for Jeff meant allowing myself to feel the painful emotions of my inner child when I recalled the shattering episodes with my own father. Unconsciously, I wanted to avoid those memories, so I used my role and my authority as a father to make Jeff feel what I did not want to feel. In other words, by relating to Jeff as my father had related to me, I put Jeff in the position of experiencing the same hurtful feelings I had experienced. In a sense, I was placing my own inner-child feelings into Jeff.

PERSONAL REFLECTION

■ Does the pattern Dr. Dickinson describes in the previous two paragraphs make sense to you? Can you think of any feelings you are carrying around today that really belong to your parents? What are they?

_____

_____

_____

■ FOR PARENTS ONLY. What, if any, hurtful feelings are you putting on your children because you have not dealt with them in your own life? Give an example of a time you did this.

_____

_____

_____

_____

Unfortunately, this happens all the time. What is the impact on our children? When they are young, they love us unquestioningly and believe we can do no wrong. They need to believe that we are infallible because they are completely dependent on us for love, security, and protection. But what happens when things go wrong, when the chinks in our armor become evident, when relationships break down? The child is convinced that it's all his fault; he must have done something bad to cause the problem.

PERSONAL REFLECTION

■ When something goes wrong in a relationship, are you convinced that it is all your fault—that you must have done something *bad* to cause the problem? Cite one or two examples of your thinking this way.

_____

_____

_____

In Jeff's case, I couldn't admit that the real issue was my unclear teaching methods and my intolerance of his apparent inability to learn. No wonder he began to feel stupid and concluded that I was disappointed in him. Still, he loved me and wanted my approval. So what did he do to get it? He tried harder. If I hadn't seen what I was doing, the destructive cycle would have continued.

Do you see the process? I give poor instructions, so Jeff tries harder to win my approval. The harder he tries, the worse he performs and the angrier I become, until finally he feels totally defeated and I am thoroughly frustrated. I begin to think he really is stupid; he feels like a complete failure. Thus, I have managed to create my son in the self-defeating image I had of myself as a child. *And what has it cost me? My relationship with my son!*

If this concept is new to you, you may be puzzling over what I mean when I say I managed to create my son in my own image. For clarity's sake, let's analyze this process a little further. My inner child feels stupid and humiliated, but I can bury those feelings by playing my parent role. I unconsciously model my parenting behavior after the patterns I observed in my own father. When my son responds in the same way I responded to my dad, I am reminded of my own inner child's feelings of stupidity, humiliation, and sense of failure. But now I am the adult. I can hide my childhood pains behind my role as the authority figure. I can wield power. I can be my dad, booming commands and being invincible. How does my son feel now? He feels stupid and humiliated, and sure that he is a failure. In other words, I have managed to create a little replica of myself. How do I know how my son feels? I don't at first, because I am too blind to the feelings of my own inner child. Unconsciously I refuse to identify with my son and his pain; to do so would require me to relive the dark feelings of my own wounded inner child. It is only when I become aware of the feelings of my own child within that I can gain insight and develop empathy for Jeff.

CYCLE OF REPEATED PATTERNS

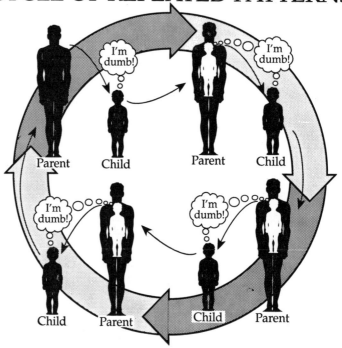

Do you find yourself parenting your youngsters the same way you were parented? In some cases that works well, especially if your parents were sensitive and perceptive people who spent time getting to know you and helping you to develop as a person in your own right. In a positive sense, we create children in our own image when we instill virtues like honesty, industriousness, courage, compassion, and generosity. As Christians we also attempt to mold our children to God's image—that is, in the image or design He created them to be, possessing godly attributes and their own unique combination of abilities.

PERSONAL REFLECTION

■ No parent is all bad or all good. In what ways did your parents positively "create you in their own image"? What virtues and values did they instill in you? What, if any, godly attributes do you possess today because of your parents?

_____

_____

_____

_____

_____

_____

Because the problem is so widespread, we will focus only on the negative aspects of creating our children in our own image.

Margaret, one of my patients, concerned about her teenage daughter's sexual behavior, became very restrictive, forcing Candy to attend every youth meeting at church, lecturing her often about sexual diseases, and warning her that God would punish her for her sexual sins.

This is not to imply that parents shouldn't warn their children of the dangers of sexual misconduct or teach them biblical principles for sexual behavior. The key is in how this is done. In time, Candy became sexually active, perhaps deliberately trying to hurt her mother. Margaret tearfully admitted that Candy was behaving just like she did when she was in high school, and that her mother had treated her exactly the same way she was treating Candy. When Margaret realized what she was doing, she told me, "I remember saying to myself that I would never do to Candy what my mother did to me. But here I am doing the same thing."

Margaret also confided that she never felt loved by her mother because she interpreted the lectures as her mother's way of saying that she was a promiscuous person. Now Margaret's daughter felt the same way about herself. What Margaret needed to do was sit down and encourage her daughter to talk about her feelings and attitudes toward boys, dating, and sex. By showing genuine interest in Candy's point of view, she would be saying, "I care about you, Candy, and want to understand how you think and feel because you are important to me." This approach would acknowledge that she respected Candy as a person in her own right, and that she felt Candy was capable of thinking through the implications of her own behavior, especially once she had reached the age where parental control and influence are more indirect than direct. A teenager who feels good about who she is and respected by her parents is in a much better position to make wise decisions about the way she will live her life than one who is not.

PERSONAL REFLECTION

■ FOR PARENTS ONLY. In what ways do you relate to Margaret's parenting experience? What secret fears from the past may be unconsciously driving you to repeat destructive patterns in the present through your children?

_____

_____

_____

_____

_____

Many years ago my mother took me to the open-air market near Lincoln Park in downtown Long Beach. In the middle of the park stood the Long Beach Library, an old structure filled with what seemed to me a bountiful supply of ancient books and ancient people. But what fascinated me most was the park. It was teeming with plump gray pigeons and scruffy old bums who called the park home. I recall one shabbily dressed gentleman sitting next to a large tree creatively "fishing" for pigeons. He tied one end of some string to a piece of bread and held the other end in his hand. Then he threw the baited bread on the grass and waited for the unsuspecting pigeon to walk over and peck at the bread. Slowly he drew the bread closer while the pigeon engaged in lunch, blissfully unaware that it would shortly be lunch for someone else. Finally, the old man had the pigeon right next to him. Before the bird knew what happened, he found himself in bird heaven, and shortly dinner was served. The message here? The pigeon's need for food caused him to be entrapped by someone who wished him harm.

In a similar way, a child's need for love and approval makes him susceptible to mistreatment from others. This problem occurs most often between parent and child. Because of the child's conflicting needs for love and independence, significant tensions can develop in families as a child enters what some psychologists call the stage of autonomy. At about age two the child becomes more mobile, better coordinated, and immensely curious and ready to explore the world around him. He wants to do things for himself—dress himself (even though his pants are on backward) and feed himself (no matter that the sticky oatmeal hits everything in a 10-foot radius). When he discovers that all his body parts belong to the same person, an individual begins to emerge!

The word _no_ becomes his favorite; he says no to everything: "It's time for dinner, Johnny." No!

"It's time to go to bed, Mary." No!

"Time for a bath, Penny." No!

The way the child's budding independence is handled during this critical time in his life will determine, to a great extent, how well he grows into a person in his own right instead of a child created in his parents' image. What do I mean?

Suppose your mother was extremely overprotective with you as a child. She fretted over your health, your scrapes and cuts, your sleep habits, your bowel movements, and your emotional well-being. Like a large bird hovering overhead, she was ready to rescue you at the slightest hint of trouble.

Kathy and I had a neighbor who was an overprotective mother. She constantly warned her three-year-old daughter, "Don't climb up in the tree or you'll fall down. Don't swing on the gate or you'll get hurt! Don't play with the dog or you'll get germs." On and on she went, creating within her child a great fear of the world.

Now I am not suggesting a disregard for the child's safety. But there is a point at which concern can cripple the child's growth. When this happens, we are looking at overprotectiveness. What is the impact on the child's development when a parent is overprotective? The child becomes unduly fearful and cautious and hesitates to venture out on his own. He develops an increased dependency on his parents' protection and direction. His confidence in his ability to solve problems and develop mastery over his world is replaced by overdependency on others to take care of him. The need for love, approval, and security is so strong within the child that he will do whatever is necessary to secure the approval of his parents. This type of environment often produces the "adapted child response" of compliancy, withdrawal, or procrastination that plagues the child into adult years. In other words, the child puts on the mask of dependency or compliancy to make himself "acceptable" to others. It is important to keep in mind that the adapted child is not the real inner child, but rather a facade to protect the inner child from harm by avoiding disapproval or criticism from significant others.

I always worry about the youngster who seems to be the perfect child. I know many teachers hope for a classroom full of these kids. They never get into trouble; they're always polite and eager to please. I'm not opposed to these characteristics, but there is a point beyond which these behaviors are unnatural for average children. They are literally too good to be true. Such children have often been created in the image of their parents to be good and obedient so they may gain the approval of all the significant adults in their lives. Parental overprotectiveness tells them, "You cannot take care of yourselves on your own; you need us to take care of you, to make your decisions, and to live your lives for you. If you follow our rules, you will receive our love and approval."

These children become adults who continue the dependent pattern with friends, then girlfriends and boyfriends, and eventually with marriage partners. When they have children, they parent as they have been parented, thus overprotecting their children too, building in them the same dependency they experienced. On and on the story goes, and where it stops nobody knows. Does it sound discouraging? Yes, but this destructive pattern doesn't have to continue if we become aware of the wrong ways we create children in our own image.

PERSONAL REFLECTION

■ Dr. Dickinson reminds us that "the need for love, approval, and security is so strong within a child that he will do whatever is necessary to secure the approval of his parents." How much time did you spend as a child seeking the approval of your parents? What behaviors brought approval from them? How did your parents communicate disapproval to you?

_____

_____

_____

_____

_____

■ Would you describe yourself as a people-pleaser? To what extent are you willing to go to keep other people happy? What has it cost you to be a people-pleaser?

_____

_____

_____

_____

■ In his book *Love: No Strings Attached*, Rich Buhler states that we often confuse *love* and *approval*. Approval must be earned and is granted because of what we do. Approval can be lost. Describe a time when you lost the approval of someone who is important to you. How did you feel in relation to that person afterward?

_____

_____

_____

_____

_____

■ Love is anything that is done for a person because of what the person is. There are no strings attached. It is unconditional. Give an example from your life of being *conditionally* loved. What did it cost you to get that love? Then cite an example of someone loving you *unconditionally*.

_____

_____

_____

_____

_____

■ FOR PARENTS ONLY. Would you say you love your children *conditionally* or *unconditionally?* Explain.

_____

_____

_____

_____

_____

■ Did you relate to Dr. Dickinson's description of the *overprotective* parent? In what ways? How often do you use "be careful" or "don't do" messages with your children? Jot down any messages you recall using.

_____

_____

_____

_____

_____

_____

_____

Another negative way we create children in our image is to be extremely critical of their behavior. While many parents feel that criticism is a way to help a child avoid making mistakes and improve behavior, from the child's perspective frequent and insensitive criticism can be very discouraging and demoralizing. It often carries with it the message that the child has failed to please Mom and Dad and is not good enough.

Mom, suppose your five-year-old child comes running to you bursting with excitement and clutching a drawing he has made of a horse. As he thrusts the picture proudly into your hands, what do you say? Imagine the conversation going something like this:

Mom: Well, Ted, what do we have here?

Ted: It's a present, Mom. I made it just for you.

Mom: Why, how nice. But what is it?

Ted: (Disappointed) Can't you tell, Mom? It's a horse.

Mom: But, Ted, horses don't look this way.

Ted: They do so!

Mom: No, I'll show you how to draw a horse the right way.

Ted: (Angrily grabs the picture back) I don't want to!

The important issue here is that Ted used his own initiative and creativity to do something nice for his mother. He wanted to please her and receive her love and approval for the picture he gave her. Mom, perhaps wanting Ted to develop his skills in art, felt the need to turn this gift into a drawing lesson. The message Ted received was, _I didn't please my mother; I did it wrong; I disappointed her._

Mom missed an opportunity to encourage Ted to use his own ideas and abilities. Repeated experiences of this type can cause a child to abandon all attempts at self-expression; instead they produce a child whose primary goal is to please significant people by being what they want him to be. This becomes the child created in the parents' image. The Apostle Paul addressed this very issue in his letter to the Ephesian Christians: "Fathers, do not provoke your children to anger; but bring them up in the discipline and instruction of the Lord" (Ephesian 6:4).

Paul was warning parents not to use harsh criticism in the training of their children because it produces anger and discouragement. Anger comes from the child's inability to please, which produces a sense of hopelessness. This is not to say that when you discipline a child with sensitivity and consistency he won't be angry with you. That would be unrealistic because discipline will produce some frustration when he can't do what he wants to do. But this kind of anger is different from the one Paul wrote about, which results from critical treatment that discourages the child.

PERSONAL REFLECTION

■ Did you grow up in a home where a lot of criticism was expressed toward you as a child? Try to recall some ways in which you were criticized. Write down what you remember hearing.

_____

_____

_____

_____

_____

■ What has been the result of critical treatment in your life? Do you struggle with being critical of yourself? Are you critical of other people?

_____

_____

_____

_____

_____

■ FOR PARENTS ONLY. Are you critical of your children? How has your criticism impacted your relationship with them?

_____

_____

_____

_____

_____

_____

■ What steps might you take to become a less critical person?

_____

_____

_____

_____

Before we consider how to help children grow up to become the persons God created them to be, let's summarize some key points about raising children in our own image.

√ *Each child God has lent us was created to be a unique person in his or her own right.*

√ *A child needs love, approval, and security in order to develop a unique identity.*

√ *Around the age of two, a child begins to move toward doing more for himself, exploring the world he lives in, and developing a sense of identity as a separate person from Mom and Dad.*

√ *As parents we can unwisely use our love and approval as candy on a string to reward compliant behavior and create children in our own image. Or we can use the power of love and approval to encourage our children to grow and develop into unique persons with their own abilities and ideas.* This does not mean that we do not discipline our children, but that our discipline is custom-made for each child, providing realistic boundaries for protection, yet at the same time offering enough flexibility for personal growth.

PERSONAL
REFLECTION

■ FOR PARENTS ONLY. As you've read through the material in this chapter, have you come to see anything about the way you parent that needs to change? Before going on, stop for a minute and ask God to confirm in your heart how you need to change. Then write a prayer of commitment, expressing to Him the ways you want to change as a parent.

_____

_____

_____

_____

_____

_____

The first step in helping a child become the individual God designed is to realize how easy it is to mold the child into what you want, rather than what God has designed.

The second step is to recognize that the whole concept of helping a child develop a unique identity is God's idea, not the product of psychology. Psychologists have recognized the importance of this principle because God has placed the need in every person as His image-bearer.

In Proverbs 22:6, we read: "Train up a child in the way he should go, even when he is old he will not depart from it." The *Amplified Bible* helps us to understand this passage more clearly when it states: "Train up a child in the way he should go [and in keeping with his individual gift or bent], and when he is old he will not depart from it."

The key phrase here is "the way he should go." Many think this refers to training a child in the things pertaining to God. In various places in Scripture we are admonished to do just that, but in this verse the emphasis is on the natural bent or aptitudes of the child. When he is old he will continue living consistently as the unique person God has gifted him to be. Mom and Dad, are you actively looking for the unique qualities of your children? You might ask, "How do we discover our children's natural aptitudes?"

One of the first steps in this process is the discovery of your own inherent giftedness. These natural aptitudes make up your identity as a person; they are a part of your inner child, the real you. Natural aptitudes are those qualities you are born with; you did not learn them, train to obtain them, or acquire them through practice. They are God-given just like your height, hair and eye color, basic body build, and the size of your nose or ears.

In the previous chapter we looked at the three general areas of natural talent: communicational talents, relational talents and functional talents. It is important to recognize your own talent strengths so that you can help your children discover theirs.

Age is one factor in identifying a child's natural aptitudes. While your child is at home, the environment you provide reflects your interests and values and, as a result, your child, being eager to please you, may show an interest in what you like rather than in what he naturally does well. It's often only after a child reaches the late teens and then leaves home that he begins to discover his own natural talents. This doesn't mean that your child's inherent aptitudes won't in some way be visible early on, but that you need to be careful not to see only what you want to see in your child, especially when it comes to your favorite strengths, like athletics, music, performing, and so forth.

My son followed in my footsteps and grew up doing almost everything I did, right down to choosing the same sports, college major, and summer work. I was on the swimming and water polo team in high school and so was Jeff. I worked as a lifeguard in college and so did he. I majored in psychology in college and so did he. That's enough to make a father proud. I think in many ways he wanted to be like me . . . but God made him different from me.

I discovered this fact when he left home for college and more so after his graduation. I came to realize that Jeff is more comfortable with a group of people than I am. He is much more organized in setting priorities and using his time effectively. He has more supervisory talent than I do, especially in initiating and developing new ideas and getting people involved. Jeff's interest in business led him to become an insurance broker, whereas my talents led me into counseling, teaching, and music.

At first I was a little disappointed that we took different paths, for I thought I knew my son so well. Now I know I was influenced more by what I wanted to see in Jeff than by what he really was. How easy it is to create a child in our own image! These days I have come to appreciate the real Jeff, and I take pride in seeing him develop his own natural aptitudes in a career of his choice.

PERSONAL REFLECTION

■ Think about your family of origin. What interests and activities did your parents encourage? What things did you do that caused them to compliment you?

_____

_____

_____

_____

■ Were the things your parents focused on and praised you for really your talent strengths or did you do them just to please them?

_____

_____

_____

_____

■ FOR PARENTS ONLY. Which of your children do you feel closest to? Why do you think you feel closest to that child? In what ways are you alike? How are you different?

_____

_____

_____

_____

_____

As your children seek out their unique strengths, you need to teach them some basic survival skills that may not be natural to them. Survival skills are behaviors needed to get along in this world and to live effectively with others. They are learned over a period of time by persistence, practice, and patience.

An illustration may clarify this point. Suppose you have a little girl named Susie. Among her other talents, Susie has a strong creative bent. You show her how to fix her hair, and she creates an unusual style that looks good. Susie always seems to do things differently from her peers and with a unique touch. As she grows older, she enjoys helping in the kitchen but she doesn't like to follow recipes. She prefers experimenting with a variety of ingredients, and her culinary creations always taste good. One problem: Susie doesn't like to clean up the kitchen; in fact, she usually leaves it a mess.

How do you, her parent, approach this problem? You might say, "I'd march her out to the kitchen and make her clean it up properly." This will surely be your response if you are a highly organized person with a natural aptitude for ordering your space. So you resolve, "I'm going to teach Susie to be as organized as I am!" Good luck! You'll need it.

What you need to understand is the difference between neatness, which is learned, and a natural aptitude for organization of space, which is unlearned. You also need to recognize that creative people often have little talent for organization of space. For them it's a nonstrength. Just look at Susie's room—it's a disaster!

Does this mean that you should simply ignore Susie's mess, chalking it up to her "natural bent" for chaos, and clean up the kitchen yourself? Definitely not! As you come to understand how people differ in their natural aptitudes, you realize that Susie will never be as organized as you are; but, equally important, she doesn't have to *like* being neat in order to learn the skill of neatness.

The tension comes when we try to force our children to be just like we are when they don't have our particular talents. Somehow we assume that something is wrong with them because they aren't able to do exactly what we do. Remember, your children want very much to please you and they need your love, support, and approval. The more you recognize your children's natural bents and distinguish them from survival skills, the more you will validate and encourage them to be what God has gifted them to be. Keep in mind also that siblings may have very different talents from one another.

Encouraging a child to develop his abilities in the area of physical activities is another example of survival skills. Even if he isn't highly talented with physical coordination, he can enjoy such socially oriented sports as tennis, baseball, swimming, badminton, bicycling, and volleyball. If your child doesn't have athletic ability, don't push him to excel; rather, encourage him to enjoy the activity and to have fun with the family. Likewise, your child may not have any natural talent in music or art or literature, but that doesn't mean he can't learn to appreciate good music, art, and literature for his own enjoyment.

PERSONAL REFLECTION

■ FOR PARENTS ONLY. What do you already know about your children's natural abilities and survival skills? Record what you know in the space provided below. *Additional space for writing is available in Appendix Three if you need it.*

Child's name and age: _____

_____

The natural abilities I've noticed in my child: _____

_____

_____

One thing I will do to encourage my child's natural abilities:

_____

_____

The survival skills my child still needs to acquire: _____

_____

Steps I plan to take to help my child acquire these needed skills:

_____

_____

_____

_____

Child's name and age: _____

_____

The natural abilities I've noticed in my child: _____

_____

_____

One thing I will do to encourage my child's natural abilities:

_____

_____

The survival skills my child still needs to acquire: _____

_____

_____

Steps I plan to take to help my child acquire these needed skills:

_____

_____

_____

_____

Child's name and age: _____

_____

The natural abilities I've noticed in my child: _____

_____

_____

One thing I will do to encourage my child's natural abilities:

_____

_____

The survival skills my child still needs to acquire: _____

_____

_____

Steps I plan to take to help my child acquire these needed skills:

_____

_____

_____

_____

Let's look at a number of things you as a parent can do to discover and encourage the natural aptitudes that make up part of your youngster's inner child.

√ *Encourage your child to try new and different things.* Do you have a comfort zone? What's that, you ask? Your comfort zone represents those things you are comfortable doing and do well. My comfort zone includes public speaking, counseling, jogging, bicycling, working on my boat, and doing things by myself or with a few close friends. My discomfort zone includes attending large parties where I don't know anybody, singing a solo, having to be responsible for many people, and doing repetitious activities.

Children also have a comfort zone with activities they enjoy. But it's important that we as parents challenge them by pushing them out of their comfort zones so that they may experience more of the world.

They are more likely to discover their natural talents if they stretch and try new things. For example, if your child likes to stay at home most of the time, persuade her to go to summer camp. Encourage her to stay overnight with her friends occasionally, so she can see how other families live. If your child tends to vegetate in front of the TV, encourage him to try new hobbies, take music lessons, build model airplanes, or experiment with home computer games—whatever it takes to nudge him out of his comfort zone.

PERSONAL REFLECTION

■ What is your comfort zone? What things are you comfortable doing and do well? How willing are you to try new and different things? Make a list of new things you want to try in the future.

_____

_____

_____

_____

_____

■ FOR PARENTS ONLY. What are your children's comfort zones? How do their comfort zones differ from yours? What are you doing to encourage your children to try new and different things? What more might you do?

_____

_____

_____

_____

_____

√ *Purchase toys that help develop talents.* A word of caution. The toys you buy are for your children, not you—to develop their talents, not yours. Our children give us an excuse to be kids again, so what do we adults do? We rush out and buy them all the things we like, not what they want. When you purchase toys, keep your child's talents in mind. If your daughter is artistic, buy her crayons and paint sets and modeling clay. Does your son like to build things? Then buy building blocks and modeling kits for him. Does your daughter like the mental challenge of puzzles and games? Then provide them for her. Does your son like to perform? Then puppets or a musical instrument may be in order. Or would he prefer a football or running shoes to hone his athletic skills? Maybe she would rather have a cuddly doll to nurture and love. Or maybe your son would prefer the doll and your daughter the football. Do you unconsciously limit your child by forcing him or her into typical male or female stereotypes? Or are you willing to let your child express interests freely, even when these contradict traditional stereotypes?

If possible, provide a play area for your child where he can make a mess—maybe an extra room or a corner of the basement or garage—a place he can consider his own, where he can experiment and create without being hassled about spilled paint or clutter. If you happen to be a noncreative parent with a creative child and you're not sure what sort of toys to buy, talk to a teacher or to other parents you consider creative. They'll be glad to give you ideas.

PERSONAL REFLECTION

■ As an adult are you free to play, or have you gotten so absorbed in work that play is a lost art to you? What might you need to do to balance out your life in the areas of *work* and *play?* What are some ways you like to play?

_____

_____

_____

_____

_____

■ FOR PARENTS ONLY. How much time do you encourage your children to spend playing? What are you doing to encourage your children to be *creative* in their play?

_____

_____

_____

_____

_____

√ *Keep an accomplishment notebook for each child.* As you watch for natural aptitudes in your child, occasionally you will notice an ability that is truly outstanding. Even at a very early age, an inherent talent may shine through. As a child in school, I often had the choice of doing oral or written reports. I always chose the oral report. Not only was speaking easy for me, but I was also a performer at heart. My mother forced me to take piano lessons for six long and painful years, assuring me I would thank her profusely in years to come. (I'm 50 now. Sorry, Mom, still no thanks!) But all the mothers loved to hear me play at the annual recitals. Why? Surely not because of my skills at the piano. No, it was my performing—Dick, the natural show-man—that did the trick.

When you attend open house at your child's school, take time to notice his papers or drawings on the wall or her projects on display. How does the work compare with the offerings of others in the class? Does he draw better than the others, write creative stories, create a winning science project? What does her teacher say about her skills and performance in class? About his efforts, his sportsmanship, his interests? A child's early accomplishments offer clues to natural aptitudes and future career goals.

Even before your child starts school, start a scrapbook of his work. Keep the book up-to-date throughout his student years, adding drawings or photographs of special events, perfect papers or reports, and ribbons or awards for significant achievement. Then, whenever your child complains about how dumb or untalented he is, bring out the book and let him see for himself the evidence of his natural aptitudes. It's a great self-esteem enhancer.

Mom and Dad, these principles for raising healthy, creative children will work for you. They're not complicated or mysterious. They're sound and scripturally based. As parents, learn to appreciate who you are as image-bearers of God. Look carefully at how God has gifted you with natural abilities. Then identify and nurture your children's special talents. Encourage them to become the unique individuals God created them to be.

PRAYERFUL REFLECTION

■ The goal of parenting is not to be a *perfect* parent, but simply, a *good-enough* parent. All parents make some mistakes. One thing good-enough parents do is recognize and appreciate their own God-given natural abilities and also those of their children. Commit yourself to being a good-enough parent this week. Express your commitment to God in the form of a prayer, thanking Him for the natural abilities he has blessed you with and also your children.

_____

_____

_____

_____

_____

_____

PERSONAL RENEWAL

■ Daily renew your commitment to be a good-enough parent by memorizing Proverbs 22:6 (AMP). Try personalizing this verse for each child who is part of your household. Insert each one's name in the verse in place of the words *a child*.

I will . . .

Train up a child in the way he should go [and in keeping with his individual gift or bent], and when he is old he will not depart from it.

If you are interested in learning more about your natural talents, especially as they relate to finding your niche in the work world, contact the office listed below for helpful information:

IDAK Group, Inc.
7931 NE Halsey
Banfield Plaza Building
Portland, Oregon 97213-6755
Ph. 503-252-3495
Ph. 503-257-0189

Chapter 7
Creating Our Own Stress

Toby was your typical corporate man—polished shoes, freshly starched button-down shirt, dark suit, every hair in place. His speech was rapid and businesslike. He checked his watch often and seemed always in a hurry. His anxiety was contagious. Whenever I was around Toby, I felt like I was in a hurry too.

Toby didn't know it, but he was on the verge of burnout. A few months before, he had been promoted to general manager of a large automobile agency and moved his family into an expensive home in an exclusive neighborhood. Although his income had increased, his house payments doubled. Toby seemed to have it all, but he was not a happy man. He worried constantly about his job and his ability to maintain his standard of living. He couldn't enjoy his success, his home, his wife, children, or friends. His sleep was restless and his physician informed him he was working on an ulcer. Reluctantly, he decided to try counseling.

After a few sessions it became clear to me that in spite of his abilities and outward successes, Toby felt inadequate as a man. He had set out to prove to the world—and himself—that he could make it to the top. What he lacked in natural talent he made up for with hard work. Now at 35 he began to realize his sad mistake of making his career his identity. For Toby, admitting that he wasn't happy in his career meant he was failing as a man; by denying his feelings he was creating such stress that his physical and emotional health was in jeopardy. Over and over, Toby asked me to give him some quick solutions to his stress-related symptoms; he didn't want to face the painful realities within his own personality.

There are many Tobys in this world—men and women—suffering from excessive stress. Stress-related problems have reached epidemic proportions in our society, invading the workplace, the home, and personal life. In Toby's case, he denied his inner child's feelings of fear and inadequacy. To avoid these painful emotions, he developed a strong "adapted child response." He put on what he considered a more acceptable "face" to prove to the world, to himself, and especially to his critical inner parent that he could be successful if he just tried hard enough.

The problem is that whenever we lose touch with our inner child and hide behind the expedient mask of the adapted child, our critical inner parent always wins. We will kill ourselves with stress to prove our inner parent wrong, but it never works, for in the end we lose our health, family, friends, and perhaps even life itself.

PERSONAL REFLECTION

■ Does your story resemble that of Toby's? In what ways?

_____

_____

_____

■ Richard Ecker in his book, *The Stress Myth* (InterVarsity Press, p. 10), states:

The thousands of people who succumb to fatal Monday [heart] attacks are but a handful compared to the hordes of Americans who daily suffer discomfort, inconvenience, disability or death as the result of stress. . . . Stress has become the most common cause of job dissatisfaction, of reduced productivity in the workplace, and of family conflict and divorce. Unquestionably, stress is the most significant health influence at work in American society today, and the problem grows more serious every day.

List 10 things that cause you to feel stress. Then go back and number your stress list in order, 1 being the *most* stressful and 10 being the *least* stressful item on the list.

_____

_____

_____

_____

_____

_____

_____

_____

_____

_____

At this point, you may be thinking that all stress is bad; it isn't. Stress does have a good side. "Life is difficult." That's the very first sentence in M. Scott Peck's best-selling book, _The Road Less Traveled._[1] Just what we want to read! Everyone already knows that life is difficult. What we really want to hear is that life is rosy . . . a bowl of cherries. We want to read about 10 steps to a stress-free life or how to get rich while playing all day. Make it easy and simple.

The fact is that life isn't simple; it's usually challenging and difficult. Our inner child likes to believe in the tooth fairy, Disneyland, and the world of make-believe where all our wishes come true just by thinking about them. It's hard for many of us to accept that life is difficult because it scares our inner child. But if we avoid the problems that cause stress, we will stay frightened and never develop into mature, fully functioning adults.

Without stress, there is no growth. In the Bible, we have an excellent example of the benefits of stress:

> Therefore having been justified by faith, we have peace with God through our Lord Jesus Christ, through whom also we have obtained our introduction by faith into this grace in which we stand; and we exult in hope of the glory of God.
>
> And not only this, but we also exult in our tribulations knowing that tribulation brings about perseverance; and perseverance, proven character; and proven character, hope; and hope does not disappoint, because the love of God has been poured out within our hearts through the Holy Spirit who was given to us (Romans 5:1-5).

When the word _therefore_ appears in a Scripture passage, it indicates a relationship to the previous verse or verses. In the passage above, the Apostle Paul tells us that our standing before God is not based on the law or ordinances but rather on the finished work of Christ on the cross when He became our substitute for sin. By placing our faith and trust in Him we have peace with God.

Then we come to the character qualities that result from stress. Notice that we are to rejoice in tribulation. Some might claim that such advice makes Christians appear masochistic. Unless we understand what this passage means, it appears to suggest self-punishment. The word *tribulation* means "affliction, pressure, distress, the normal, unavoidable pressures of daily living." We rejoice because God uses these stressors for our character development.

Notice the progression. First, there is tribulation, which produces perseverance, or the ability to hang in there and not quit. You've heard the saying, "When the going gets tough, the tough get going." That's what this passage is saying. Notice what follows next: Proven character, or the ability to carry on in the face of hardship, to be effective under pressure. It's the equivalent of the Underwriters Laboratory approval (UL) applied to human beings. You cannot have proven character without perseverance. What follows next is hope. The hope here is based on what has preceded in this passage. Out of stress comes perseverance, out of perseverance comes proven character, and as a result, your hope in God is strengthened. God uses stress in your life to build character.

PERSONAL REFLECTION

■ Without stress in our lives there is no growth. Discover the good side of stress by applying the principles of Romans 5:1-5 to a particular tribulation you've faced in the past.

TRIBULATION: What is one unavoidable pressure of daily living you've faced?

_____

_____

PERSEVERANCE: How has that unavoidable pressure increased your ability to hang in there and not quit?

_____

_____

PROVEN CHARACTER: Describe specific ways you became more effective under pressure because you didn't give in to it.

_____

_____

_____

HOPE: In what ways did you learn to trust God and hope in Him because of the pressure you were under?

_____

_____

_____

REMEMBER: God uses stress in our lives to build character!

√ *Stress increases coping skills.* My client Martha was talented and intelligent but lived in a sheltered world. She had always depended on her husband Bill to take care of her. She let him handle the "annoying details" of her life, like paying bills and balancing a checkbook, while she spent her time taking art classes and designing jewelry. She thought life would go on forever this way until Bill died of a heart attack at 41. With his death, Martha's rosy world came to a crashing halt. Not only had she lost her husband, but she felt helpless to take care of herself. Deep depression led her to my office for therapy.

It took Martha six months to work through her grief. As her depression lifted, she began to face the difficult task of putting her life back together. At first, running her household and managing her personal finances overwhelmed her; but the more she talked out her fears and sense of helplessness, the closer she moved toward taking care of herself. I encouraged her to make a list of skills she needed to manage her life effectively. Then I had her prioritize them from the simplest to the most difficult. With the help of supportive friends who encouraged her but refused to feed her dependency, Martha stepped out, tackled the tasks, and began to grow.

It was exciting for me to see the change in her over the next months—and exciting for her as well. In the two years since Bill's death, Martha has developed into an excellent manager of her home. She has also developed a business making custom jewelry which she sells to exclusive women's shops. For Martha, the stress of her husband's death motivated her to develop her own talents, skills, and coping capacities so that she was able to grow as a person. But I'm not suggesting there has to be a major catastrophe in your life in order for you to grow. Even daily stress can be viewed as an opportunity for personal growth rather than as a meaningless series of headaches and hardships.

PERSONAL REFLECTION

■ Take some time to think over the last six months of your life. Have you had some very stressful experiences? Write a brief statement of each of those stress situations in the left-hand column; then in the right-hand column record some positive lessons you have learned from the experience. If nothing comes to mind, try to think of a positive benefit that could result from the experience.

STRESS SITUATION	POSITIVE LESSONS LEARNED
_____	_____
_____	_____
_____	_____
_____	_____
_____	_____
_____	_____
_____	_____

√ *Stress develops patience.* Unfortunately, we do not develop patience by reading a book on the subject. We learn patience during the daily experiences of life as we encounter normal frustrations and conflicts. The New Testament writer James tells us that without trials—the stress and strain of daily life—we will never develop patience. I tend to be very competitive in athletics, but as I've aged, I have modified my competitive urges so that I can enjoy sports without turning them into a contest. But years ago, golf really challenged my competitive spirit. I developed a healthy slice (curving the ball to the right when it's supposed to go straight), so I was forever playing the fairways to the right instead of the one I was supposed to play. Whenever I sliced the ball, I got so mad I'd throw my club, sometimes achieving more distance with it than I did with the ball.

One day, when Jeff was about nine, he and his mother and I played golf at a pitch-and-putt course. I had just hit the ball miserably and in my anger was about to launch my club into outer space. For an instant I glanced down at my son and was stunned by the horrified look on his face. I resolved then to either give up this "relaxing game" or develop better control of myself. I chose the latter. To continue to play golf, I had to develop patience and change my attitude toward the game. Since I didn't play often enough to perfect my game, I needed to be more tolerant of my bad shots. I also learned to enjoy the good shots and focus on the lovely environment and the warm companionship of friends or family.

PERSONAL REFLECTION

■ Would you describe yourself as patient or impatient? What kind of things "exercise" your patience? *EXAMPLE: Waiting in line. Slow traffic.*

_____

_____

_____

_____

■ Describe a situation God used in your life to teach you to be more patient.

_____

_____

_____

_____

√ *Stress produces needed change.* Change is stressful, even good changes like a vacation, a marriage, a promotion at work, or a move to a new house. Change elevates our anxiety, which is a form of stress. Our inner child would like to avoid anxiety, so we often stay in the same old rut we're in; at least it's safe and secure.

Maybe you've been at the same job for years. You're bored, yet when a new job opportunity comes along, your inner child cries, "What if I fail? What if the work is too hard? What if I have to move?" Even though the new position may be right for you and would stretch your abilities, the potential change causes you to experience stress. It's much easier to stay where you are.

What's interesting is that change is often the result of stress. Essentially there are three reasons for change:

• *Boredom.* The need for security holds you captive until you become so bored with your situation that you decide to do something about it. Boredom prompts you to make a change.

• *Enlightenment.* The second reason for change is a new understanding or fresh insight into yourself or your situation. For example, knowledge of who God is sheds light on the changes God desires for us in our daily walk with Him. The psalmist said, "Thy word is a lamp to my feet, and a light to my path" (Psalm 119:105).

• *Emotional or physical pain.* People usually come for therapy only after suffering the psychological pain of deep anxiety because they can't cope with life, just as people who suffer from physical pain often wait until the pain is unbearable before consulting a doctor. It is interesting that two of the three reasons for change—boredom and pain—are also caused by stress.

Jess Lair was a high-powered advertising executive who at 36 suffered a near-fatal heart attack. During nine months of recovery, he reevaluated his life and decided to leave his high-paying job and return to school to finish a Ph.D. in psychology. After completing his degree, he secured a teaching position at a university and authored a number of books. Two of them related to the course he taught and to his own life experience: *I Ain't Much, Baby, But I'm All I Got*, and one coauthored with his wife, *Hey, God, What Should I Do Now?* It took a heart attack to wake Jess up to the fact that stress can kill. Fortunately, he changed his lifestyle in time. How about you? Have you tolerated enough stress? Is it time to change something in your life for the better?

PERSONAL REFLECTION

■ How do you react to change? Think about a change you've made in your life and/or behavior in the last year. Which of the three reasons for change mentioned in this chapter—boredom, new understanding or fresh insight, emotional or physical pain— prompted you to make that change?

_____

_____

_____

_____

√ *Stress builds stress tolerance.* The maxim is true: The only people without stress are six feet under. Part of daily living is stress. So it's important that you learn how to build up a tolerance for stress just like an athlete builds up a tolerance for pain and fatigue. When you start an exercise program, you notice that in several weeks you have built your stamina. Repeated sensible exercise can give you a faster pace with less fatigue. And the more we persevere without quitting during stressful times, the more we develop our stress tolerance.

√ *Stress helps us to recognize our nonstrengths.* Let's face it—we all have nonstrengths or weaknesses. Just as God has gifted us all with natural aptitudes, so He has also seen fit to create us with "nonaptitudes" as well. If we all could do everything exceedingly well, we would not need one another. But God's choice for us is that we work together. For example, when Kathy's strengths complement my nonstrengths, and vice versa, we make a very effective team. When married couples realize this fact, what a difference it makes in their families!

How do you recognize your nonstrengths? Your stress level gives you a good indication of what you don't do well. One of the significant causes of stress is working over a period of time at a task for which you are not naturally gifted.

Think about Toby, the businessman you met at the beginning of this chapter. Shortly after landing his big promotion, he wound up in my office, a prime candidate for stress overload and burnout. Why? He had been promoted to a position for which he was not naturally talented. He believed the myth that you can do anything you put your mind to, if you just work hard enough. Don't you believe it! That myth can set you up for enough stress to seriously affect your emotional and physical health.

Toby was a successful salesman who often found himself at the top in yearly sales. His big mistake was in not recognizing that he was good in sales, working alone. When he stepped into management and tried supervising others, he discovered he lacked the natural aptitude to work effectively with the people under him. As his frustration increased, his stress level shot up. Rather than stepping back for some serious evaluation, he worked harder—until his stress level reached the breaking point.

Toby's stress was teaching him something vital about his nonstrengths. Is there a lesson in Toby's experience for you too? The harder you work to achieve excellence in a task for which you have no natural aptitude, the greater your personal stress will be. Are you facing a situation similar to Toby's? Then don't just push yourself to work harder. Take time to step back and ask yourself some hard questions about whether this is really your area of giftedness. Seek the advice of a close friend who is willing to speak frankly about your strengths and nonstrengths. Then focus on what you do well naturally and let others help carry the load by complementing your nonstrength with their strengths.

Remember Moses and the Children of Israel after the Exodus? Moses was stressed to the breaking point trying to be all things to the Israelites—teacher, judge, counselor, and arbitrator. Do you think he was naturally talented in all those areas? I doubt it. His father-in-law, Jethro, noticed the heavy toll stress was taking on Moses and said to him, "The thing that you are doing is not good. You will surely wear out, both yourself and these people who are with you, for the task is too heavy for you; you cannot do it alone" (Exodus 18:17-18).

Jethro wisely suggested to Moses that he delegate responsibilities to others who were sensitive to God, who stood for that which was right, and who were *talented* for the job.

PERSONAL
REFLECTION

■ Are there any tasks you are doing at present for which you lack the motivation or which drain you of energy? What are they? What has stress taught you about these nonstrengths? Be specific.

_____

_____

_____

_____

_____

GENERAL RULE OF THUMB: For each task you do, ask yourself this question—"Is this a weight *or is it a* wing?" *(Weights will reveal your nonstrengths; wings will show you where you're naturally gifted.)*

Regardless of how strong you may think you are, or how effectively you are using your inherent aptitudes, you do have stress limits. Several years ago a group of psychologists in private practice were shocked when one of their colleagues committed suicide. Apparently no one had noticed their friend's increasing signs of stress and depression until it was too late. We all have our limits and we need to be aware of them.

There are many factors in our hectic, fast-paced world that can cause us to reach and often exceed our stress limits, even though our inner child is screaming for relief. Let's take a look at some of the causes of excessive stress.

√ *Unrealistic expectations.* I find it helpful to distinguish between the actual demands I face in life, whether on the job or in the home or in relationships, and *the demands I place on myself* that go far beyond what is actually expected. This brings me back to the power of the inner critical parent that demands perfection and is demeaning and critical about anything less. The inner child never has a chance to succeed because nothing will satisfy the demanding inner parent. To satisfy this inner parent, I must be perfect. This attitude adds incredible stress to my life because I will never be satisfied with anything I do, since it falls short of perfection.

It has been only in the last several years that I have been able to come to grips with the unrealistic demands of my inner critical parent. For years nothing I did was good enough. I didn't care what others said regarding my accomplishments; my efforts could never satisfy my inner parent. In physical exercise I pushed myself until I experienced more stress from exercise than I did from my job. If I rode my bike, my goal was to see how fast I could go, or how many bikers I could pass. The pressure I felt was internal, not external; self-generated, not others-generated. I had an incredible capacity to take something enjoyable and turn it into drudgery.

What about you? Are your expectations realistic? Do you demand more from yourself than is required? I'm not suggesting that you shouldn't set standards of excellence. But standards must be realistic and obtainable.

PERSONAL REFLECTION

■ Do you demand more of yourself than is required? Give one or two specific examples of your doing this.

_____

_____

_____

_____

_____

■ How can you maintain personal standards of excellence without setting unrealistic expectations for yourself?

_____

_____

_____

_____

■ If you are a person who expects too much of yourself, you may also expect too much of other people. Are you aware of any unrealistic expectations you may have of other people in your life? What are those expectations?

_____

_____

_____

_____

_____

√ *Unbalanced parental modeling.* One of the most significant ways we learn about life is by watching what our parents do, as opposed to listening to what they say. Some of the behaviors we observe in Mom and Dad may lead us to develop habits that increase negative stress. One such behavior involves the workaholic parent, usually the father. The son and daughter watch Dad bury himself in his work. He is gone before the kids are up and comes home after the kids are in bed. Mother explains Dad's absence as his way of providing for the family, but the kids don't understand. They would rather play with Dad than live in a fancy house or ride in an expensive car. When son and daughter grow up, their concept of work is to bury themselves 24 hours a day until they experience burnout, all for the sake of the family.

I learned some important lessons about life from my father, but he never taught me how to relax and enjoy myself. He was perpetual motion on the weekends, making lists of chores for me to do before I could have fun with my friends. I wish Dad and I could have had more fun together; I missed that. Even when I became an adult, I felt guilty if I sat down on Saturday to watch a football game on TV. I thought I should be doing something more productive.

Mom and Dad, what messages are you communicating to your children? Do you live a balanced life before them? Do you work hard but also take time to relax and enjoy life? Your priorities will become their priorities without you even saying a word.

PERSONAL REFLECTION

■ Were either or both of your parents workaholics? What "silent messages" about work did they communicate to you by their example?

_____

_____

_____

_____

_____

■ Would you describe yourself as a workaholic? Why or why not?

_____

_____

_____

■ FOR PARENTS ONLY. What attitudes toward work are you modeling for your children? What attitudes toward play? What can you do to teach your children to relax and enjoy life more?

_____

_____

_____

_____

√ *Unbridled ambition.* Have you seen the bumper sticker that says, "The person who dies with the most toys wins"? This mentality causes stress that can push you to your limit. In order to afford all the good things in life, you spend more time working. Are all those extra things worth the cost of your health, your family, and friends? You may find it helpful to think through what's really important in life and ask yourself, "Are all the things I strive for really worth the energy that is required to get them?"

What are your priorities? Do you evaluate how you spend your time? If not, it's easy to find yourself in the rat race of unbridled ambition, desperately seeking to acquire things while ignoring your inner child's crying, "Give me a break! I'm pooped!"

PERSONAL REFLECTION

■ Write your own definition of the word *ambition*.

_____

_____

■ Would you describe yourself as a person of "unbridled ambition"? Why?

_____

_____

_____

■ What is really most important to you in life? (Look at the areas of your life where you spend the most time and money.) Make a list of your priorities. Be honest.

_____

_____

_____

_____

√ *Unstable economy.* Another cause of stress that pushes us to our limits is the high cost of living. Our son Jeff married three years ago, and there is no way he can afford to buy a house on his insurance broker's salary unless his wife works too. For many couples, both husband and wife must work to afford even the basics. This dilemma causes additional stress, especially if there are children in the home. By the time Mom and Dad come home from work, they're tired and have little energy or patience to give quality time to the kids.

√*Unrelenting job demands.* Some occupations are more stressful than others. If you are a nurse, teacher, law enforcement officer, doctor, air traffic controller, pastor, or mental health professional, you need to develop some stress safety valves, like engaging in hobbies that provide a complete change of pace. I mess around with the engines on my boat. My fingernails get dirty, my clothes get grimy, and I smell of diesel fuel, but it's relaxing because engines don't talk back. In fact, I don't even have to talk to my engines, except for an occasional monologue when they don't run after I've tried to fix them.

Another safety valve, exercise, is a great way to burn off job stress. But be careful not to overdo it or you'll find yourself looking forward to work just to relieve the stress of too much exercise. Take more frequent vacations. Rather than one long one each season, schedule a week at Christmas and a week in the summer. If possible, take off a day or so every six weeks. And don't forget your friends—they can provide wonderful emotional support if you're willing to be open and transparent with them. Remember, Lone Rangers never do well at the stress game; they usually bite the silver bullet in the end.

PERSONAL
REFLECTION

■ What stress has our unstable economy produced in your life? How have you dealt with this cause of stress?

_____

_____

_____

_____

_____

_____

■ What "safety valves" have you built into your life to offset unrelenting job demands? What more might you need to do?

_____

_____

_____

_____

√ *Unsuitable work environment.* Have you considered the possibility that you are in the wrong job? I frequently talk to people who are suffering negative stress because they're in the wrong occupation.

Phil, a computer salesman, originally came to counseling for marital therapy. But as we talked, I could see that finances caused much of the tension between him and his wife Debbie. Living on straight commission and always behind in his monthly quota, Phil simply wasn't earning enough.

Debbie, meanwhile, was a mover by nature. When the unpaid bills piled up, she prodded Phil to work harder or put in longer hours. Debbie's nagging forced Phil to face the fact that he just wasn't making it on the job, so he took his anger out on her. Instead of working longer hours, he found excuses for not making his calls. When his confidence diminished, he made more excuses. And as his calls fell off, so did his sales. It became a vicious circle that robbed Phil of his self-esteem. He made the mistake of equating his identity with his job description. Then, when his wife suggested he work harder and make more money, it was an even deeper blow to his masculine pride.

The problem wasn't that Phil was untalented; rather, he was in the wrong place to utilize his talents. He wasn't a born salesman, but was gifted in promoting and teaching. When his company transferred him to another position training employees, Phil's stress level decreased and his job satisfaction increased markedly.

PERSONAL
REFLECTION

■ Describe the "perfect job" for YOU. Think about specific tasks you do well or that come easily for you, the kind of people contact you prefer on the job, how large an organization you want to work for, and how you see your work contributing to your overall life purpose.

_____

_____

_____

_____

_____

_____

_____

_____

■ Does the description you just wrote match the work you are doing at present? If so, in what ways? What more are you looking for in your work?

_____

_____

_____

_____

■ If you feel you are in the wrong job, what steps are you willing to take to find a more suitable job for yourself? Be specific.

_____

_____

_____

_____

If you want a surefire formula for exceeding your stress limits and totally exhausting your inner child, try *combining* some of these stress factors we've just considered. For example, when you are unrealistic in your expectations, plus overenthusiastic and convinced you can do anything with hard work, you are well on your way to exceeding your stress limits. Suppose you combine the model of a workaholic father with a high-stress job that happens to be wrong for you. Congratulations, you're on the way to burnout.

Remember Toby? He combined a workaholic father with a high-stress job that was wrong for him and topped it off with unchecked enthusiasm. The job was killing him, and yet his pride would not let him admit that he was not in the right place for his talents. Toby became a classic example of the Peter Principle, which claims you are promoted into higher and higher levels of incompetency if you are not in your talent area.

How do you know if your inner child is being abused by excessive stress? Let me suggest some symptoms:

√ *Depleted energy reserves.* You notice that you don't have the energy it takes to perform even the simplest activities. You are always tired. Your sleep is restless and you wake up tired.

√ *Lowered resistance to illness.* Colds, coughs, sore throats, or nasal drip hang on forever. You don't throw off routine illness as you once did. You seem to catch everything that flies by.

√ *Increased dissatisfaction, pessimism, and irritability.* People comment that you seem to be more negative, impatient, or irritable than you used to be.

√ *Increased absenteeism and inefficiency at work.* You arrive late more often. You watch the clock. Your usual work output is markedly decreasing. You have lost your desire to do the work you are dong. You can't wait for the weekends and you hate Mondays.

Of course, these symptoms are not always caused by stress. There may be something wrong with you physically. Whenever physical symptoms are present, it is a wise idea to check out possible physical causes before concluding that the symptoms are stress-induced.

PERSONAL REFLECTION

■ When stress is not being managed properly in our lives, we end up being burned-out. Do any of the symptoms of burnout Dr. Dickinson suggests apply to your life at present? Check all that apply.

Burnout Checklist

❑ I lack the energy it takes to perform even the simplest activities.
❑ I am always tired.
❑ My sleep is restless and I wake up tired.
❑ I seem to catch every illness that is around.
❑ Routine illnesses seem to hang on for long periods of time.
❑ I feel more dissatisfied, pessimistic, and irritable than I used to.
❑ I arrive late for work more often.
❑ I find myself watching the clock more.
❑ My usual work output is markedly decreasing.
❑ I have lost my desire to do the work I am doing.
❑ I can't wait for the weekend and hate Monday mornings.

■ Jot down specific ways you are abusing your inner child by exceeding your stress limits. Let your inner child talk back to the adult you about the abuse he or she feels. Write down what you hear your inner child saying to you in the form of "I" statements. *EXAMPLE: I never have time to play anymore because you are always working.*

_____

_____

_____

_____

_____

_____

In this chapter we have explored a number of ways we abuse our inner child by exceeding our stress limits. This chapter concludes the first section of the book in which our goal is to understand the inner child and the many ways our child within experiences pain. Now we move to the second section which focuses on ways that we can nurture our inner child.

PRAYERFUL
REFLECTION

■ Go back and review the stress list you compiled on pages 158–159. What things are your greatest sources of stress right now? Write a short prayer asking God to show you what steps you need to take to manage it better in your life. Trust Him to show you how He can use that stress for good in your life.

_____

_____

_____

_____

_____

_____

PERSONAL RENEWAL

■ Renew your thoughts and feelings this week by meditating on Romans 5:1-5 (NCV).

Since we have been made right with God by our faith, we have peace with God. This happened through our Lord Jesus Christ, who has brought us into that blessing of God's grace that we now enjoy. And we are happy because of the hope we have of sharing God's glory. We also have joy with our troubles, because we know that these troubles produce patience. And patience produces character, and character produces hope. And this hope will never disappoint us, because God has poured out His love to fill our hearts. He gave us His love through the Holy Spirit, whom God has given to us.

Chapter 8
Releasing the Inner Child

The story is told of a young naturalist who visited a chicken farm. As he inspected the pen, he noticed an eagle strutting around acting very much like a chicken. The naturalist mused to himself, "What is the king of birds doing in a chicken coop behaving like a chicken?" His curiosity mounting, he inquired of the owner, "How is it that a mighty eagle is cohabiting with these lowly chickens?"

The farmer replied, "Well, sir, I'll tell you. One day I came on this baby bird, and not knowing what kind of bird it was or what to do with it, I decided to put it in with my chickens. It's been there ever since, and it behaves just like all the other chickens."

"But it's not a chicken, it's an eagle," cried the naturalist. "It belongs in the sky, not in a chicken pen!"

"As far as I'm concerned it's a chicken," replied the farmer.

"Would you permit me to release this eagle so it can fly and be what it was created to be?" the naturalist asked.

The farmer shrugged. "It's fine with me, but you're wasting your time. That bird really thinks it's a chicken."

Gently the naturalist reached into the pen and placed the eagle on his arm. Lifting it up toward the sky, he spoke quietly to the king of birds. "You are an eagle. You were meant to fly." But the eagle remained on his arm looking at the pen, then hopped down and promptly rejoined the chickens.

The next day the naturalist returned to the chicken coop, carefully picked up the eagle, rested it on his arm, and carried it out of the pen. Raising his arm in the air, he gave the eagle a gentle push, but the eagle glided to the ground and darted back to the chicken pen again.

The naturalist returned on the third day, but this time he took the eagle up to a high mountain away from the chicken pen. He placed the bird on his arm and said, "You are an eagle. You were created to fly." He held his arm up high and gave a gentle nudge. The eagle trembled. Then, spreading its wings, the graceful bird began to fly. Higher and higher it soared until the naturalist could no longer see it. At last the eagle had found its true identity—with the help of one who respected the difference between a chicken and an eagle. With compassion and patience, the naturalist had encouraged the eagle to be all that God designed it to be.

Do you realize that God has designed you with a unique identity, feelings, and natural aptitudes? In other words, you have an inner child who needs to be released just as the eagle needed to be released from the chicken coop. You cannot release your inner child by yourself. Sheer determination won't do it. You need the help of others, especially loving, caring friends and family and above all, the help of God, the One who created you.

PERSONAL REFLECTION

■ What, if any, thoughts and feelings were you aware of as you read the story of the eagle? Did your inner child identify with the need of the eagle to be released? In what ways?

_____

_____

_____

_____

_____

In this chapter we'll explore why having a personal relationship with God through His Son Jesus Christ provides the only sure foundation for releasing your inner child and building a healthy self-esteem. I realize that the terms self-esteem and self-image may raise a red flag in the evangelical world. A number of Christian writers and pastors have made vociferous attacks on the use of such terms and have gone so far as to blame psychology for seducing Christians away from God.

I am well aware that many secular psychologists have no time for God, but I also know of many dedicated Christian professionals in psychology who have been called into this unique form of Christian ministry. Daily we confront pain-wracked Christians who desperately want to reach out to God but find it difficult because of the damage they have experienced in their early lives. Unfortunately, in many churches the message from the pulpit simply does not reach that deep, inner core where people struggle emotionally. Hurting people are often told that they need more faith, or there is sin in their lives, or all they need to do is trust God more. There may be truth in these statements, but heaping more guilt on such wounded people does not turn them into victorious Christians.

Caring, concerned Christians can help these people turn their hearts toward a loving Heavenly Father who can take their damaged lives and nurture their frightened inner child back to health and vitality. This takes time and knowledge about human behavior, but above all it requires unconditional love that enables the hurt one to look inward and then upward to find restoration. Let's talk abut this unique love and its power.

PERSONAL REFLECTION

■ How do you see yourself? Find a quiet place. In the space provided below, write down spontaneously the thoughts that come as you think about your view of yourself. Don't censor what you write. Write as long as you can. *If you need more space for writing, use the supplemental journaling pages provided in Appendix Three of this workbook.*

My View of Myself

_____

_____

_____

_____

_____

_____

_____

It was obvious that the farmer didn't care that an eagle was living with chickens. To him, birds were birds. Have you ever felt that way? You're just a Social Security number, a zip code, a license plate number, a resident occupying a house, or just part of the herd. People walk by as if you aren't there. Have you ever stood in a checkout line at the grocery store where the cashier never even looks at your face, then glibly wishes you a nice day? The mark of impersonality seems to be everywhere.

PERSONAL
REFLECTION

■ Do you ever feel "invisible"—like you're just a number? When was the last time you felt that way?

_____

_____

_____

_____

_____

■ What is it that makes you feel loved and valued as a person? Who is the person that most often makes you feel valued? What does he or she do to make you feel that way?

_____

_____

_____

_____

My friend, do you know that there is one Person who knows you better than you could ever know yourself? Yes, better than your mate, your friends, your parents, or anyone else in your life? That Person is Jesus Christ. Listen to His words:

> My sheep hear My voice, and I know them, and they follow Me; and I give eternal life to them, and they shall never perish; and no one shall snatch them out of My hand (John 10:27-28).

If you have placed your faith and trust in Jesus as your sinbearer and Lord, He knows you in a special, approving way. God has entrusted you to His Son as a love gift and Jesus prizes you highly. To Him you are never a number, a nonentity. Rather, you are always in the mind of Jesus because you are one of His. As we experience being known by God the Father and His Son Jesus, we begin to treat others with this same compassion and respect for their unique personhood. In my counseling practice I often marvel at how well people respond when I take time to really get to know them.

JESUS KNOWS YOU AND VALUES YOU!

Jesus knows you. His loving, caring eyes gaze right through the many masks you wear to protect yourself from the hurt, shame, and humiliation. Jesus reaches beyond the defensive barriers you've built and finds the fragile inner child hidden in the attic of your mind. He knows how you long to release that child from the bondage of pain and fear so you can be the whole authentic person God created you to be. God is able to deliver you. He is able.

PERSONAL REFLECTION

■ Picture in your mind what it would be like to experience the release of your inner child. What frightens you most about the thought of finally being released? Ask God to help you trust Him enough to actually experience the release of your inner child.

_____

_____

_____

_____

_____

Another unique feature of your relationship with God is that your life has immeasurable value to Him in a way that differs from all other personal relationships. I believe that my genuine caring, loving, and valuing of my patients is a significant healing agent in their therapy. Human caring is not always easy, for we tend to place higher value on those who are especially attractive, charming, successful, or intelligent.

Chuck came to my office for help because of conflicts with his employer. He worked in a warehouse for a large manufacturing company where his boss and fellow employees ridiculed him for his religious beliefs, his mental slowness, and his poor communication skills. When I saw Chuck for the first time, he was depressed, discouraged, and feeling worthless. It was evident that he was functioning at a below-normal intelligence level and would probably never go beyond factory work.

Phil, on the other hand, came to see me because of periodic bouts with depression. He was in his late 40s, handsome, intelligent, wealthy, creative, and articulate. He owned a thriving business and was a whiz at putting together big deals for big bucks. Except for his periodic depression, his life was a whirlwind of excitement.

If you were in my place as a psychologist, which of these two people, Phil or Chuck, would you appreciate more? Answer honestly—your gut-level reaction, not just what you think you should say. I imagine your response would be like mine—Phil gets the vote because he has many more qualities that we value. As much as I dislike my very fallible and human reaction, I must be honest with myself before I can change my perspective on valuing others.

Here's another tough question: Do you believe that your life and the life of every human being has intrinsic worth? Let me put it another way. Is human life valuable to you regardless of what a person may have accomplished on this earth? I trust you said yes.

Now I want you to go on an imaginary trip with me to the place in your town or city that houses the poor, transients, bag ladies, hobos, and bums. Dopers and drunks lie on the sidewalk or in the alley or gutter, while the mentally ill walk the streets talking to themselves or to trees or the ocean or nothing at all. As you step gingerly around the debris that surrounds them and close your nostrils to the stench, you stare down at a soiled, unshaven man who reeks of alcohol and has just vomited on himself. Trace every detail of this man upon your mind. Then ask yourself again: "Do I believe that every human life has value, regardless of what he has accomplished on this earth?" If you answer honestly from your innermost self, my guess is that now your answer is no. Humanly speaking, that's how I would answer. I'm not proud of how I feel, but what I find within myself is that value and worth are conditional. I value those people who make some sort of contribution to society. The bums, alcoholics, dopers, and mentally ill are taking up space with no measurable purpose or contribution to my welfare or the welfare of others. In fact, I pay taxes to fund programs to "help" them.

Are you offended by my frankness? Look deep within yourself—you may find the same attitudes that I have, although you may try to sugarcoat them so they don't sound so bad.

PERSONAL
REFLECTION

■ During His earthly ministry, Jesus continually demonstrated the reality that He knew and valued people as individuals. Examine each of the following Scripture passages to see how He did this. Then answer these questions: How did Jesus communicate to the person(s) in this passage His *deep understanding* of them and His *unconditional acceptance* of them? What was each one's response to Jesus?

Luke 7:36-50 _____

_____

_____

_____

John 4:4-26 _____

_____

_____

_____

John 1:43-49 _____

_____

_____

_____

Luke 19:1-10 _____

_____

_____

John 8:1-11 _____

_____

_____

_____

_____

■ Can you think of anyone in your life who has expressed to you the kind of understanding and acceptance Jesus did to people? Who is it? How has that person demonstrated his or her understanding and acceptance of you?

_____

_____

_____

_____

■ Do *you* believe that every human life has value, regardless of what he or she has accomplished on this earth? If you answered yes, give an example of how you've lived out that belief.

_____

_____

_____

_____

Without God as creator of human life there can be no logical foundation for making the statement that your life, my life, or anybody's life has intrinsic value, apart from what we have accomplished here on earth. God has declared this in His self-revelation, the Bible.

The other option is evolution, a position that suggests we start as nothing and over a period of time become something. Not just anything but something personal that can think about supernatural things. And all that is needed is time—lots and lots of time.

The theory of evolution requires one giant leap of faith. In fact, it's a suicidal leap because life loses any basis for intrinsic worth. According to the evolutionary position, value and worth are based on utilitarian function. The question evolution asks of us is, "What can you do that has utilitarian value?"

Only God offers a basis for knowing that your life has great worth, regardless of what you accomplish on this earth. *God has placed that value on you!* You can't earn it, work for it, deserve it, buy it, steal it, borrow it, or beg for it. It's yours because God created you and freely chose to place great value on your life. It comes down to this: If I am going to see my life as inherently valuable, I must see myself and others *from God's perspective.* If I take a human perspective that leaves God out of the picture, there is no such thing as inherent value to life. It's obtained the hard way—*you earn it!* If you don't think that's true, take a look at your own inner parent. What's the major thing that keeps you feeling inadequate? It's that you don't measure up to your inner parent's standards, right! Humanly speaking, the bottom line is that your value is based on what you do, not on who you are.

PERSONAL
REFLECTION

■ Are you absolutely convinced—feel it deep in your heart—that your value is based on who you are and not on what you do? Let the truth of God's Word remind you of your intrinsic value. Look up each of the Scriptures listed below and after reading the passage, complete this statement:

I am valuable because . . .

Genesis 1:27, 31 ———————————————————

————————————————————————————

Jeremiah 1:5 ————————————————————

————————————————————————————

Psalm 103:13-14 —————————————————

————————————————————————————

Psalm 119:73 ———————————————————

————————————————————————————

Psalm 139:1-16 —————————————————

————————————————————————————

_____

_____

_____

_____

_____

_____

John 10:3, 14-15 _____

_____

John 10:27-28 _____

_____

Romans 5:8 _____

_____

■ God entrusted you to His Son Jesus as a love gift. Jesus highly prizes you! Go back to the illustration on page 180 in this chapter and in bold letters write your name across the gift, in that way personalizing this message to yourself.

Jesus constantly encountered people who based their value on human effort and rigidly imposed standards. His Parable of the Pharisee and the Tax Collector is a nice study in contrasts—a religious bigwig and a shady member of the IRS. He told the parable "to certain ones who trusted in themselves that they were righteous, and viewed others with contempt" (Luke 18:9).

Guess who He's talking to. The Pharisees, you say? You're partially correct, but there is another group to whom this parable is directed—you and me. For we also judge our value on what we do, not on who we are before God. Jesus then told a story to show them what He meant:

Two men went up into the temple to pray, one a Pharisee and the other a tax gatherer. The Pharisee stood and was praying thus to himself, "God, I thank Thee that I am not like other people: swindlers, unjust, adulterers, or even like this tax gatherer. I fast twice a week; I pay tithes of all that I get."

But the tax gatherer, standing some distance away, was even unwilling to lift up his eyes to heaven, but was beating his breast, saying, "God, be merciful to me, the sinner!" (vv. 10-13)

The same qualifications for worth that the Pharisee used to elevate himself were the very ones he used to value the tax gatherer. The Pharisee thought he was a great asset to God while the tax gatherer was junk. There is some Pharisee in all of us. We use conditions of worth to judge ourselves and others, but this is not God's perspective. Notice Jesus' words about the tax gatherer:

I tell you, this man went down to his house justified rather than the other; for every one who exalts himself shall be humbled, but he who humbles himself shall be exalted (v. 14).

PERSONAL REFLECTION

■ Which of these characters are you most like—the Pharisee or the tax gatherer? Why? Be honest.

_____

_____

_____

■ The Pharisees conformed to the letter of the law—they *did* all the right things—but in their hearts they were like "whitewashed tombs" (Luke 23:27-28, NIV). Their sense of value was based on what they did, not on who they were. What kind of "doing" have you gotten caught up in to find your sense of value? Has your "doing" brought you the sense of value you've sought? Explain.

_____

_____

_____

_____

_____

■ What do you think it means to "humble yourself"? Describe a time when you felt humbled. What was the attitude of your heart at that time?

_____

_____

_____

_____

_____

We humble ourselves when we come to our Heavenly Father and with open hands of faith acknowledge that life has value and worth only because God has chosen to make it so, not because of anything we can do for ourselves or for God. He demonstrated the value He places on us by sending His beloved Son to bring us into a personal relationship with Himself. Do you have a personal relationship with God through His Son Jesus? When you understand the basis of intrinsic worth, you can open the door of the mind's dark attic and let your inner child move out to the sunlit living room. Your Heavenly Father values you and that inner child you have managed to hide for so many years. Let Him help you release it.

PERSONAL REFLECTION

■ Have you ever invited Jesus Christ into your life as your personal Savior and Lord? If not, would you like to? Then in the quietness of your own heart repeat the following prayer:

Lord Jesus,
Right now I invite You into my life. I recognize that I am a sinner and fall far short of Your perfect standard. I acknowledge my need of a Savior. Dear God, I believe that You sent Your beloved Son Jesus to die on the cross for my sin and I receive Your Son into my life to be my Savior and Lord. Thank You, Lord Jesus, for loving me.

■ If you prayed that prayer, tell someone you know who's a Christian, or please write to Dr. Dickinson at the following address:

Dr. Richard Dickinson
IDAK Inter-face
10900 Los Alamitos Boulevard, Suite 201
Los Alamitos, California 90720

I met 26-year-old Marsha in the hospital during my doctoral internship. She had been admitted after a near-fatal suicide attempt. She was sullen, angry, sarcastic, and she fluctuated between depression and manic behavior. She was also bright, attractive, talented in art, and quite athletic. Now she was assigned to me as a patient, and so we began several months of very difficult counseling. She didn't trust doctors and was often uncooperative in therapy, refusing to talk for long periods of time. It was clear from the start that nobody was going to get close to Marsha; if anyone tried, he would pay a price for risking it.

Because I was new at hospital work, I vacillated between being angry with Marsha and feeling totally incompetent to help her. Still, there was something about her that drew me to her; I could hear her inner child faintly crying for help.

I quickly learned that Marsha lived in two worlds. One was the world of her adapted child or false self, in which she pretended to be confident, self-sufficient, and able to handle anything life threw at her. People who knew her considered her a "together" person. But her other world was a very different picture. It was the world of a very hurt, abused, frightened, confused little girl who had decided never to let anyone get close enough to hurt her the way her mother did when she was growing up. She felt guilty and worthless, and saw herself as a bad person. It took several years of working with Marsha before she trusted me enough to reveal her frightened inner child, but finally she came to believe within her deepest self that she was indeed a person of value and worth.

While Marsha's case is extreme, it illustrates the fact that many of us live in two worlds—the artificial persona with a bright facade that we create for others, and the real, wounded, broken child that we hide in shame. In the first section of this chapter, I talked about our being known and valued in a unique way by God. You may have found that idea uplifting. Or, you may have read the words and understood the ideas, but the truth never penetrated emotionally so that you could really feel it. Why? Because you feel unworthy as a person and are convinced even God cannot value you or take time to know you.

PERSONAL REFLECTION

■ Do you, like Marsha, live in two worlds? What is the "public version" of yourself that you present to the world? Describe it. What is the *inner you* like? What silent self-concepts keep the *real you* hidden inside?

_____

_____

_____

_____

_____

You might be asking, "Wait a minute. Doesn't Scripture say that all men are unworthy to stand before a Holy God, on the basis of their own self-righteousness?" You're right. That's what the Bible says. But that's only half the story. From my experience as a psychologist working with Christian clients, I've noticed that many of God's saints feel unable to take hold of God's love so that it truly impacts their lives. The typical rejoinder of many well-meaning brothers and sisters in Christ is, "Read your Bible more . . . memorize Scripture verses . . . have more faith . . . trust God more." This kind of advice tends to heap more guilt on Christians who already feel unworthy. They consider themselves failures as Christians.

A key issue here is the self-image or self-concept problem, which brings us back to our two worlds—the person we show to others on the surface and the person we know ourselves to be inside. How we really think and feel about ourselves inside forms our self-image or self-concept. Our past life experiences exert a powerful influence on how we see ourselves, thus shaping our self-image prior to our coming to God through His Son, Jesus Christ. In other words, you bring into your relationship with God a self-image that does not disappear at the moment of conversion. You have already formed a way of seeing yourself based on the treatment and responses of significant people in your life, especially during your early years.

Even though Marsha was a Christian, she saw herself as a bad person. She read Scripture, but it stayed in her intellect, never reaching the damaged inner child that longed for love. Is your experience similar to Marsha's? Often the church is not prepared, nor does it understand how to reach people with damaged self-concepts.

I spent many of my early Christian years struggling with the question of whether God could be trusted and could really love me. Having faced these issues myself, I have a sensitive place in my heart for those who experience the same struggles. You wonder if anybody understands what it's like to be caught between two worlds. On one hand, God tells you He loves you and you are secure in His love; you are valued for who you are and not what you've accomplished. On the other hand, you struggle with self-doubt and fail to live up to your own expectations. You wonder if people, even God Himself, can be trusted; and you question whether your past life and behavior can ever be forgiven.

My friend, God is able to help you change your view about yourself so that it begins to conform to the way He sees you. And as you change your self-image, you begin to free your inner child.

PERSONAL REFLECTION

■ In what ways do you identify with the struggle Dr. Dickinson describes in the preceding two paragraphs? Have you, as a Christian, questioned whether God could be trusted and if He could ever *really* love you? Admit your self-doubts, fears, and concerns to Him. He knows your struggle and understands. He is full of compassion for you. Spend time journaling the thoughts and feelings you are in touch with at this moment.

_____

_____

_____   _____

_____

_____

_____

There are two possible reasons why we do not allow God's love to penetrate our inner self. One reason is a negative self-image; the other is sin. The word *sin* is not very popular today in either psychology or theology. The tendency for most secular psychologists is to see sin or evil as environmental rather than intrapersonal. Yet, we tend to project our sinful behavior on others or direct it against ourselves in a destructive manner. Many pastors don't talk about personal sin; if they did, they would lose their congregations.

My friend, sin is a reality. The Bible speaks directly about it, and we instinctively know of its existence within ourselves. While we would rather not think about sin, it nevertheless touches every area of our thought life and our behavior.

The primary question is: "How can I face the truth that I am a sinner and yet still feel loved and accepted by God? How can I enjoy a healthier self-image and feel guilt-free without denying the sin issue?" The exciting news is that it is possible.

First, let's take a look at your inner child again. As you recall, your inner child contains your feelings, your natural aptitudes, and your uniqueness as a person created in the image of God. The bad news is that your inner child and my inner child have, in addition, an inherent tendency to sin. Sin, as defined in Scripture, generally means to miss the mark.

Think of it this way. You are standing 50 feet from a target. You take a bow and place an arrow in it, pull the string back, take aim, and release the arrow. The arrow sings through the air and hits the target, but it misses the bull's-eye. Whether you missed by an inch or a mile, you missed the mark. In the biblical sense, the bull's-eye is God's standard of perfection.

What do I mean by God's standard of perfection for us? It can be summarized in the Ten Commandments, found in Exodus 20:1-18:

√ *You shall have no other gods before Me.*
√ *You shall not make for yourself an idol, or any likeness of what is in heaven above or on the earth beneath or in the water under the earth.*
√ *You shall not take the name of the Lord your God in vain.*
√ *Remember the Sabbath Day to keep it holy.*
√ *Honor your father and your mother.*
√ *You shall not murder.*
√ *You shall not commit adultery.*
√ *You shall not steal.*
√ *You shall not bear false witness against your neighbor.*
√ *You shall not covet.*

These are God's standards of perfection. One mistake anywhere in your life and you have blown it. It is impossible to make yourself righteous by keeping God's law. A quick look at these commandments shows us just how far people in today's society have fallen from taking God's absolutes seriously.

If you are uncomfortable with God's standards, try your own. Suppose that God has recorded every moral judgment you ever made in your life, and someday when you stand face-to-face before Him, He will ask, "What right do you have to enter My kingdom?"

You answer, "I have been a good person."

God replies, "Have you kept all your own moral judgments you ever uttered?" Then He plays back all the moral pronouncements and declarations you have spoken. How would you stand? Not so good, right? I know I wouldn't.

But what most people fail to realize is that God never intended that we should try to make ourselves acceptable to Him by keeping the Ten Commandments. Rather, He gave them as a mirror so that we could look at ourselves in His holy standards and see how far short we have fallen. The Apostle Paul speaks to this:

> Now we know that whatever the Law says, it speaks to those who are under the Law, that every mouth may be closed, and all the world may become accountable to God; because by the works of the Law no flesh will be justified in His sight; for through the Law comes the knowledge of sin. . . .
>
> For all have sinned and fall short of the glory of God (Romans 3:19-20, 23).

The reason we sin is that we have an inherent sin nature which refuses to bow the knee in humble subjection to God's will.

I watch my grandson Andrew with fascination. At age two he does not like to submit his emerging sense of self to his parents' will. When they discourage him from doing what he wants to do, he readily demonstrates his robust temper. We're a little more sophisticated about it, but we respond in the same way. Inside we too want to do exactly what *we* want to do.

PERSONAL REFLECTION

■ In his book, *A Hunger for Healing,* Keith Miller says this about sin:

At an existential, everyday level of thinking, sin is thought to refer to "bad things one does" such as theft, adultery, murder, gossiping, judging, and so forth. But as William Temple pointed out, these things are only symptoms of a deeper disease. He says 'there is only one Sin (with a capital *S*), and that is putting ourselves in the center of our lives and other people's lives where only God should be.' (*Readings in St. John's Gospel*, Morehouse, 1985). Sins with a small *s* are those specific things we do as a result of putting ourselves in the center (like stealing, adultery, and trying to control people" (*Hunger for Healing*, Harper San Francisco, p. 3).

■ In what ways have you put yourself in the center of your own life, and the lives of other people? List some specific ways you have attempted to impose your own will on the lives of other people. *EXAMPLE: When my wife talks to me about a problem she is having, I give her several "helpful" suggestions about things she can do to solve her problem, rather than just listening to her. When someone I love is upset with me, I withdraw emotionally and sometimes, physically.*

_____

_____

_____

_____

_____

_____

■ Letting go of Sin is giving up the need to control things in my own life and in the lives of other people. In what ways do you see yourself as needing to "stay in control" (of yourself) or "be in control" (of other people)? *NOTE: Control is often expressed in very subtle ways.*

_____

_____

Even knowing all there is to know about us, God loves us enough to provide a way for us to have a relationship with Him. Without ignoring our sinfulness, He offers a solution to make us acceptable to Himself. The Apostle Paul describes this provision:

> For while we were still helpless, at the right time Christ died for the ungodly. For one will hardly die for a righteous man; though perhaps for the good man someone would dare even to die. But God demonstrates His own love toward us, in that while we were yet sinners, Christ died for us. Much more then, having now been justified by His blood, we shall be saved from the wrath of God through Him. For if while we were enemies, we were reconciled to God through the death of His Son, much more, having been reconciled, we shall be saved by His life (Romans 5:6-10).

It is only through the death and resurrection of Jesus Christ that we can stand before a holy, righteous God. Since He demands perfection, and no human being is or ever has been perfect, we all fail to live up to God's standard of perfection. Jesus Christ, the God-Man who knew no sin, was the only One who qualified to meet God's standard of righteousness. There on the cross some 2,000 years ago, He took upon Himself our sin so that we could stand guiltless before God on the basis of what Christ accomplished, not on what we accomplish for ourselves.

Jesus came to earth to be my Savior and Lord. What does that mean for my self-image and the releasing of my inner child? It means a freedom to transparently be myself before God, without fear of rejection, separation, or humiliation.

It works like this. Occasionally ungodly thoughts pass through my mind. I may never act on them, but that doesn't change what goes on in the inner resources of my mind. I sometimes wonder how I can be a child of God, considering some of the things I think about. Then my mind reflects on the wonderful assurance that God knew exactly what He was getting when He brought me to Himself. He knows that I still struggle with the old sin nature inside me. Therefore, I should never be surprised at what goes in my mind.

God's concern is that I do not give sin any foothold in my life. But when I do, He is always ready to forgive, as I repent and confess my sins to Him. What a contrast to the critical inner parent that is unmerciful when we foul up. This critical parent heaps all manner of guilt and condemnation on the inner child, saying such things as, "You're going to hell for sure!" Only in the security of believing that in Christ I am known, valued, cleansed, and forgiven am I free to release my inner child and open my arms to receive all that God has for me.

PERSONAL REFLECTION

■ This indeed is GOOD NEWS—as a Christian, there is nothing you *have* ever done, or ever *will* do that can separate you from the love of Christ (Romans 8:38-39). You are free to be completely transparent before God because you stand *guiltless* before God on the basis of what Christ accomplished on the cross. Is there anything in your life you feel so ashamed of that you have never been able to admit it to anyone? Make a list of those things below. It takes rigorous honesty and humility to admit shameful things to ourselves, God, and other people. Writing them down is the first step.

_____

_____

_____

_____

_____

_____

■ Now go back and in bold letters write the words *NOT GUILTY* across your list. This is the truth—before God, in Jesus Christ, you stand *guiltless*. Because of His grace you stand free through His forgiveness. Hold on to the truth . . . it will set you free!

Writing this book, teaching Sunday School classes, speaking at Christian conferences, studying the Bible, and practicing psychotherapy as a Christian psychologist does not automatically mean that I understand the depth of God's love experientially. I've done all of the above, but it wasn't until the last 15 years of my Christian experience that I came to know in a deeper sense the power of God's love. The road has been painful but life-changing.

In previous chapters I have shared some of my personal experiences because I wanted you to know that the things I am writing about also apply to me. During the early '70s, I went through a time of turmoil, doubting, rebellious behavior, and marital conflict. As a result of those days, I finally began to comprehend the abiding love of God.

One afternoon in the middle of my life's chaos, I sat down at my typewriter and paraphrased a personal application of 1 Corinthians 13. It was as if God's Spirit took charge of my thoughts as I wrote:

Because God loves me, He is slow to lose patience with me.

Because God loves me, He takes the circumstances of my life and uses them in a constructive way for my growth.

Because God loves me, He does not treat me as an object to be possessed and manipulated.

Because God loves me, He has no need to impress me with how great and powerful He is because *He is God,* nor does He belittle me as His child in order to show me how important He is.

Because God loves me, He is for me. He wants to see me mature and develop in His love.

Because God loves me, He does not send down His wrath on every little mistake I make (of which there are many).

Because God loves me, He does not keep score of all my sins and then beat me over the head with them whenever He gets the chance.

Because God loves me, He is deeply grieved when I do not walk in the ways that please Him, for He sees this as evidence that I don't trust Him as I should.

Because God loves me, He rejoices when I experience His power and strength and stand up under the pressures of life for His name's sake.

Because God loves me, He keeps on working patiently with me even when I feel like giving up and can't see why He doesn't give up too.

Because God loves me, He keeps on trusting me when at times I don't even trust myself.

Because God loves me, He never says to me, "There is no hope for you." Rather, He patiently works with me, loves me, and disciplines me. I marvel at the depth of His concern for me.

Because God loves me, He never forsakes me even though many of my friends might.

Because God loves me, He stands with me when I have reached the rock bottom of despair, when I see the real me and compare myself with His righteousness, holiness, beauty, and love. It is at a moment like this that I can really believe that GOD LOVES ME!

Yes, the greatest of all gifts is God's perfect love!

About halfway through my writing of this paraphrase, tears filled my eyes because in a very personal way I saw God's love from a new perspective. I had read this passage many times, but this time something was different. For the first time I saw myself as I really was.

PERSONAL REFLECTION

■ It is only as we let God's love penetrate our inner child that we can be truly intimate with God and other people. Have you felt *loved* by God in the past? Do you feel *loved* by Him now? If you answered these questions no, what do you think is keeping you from experiencing the love of God in your life at a deep, heartfelt level?

_____

_____

_____

_____

■ Read Dr. Dickinson's paraphrased version of 1 Corinthians 13 again. This time stop at the end of each sentence. Wait a moment before going on. In that moment of silence let God speak to you personally, quietly about His love for you. Jot down anything you "overhear" Him saying to you as you reread this love message.

_____

_____

_____

_____

I was raised in a very conservative Christian environment. My family never danced, played cards, went to movies, smoked, drank, swore, or engaged in any other behavior that was considered unchristian. I attended a church that supported these same values regarding "Christian behavior." I accepted Christ as my personal Savior when I was seven, and I sincerely believe that my decision was real.

But one major factor significantly affected my outlook on God and that was fear. I was equally fearful of my father, and through much of my early Christian experience I unconsciously equated the two as one. My fear of both God and my father paved the way for a convincingly adapted child, which appeared on the scene while my true inner child beat a fast retreat to the upstairs closet of my personality. The adapted child in me knew all the right things to say, how to act, and even how to think in order to please God, my father, and all the people at church.

But most of my life I felt alone and frustrated because I could never feel close to others, especially to God. In chapter 4, I stressed that unless we are in touch with our inner child, and not just the "perfect" adapted child we present to others, we can never feel truly intimate with God or others, because intimacy involves self-disclosure. In other words, we must be able to share how we really think and especially feel about things which only our inner child knows.

I lost touch with my inner child because I feared the disapproval and rejection of God and of other people if I would allow them to get close to me. While the adapted child in me was behaving like a good Christian boy anybody would be proud of, my inner child was feeling and thinking about a lot of things that were not so Christian.

It was fear that kept me from acting out my desires for much of my early life, up to around age 30. Between 30 and 35, I would say that I experienced my delayed adolescent rebellion. I wanted to do what I wanted to do, even if it meant being zapped by God. It was near the end of that period that I wrote my paraphrase of 1 Corinthians 13. I was so taken by the inner sense of God's presence within me and so overwhelmed by His love—even though I was far from Him at the time—that my heart began to turn toward home.

What I needed from the Lord was comfort, caring, and love because my inner child was scared, lonely, confused, and very unhappy. But would the Lord accept me as I was? Was there comfort in His presence? Then I remembered an experience in the life of Jesus:

> They began bringing children to Him, so that He might touch them; and the disciples rebuked them.
> But when Jesus saw this, He was indignant and said to them, "Permit the children to come to Me; do not hinder them; for the kingdom of God belongs to such as these. Truly I say to you, whoever does not receive the kingdom of God like a child shall not enter it at all" (Mark 10:13-16).

What struck me about this event was the compassion Jesus had for the children. The disciples tried to restrain the children by rebuking them, but Jesus was indignant with anyone who hindered the children from coming to Him. How strangely familiar the disciples sounded to me! Like my inner critical parent who kept telling me, "Jesus doesn't have time for you. Look how little you've done with your life. How can you expect God to forgive you and take you back?" I was deeply moved by how Jesus defended the children against the critical and unsympathetic disciples, because the children could not defend themselves.

I often felt that my inner child was no match for the critical parent inside me. I desperately needed someone to stand up for me when I felt rejected or overwhelmed. This is what Jesus did for the children and what I have experienced Him doing for my inner child.

Not only did Jesus defend the children but He blessed them. Intrigued by this statement, I researched the word *blessed*. It means, "to consecrate, to declare or set apart as holy or honored, to sanction, exalt, edify, approve, smile upon." Jesus smiled upon the children, brought them comfort and joy, and a sense of total acceptance. One expositor, commenting on this word, described Jesus taking each child in His arms, one at a time, and blessing him. He fervently blessed and kept on blessing them, favoring them with His love. It was a process that took time but Jesus did not grow weary of the task.

This incident in the life of Christ spoke to me about how He comforts the inner child in you and in me. Did you notice that Jesus used touch with these children? Touching is the primary way we communicate love and care to children. It's the same for the inner child within each of us. So often I visualize myself being physically comforted by the Lord and feeling His love surrounding me when I am needy. Such special moments of intimacy with God help me to release and reveal my inner child without hesitation or fear.

If you have placed your faith and trust in His Son Jesus, God never forgets you or stops loving you or lets you go, no matter what you have done. You are in His family forever. It is that kind of compassion that leads your inner child from the darkness of fear and despair into the light of day so that you can be yourself, the genuine you, enjoying your own unique feelings, abilities, and personality.

PERSONAL REFLECTION

■ Did you find yourself responding emotionally to the description Dr. Dickinson paints of Jesus with the children? What were you feeling? In what ways does your "inner child" long to be touched and blessed like the children in that story? Tell Jesus what you need.

Loving Jesus,

_____

_____

_____

_____

_____

_____

_____

There is one more vital issue we must cover here, and that is the importance of other people in releasing the inner child.

Remember Marsha? God used my compassion for her to bring her into a closer and more personal love relationship with the Lord. She had attended church and heard sermons about God's love, but until she could trust another person who loved her inner child and listened to it and protected it, she could not, in one sense, allow God to touch it. You see, the ministry God has entrusted to us is to be the human arm of His life-changing process. This is what the Apostle Paul meant when he said, "Bear one another's burdens, and thus fulfill the law of Christ" (Galatians 6:2).

What is the law of Christ? It is to love others with the *agape* love that only God Himself can provide in the hearts of believers. It is unconditional love without regard for accomplishments. In other words, you can't earn *agape* love; it's free for the receiving. It's the love of 1 Corinthians 13.

As one trained in the discipline of psychology and called of God to minister and disciple others, I am part of the process of building up the body of Christ—the church of Jesus Christ. I minister to a special group of God's saints who live with deep emotional hurts that have seriously impaired their growth. Through emotional traumas, they have lost touch with their inner child. My job is to find that child and nurture it back to health so that person can be whole.

You too are called to minister to the body of Christ. In your own way, led by the Spirit of God, you can touch people who need love and affirmation. God wants to use your inner child to touch the inner child of others, so that people everywhere will begin the process of being made whole. What a blessed privilege we have.

PERSONAL REFLECTION

■ Think of three people you know who seem to be locked up emotionally and out of touch with their inner child. Write down their names on the next page. Then ask God for opportunities to minister to them, helping them also to release their inner child. As those opportunities present themselves, come back to this question and write down next to the person's name how God used you in that person's life.

Who I Helped	How I Helped
_____	_____
_____	_____
_____	_____
_____	_____
_____	_____

PRAYERFUL REFLECTION

■ Are you able to let God through His Son Jesus release your inner child so that you can be all God created you to be? If so, write a prayer letting God know of your readiness. If trust is still an issue, you may not yet be ready to experience the release spoken of in this chapter. God understands. Express your fears and hesitations to Him. He knows exactly where you're at. He will wait until your inner child is ready to take the next step.

_____

_____

_____

_____

_____

PERSONAL RENEWAL

■ This week take some time to read the story of the prodigal son found in Luke 15:11-32. Picture in your mind the father waiting patiently for his son. Does this describe your father? If not, picture your Heavenly Father loving you even if presently you feel far from Him. Write down in Appendix Three any thoughts that come to mind as you read this parable.

Chapter 9
Developing a Caring Inner Parent

For one week, Tammy listened to the daily five-minute Christian radio program sponsored by IDAK Inter-face, the human resource and development center where I'm the director. The radio speaker said, "God has gifted each of us with natural aptitudes for excellence. If those aptitudes are not functioning in our careers, we experience dissatisfaction and eventually become candidates for job burnout."

This hit home to Tammy. She lived through each day for 5:00 when she could leave work and go home. Yet, she felt guilty for her feelings. Her critical inner parent told her that she was lazy and irresponsible, and should work harder so she could be a good testimony to the other workers who were not Christians. In other words, just grin and bear it.

Actually, Tammy was far from lazy. If anything, she tried too hard. She had worked as a secretary/receptionist for a medical doctor for five years. She was well-liked and very efficient, but lately was showing stress on the job and feeling depressed and fatigued. She found it difficult to get up in the morning and would erupt with flashes of irritation both at work and at home. Always guilty and apologetic for her anger, she couldn't understand why she felt so out of control. She told herself she was fortunate to have a fine job and a good salary with nice people to work for. Still, her depression and irritability persisted.

PERSONAL REFLECTION

■ If you were to write out an assessment of your current job situation, would it sound anything like Tammy's? In what ways?

_____

_____

_____

_____

To better understand Tammy's conflicting feelings, let's look at the attitudes reflected in her home during her childhood. Tammy's father, Jim, a no-nonsense kind of guy, was a strict disciplinarian just like his own father had been. Jim had given up a promising career in baseball because his father considered athletics unchristian and a waste of time. Jim pursued a business career and became a bank teller—a job he hated. Although he moved up in the banking world, he always considered his job a duty to perform. He passed this attitude on to Tammy.

Tammy's mother, Anne, was quiet and never challenged anything her husband said. She felt that a good Christian wife should be submissive in all things—an attitude fostered more by her upbringing than by biblical teaching. Anne found her husband to be every bit as authoritarian in temperament as her own father had been. In fact, Anne's married life was practically a duplication of her early life—submission and obedience to the male authority figure in the home. Without even realizing it, Anne passed on this attitude of acquiescence and passivity to her daughter.

But Tammy was very much like her mother in other ways too. She was artistic, with a real knack for design and handicrafts. She was also imaginative and observant, good at reading people and adept at problem-solving. She worked best with one or two others.

Unfortunately, Tammy was in a job for which she was totally unsuited. No wonder she was depressed and irritable. Whenever she talked to me about her artistic interests, her face would light up and she would become a different person. It became clear to me that Tammy's childhood experiences with her parents had contributed to her development of a critical inner parent that suppressed her creative inner child. That inner parent echoed the words of her father, criticizing her interest in the arts and convincing her that God would not be pleased with her.

Now that, my friends, is stacking the deck—when you feel that God the Father is against you too. What chance do you have, especially if you're eager for the approval of others, as Tammy was? When Tammy heard the IDAK radio broadcast, she saw a ray of hope. Maybe, just maybe, there was still a chance for her inner child to be a part of her life and career. Today, Tammy is exploring new options for her career, but she is still not convinced that it's OK to enjoy her natural talents and that she can actually be paid for something she loves to do.

There are many Tammy's in this world. Perhaps you are one of them, suffering under the bondage of a very critical inner parent who hasn't the slightest idea what your inner child's talents are. People with critical inner parents are unduly influenced by other people's opinions of them. They may spend their entire lives trying to win the approval and acceptance of their unreasonable inner parent and never experience the joy, excitement, and fulfillment of doing what God has gifted them to do. What's even more tragic is that they may feel that God is the same as their inner critical parent and that a life lived in boredom, unfulfillment, and disappointment is somehow pleasing to Him. Not so.

Your Heavenly Father is not your critical parent. He knows you, values you, forgives you, and loves you as no one else can. To release your inner child and experience its growth requires the presence of a nurturing parent within your personality, rather than a critical, punitive, devaluing one.

PERSONAL REFLECTION

■ Write a description of your inner parent as you know him or her.

_____

_____

_____

_____

■ Write a description of your mother. What kind of person is she?

_____

_____

_____

_____

■ Write a description of your father. What kind of person is he?

_____

_____

_____

_____

■ Write a description of any other significant person in your early life—an aunt, uncle, grandparent, etc. What was he or she like?

_____

_____

_____

_____

■ Write a description of God as you understand and know Him today.

_____

_____

_____

_____

■ Compare the description of your inner parent with those of your mother and father. What similarities do you notice?

_____

_____

_____

_____

■ Compare the description of your inner parent with the significant others you listed. Again, what similarities do you see?

_____

_____

_____

■ Finally, compare the description you wrote of God with that of your real parents. What similarities do you observe?

_____

_____

_____

_____

■ What conclusions can you draw about your own inner parent from the questions you've answered above?

_____

_____

_____

_____

At this point you may be asking, "How do I develop this inner nurturing parent, especially since I'm already struggling with a critical one?" Let's explore the qualities of a healthy, nurturing inner parent and discuss how you can build this positive influence into your personality.

Based on my experience as a psychologist, I've concluded that a large percentage of my patients come from family backgrounds in which the father was abusive in one or more of the following ways:

❑ Sexually abusive

❑ Physically abusive

❑ Absent, either physically or emotionally

❑ Unable to express caring feelings to the children

❑ Very critical, often abusing alcohol

PERSONAL REFLECTION

■ Would you describe your father in any of the five ways mentioned above? Check any that apply.

It is extremely difficult for the child living in these conditions to build a healthy inner parent that guides and nurtures the inner child. Often, when there is an inadequate or abusive parent, the child has to idealize that parent, seeing him as good in order to maintain some hope in his world. Usually, the child sees himself as bad in order to make the bad parent good.

Those who have a critical inner parent need the experience of having someone who models a healthy and nurturing attitude toward them. This can be accomplished through therapy, through close, caring friends and loved ones, and especially through a personal and growing relationship with God the Father.

PERSONAL REFLECTION

■ Can you think of anyone in your life at present who demonstrates a healthy and nurturing attitude toward you? Who is it? What does this person say to you or do for you that feels nurturing?

_____

_____

_____

_____

The problem for many of us who struggle with the inner critical parent is that God becomes an extension of that critical parent. Instead of offering relief to our inner child, He seems to offer only more rules and regulations, guilt and condemnation, and deep feelings of inadequacy. What a distorted and inaccurate portrait we paint of God! What we need is a true picture of our Heavenly Father as revealed in the Bible. To begin to understand God, we must start comprehending how much He cares for us as individuals and how committed He is to our growth.

One of the most touching and revealing stories about the love of God the Father comes from the lips of Jesus in the story of the prodigal son. Every time I read it, I am deeply moved. Although the focus is often placed on the son, the main character is actually the father who loves his lost son unconditionally. The father in this account represents God the Father and, in one way or another, we are the prodigals. The story is found in Luke 15:11-32. Let me give you my paraphrased version, and then draw from the story some essential qualities of the nurturing father who is, in fact, God Himself.

There was a man with two sons. The older boy stayed home, always did the right thing, obeyed his father, and never rocked the boat. The younger son liked doing his own thing, was easily bored with the routine of homelife, had an insatiable curiosity, and was bound and determined to live life in the fast lane.

Being rather assertive, the younger son asked Dad for an advance on his inheritance. Now, an inheritance usually comes after a parent dies, so Dad was under no obligation to grant his son's request, but he did so anyway. Do you suppose Dad knew his son so well he figured he needed to learn life's lessons by direct experience? Could be.

So the boy gathered his money, packed his bags, and split for the far country, perhaps to the Las Vegas or Hollywood of his day. Get the picture now: This boy had his pockets stuffed with money and was buying drinks for everyone in the house. His roster of friends grew rapidly; he was really on a roll. "Man, this is living," he told himself. "It sure beats the dull, predictable life back home!"

But one day he turned his pockets inside out and found that his money was gone. Mr. Somebody suddenly became Mr. Nobody.

It shocked him to learn that without money, status, or material goods, "you ain't nobody." He couldn't buy friends. He couldn't even buy himself a square meal, so he took a job feeding pigs. He knew he had hit rock bottom when his employer wouldn't even let him eat the slop he was dishing out to the hogs. Painful reality hit him hard there in the pigpen. "Man, I'd be better off back home working as a hired laborer," he grumbled. "At least there I'd have three squares a day. That beats starving to death in this mess."

But the more he thought about it, the more he wondered if Dad would even take him back. After all, he had sinned against God and his father and had squandered his inheritance. "I can't really expect my father to consider me his son anymore, but maybe if I confess how wrong I've been, he'll hire me as a common laborer."

With that, he fled the pigpen and journeyed home. As he approached the familiar homestead, he saw his father watching from the doorway. When the old man spotted his son, he broke into a run, his arms wide open. The boy opened his mouth to confess his sins, but his father hugged and kissed him with such deep emotion that the boy couldn't speak. When he finally revived from the shock of his father's love, he tried to confess his wrongdoing, but his father was already clothing him in his best robe and placing a fancy ring on his finger. It was time to celebrate!

Dad proclaimed to anyone who would listen, "My son was dead, and has come to life again; he was lost, and has been found."

The best calf was roasted and everyone joined in the celebration— except the older son who went around grousing to himself, "Who does my kid brother think he is? He turned his back on the family and squandered our money and now Dad's treating him like a celebrity. I've always been good and Dad never had a party like this for me."

When the father noticed that his older son was absent, he went looking for him and urged him to join the party, but the boy refused. Instead, he spilled out his anger about the unfairness of it all. His father replied, "My son, you have always been with me, and all that is mine is yours. But we must be merry and rejoice, for your brother was dead but now he lives; he was lost and has been found."

PERSONAL
REFLECTION

■ Are you more like the older boy in this story who stayed home, always did the right thing, obeyed his father, and never rocked the boat? Or are you like the younger son who liked doing his own thing, was easily bored, and was determined to live life just the way he wanted to? Tell why you relate to the son you do.

_____

_____

_____

_____

■ What feelings, if any, surfaced in you as you read the part about the father in this story? Why do you think you felt the way you did?

_____

_____

_____

_____

My friend, don't you long for a father like this? If your internal parent was like the prodigal's father, would your inner child be released and growing? You bet it would! Let's look at the specific nurturing qualities evident in the prodigal's father—qualities that are present in our Heavenly Father as He nurtures us.

❏ *The Father's Love.* The father in our story loved both his sons, but they needed to be loved in different ways. Real love takes time to know each person as an individual. In the same way, your Heavenly Father loves you and knows exactly what you need. The father in the parable knew that freedom and the university of hard knocks were what his younger son needed. No matter what Dad would have said to him, the boy was not ready to listen. Yes, his rebellion cost his father a large portion of his material goods, but his son was worth it.

What do you suppose the father was doing while his son was away? I believe he stood for long periods of time gazing down the road, watching for him to return. That's why he was able to spot the boy while he was still a long way off. The father knew that his love would one day bring his son home. His love was so deep that he didn't even need to hear his son's confession; he knew the boy had learned his lesson the hard way; otherwise, he never would have returned. Nor did the father cast accusations, demanding, "How could you do this to me after all I've done for you?" No. It was enough that his son had come home.

Can you imagine what you would say if your child behaved like the prodigal? Would you kick the ungrateful youngster out? Make him repay the money he had wasted? Treat him with silence until he had suffered enough? So often when our children disappoint us, we cover our fear and anxiety with anger and attack the child for making us suffer.

What would your parents' reaction be if you yourself were the prodigal? What would your inner critical parent say to you about your value and worth? Would you feel hopeless and filled with despair? Would you feel so guilty that suicide would be a viable option because you could foresee no redemption or restoration?

How we need the love of God! Throughout the Bible we see the love of God directed to all persons, to bring them to repentance and restoration through the supreme sacrifice of Jesus Christ, God's love gift. Within the inner child lies rebellion and the desire to be accountable to no one. But God's love melts the hardened heart of our rebellious inner child and brings us to the foot of the cross where we reach out in faith for His love and forgiveness.

Perhaps you know the Father's love, but you are away from Him in a far country, thinking you can find excitement without God. You ask, "How could God ever love me after the things I've done?" My dear friend, He does love you and like the prodigal's father, He waits for your return. He desires to pour out His love and affection on you if only you will receive them. Jesus affirmed this when He said, "I tell you that in the same way, there will be more joy in heaven over one sinner who repents, than over ninety-nine righteous persons who need no repentance" (Luke 15:7).

As you draw near to God and rediscover His love for you, He will form within your personality an inner nurturing parent who has power to hush the critical parent messages you have lived with so long.

PERSONAL
REFLECTION

■ "Real love takes time to know each person as an individual," says Dr. Dickinson. Is there anyone in your life at present that you feel knows and loves you in the way Dr. Dickinson describes here? Who is it? Tell how this person expresses his or her love to you.

_____

_____

_____

■ Do you feel—at a heartfelt level—that your Heavenly Father loves and knows exactly what you need? Why do you feel as you do?

_____

_____

_____

_____

■ Do you feel close to or far away from God at present? Describe the level of intimacy you are experiencing with Him today.

_____

_____

_____

_____

❑ *The Father's Patience.* The wandering son was likely not the easiest person to live with. He probably questioned much of what his father told him and disobeyed his instructions. He was not cut from the same mold as his older brother—he was the younger child.

A youngest child is often labeled "baby of the family, the spoiled one, the brat." These labels are, of course, unfounded, especially if you ask any of us who are the youngest in our families. Yet there is a nugget of truth in them; by the time parents have experimented on the oldest child, they assume a much more relaxed posture with the other children who come along. When the final child arrives, Mom and Dad are veterans at child-rearing and usually let the youngest get away with things the older kids could never do.

As a rule, younger children tend to be more creative, more expressive of their feelings, and less disciplined than their older siblings. No doubt the prodigal would have fit into this category. The older son was much more responsible and was expected to set an example for his younger brother; in fact, the older son behaved much like a second father.

The father showed great patience with both of his sons. He knew he could not pressure or force ideas or beliefs on the younger son; the boy had to work things out for himself. That's why Dad gave him his inheritance and let him go to a far country to learn firsthand about life. The father's decision involved a fine balance of risk and trust—he risked the chance that the boy might never come home again; but he knew his child well enough to trust he would someday return. So he waited patiently, resisting the urge to go out and look for his wayward son.

Did you notice the patience the father exhibited with his older son, who was jealous and angry with his younger brother? Dad didn't belittle him or make him feel guilty for not wanting to join the welcome-home celebration; instead, he was genuinely concerned with his older son's feelings. He sought him out and patiently took time to talk and listen to him.

How would you react if you had a son like the prodigal? Would you be on his case, constantly trying to force him to conform? Would you repeatedly point out his mistakes and try to fit him into your mold? Were *you* ever a prodigal? How did your parents treat you? What about your inner parent? You may have experienced the pressure of a very impatient inner parent. This inner stress increases your fears of failure to the extent that you shy away from doing things that challenge you, for fear of not living up to the expectations of your inner impatient parent.

Your Heavenly Father is not like that. He is patient with you; He doesn't keep a scorecard on all your mistakes. Take a moment to reread the paraphrase of 1 Corinthians 13, in chapter 8 of this book. Notice the patience of God toward you, which frees you to be who you really are inside. He allows for mistakes, errors in judgment, blunders, and screwups without pouncing hard on your inner child. It is God's loving patience that beckons us from a far country and turns our hearts toward home. The Apostle Paul underscores this principle in writing to the Roman Christians:

> Or do you think lightly of the riches of His kindness and forbearance and patience, not knowing that the kindness of God leads you to repentance? (Romans 2:4)

As you grow in your understanding of God's patience toward you, you will experience positive changes in your feelings and attitudes. Day by day you will become aware of God forming a caring parent within you to counteract the impatient parent that has harassed you and kept your inner child in bondage for so many years.

PERSONAL REFLECTION

■ Were you ever a prodigal? How did your parents treat you?

_____

_____

_____

■ How do you feel when someone is impatient with you? Give an example of a time when someone you love was impatient with you. How did you respond to his or her impatience?

_____

_____

_____

_____

■ What message does your "impatient" inner parent send to your inner child when he or she makes a mistake, misjudges, blunders, or screws up?

_____

_____

_____

_____

■ What caring messages does your inner child need to hear when he or she messes up?

_____

_____

_____

_____

_____

❏ *The Father's Discipline.* In chapter 8, I mentioned about fear being my major motivation for good behavior. I felt that if I didn't keep my inner child in strict control, my life would be out of control. My strictness took the "inner parent" form of condemnation, guilt, humiliation, and harshness. It was as if my inner parent intimidated my inner child. But this kind of punitive control really ignites the inner child to rebellion. It's much like following a religion based on trying to fulfill the law. This approach can become very stressful because it stirs up rebellion that we are forced to suppress, thereby draining our energies for more healthy activities. Salvation by God's grace removes the need to rebel, because the basis for our relationship with God is through faith in Jesus Christ. It is in grace and love that we walk with Him, not by keeping the law.

However, even in a love relationship, there is need for the inner child to be controlled. The important question is how to do this—which leads us to the subject of discipline.

In the story of the prodigal, the father allowed the natural consequences of reality to discipline his son. That doesn't mean Dad was a softy. No doubt he disciplined his boys as they grew up, and I suspect that the younger son, with his "I'd rather do it my way" attitude, received the lion's share of correction. But the father knew his boys and understood what kind of discipline was most appropriate for each one. Once the boys were grown, the father sensed that his younger son must learn his lesson the hard way before he would be willing to bring his inner child under control.

Here's the way I see it: As the destitute youth groveled friendless and alone in the pigpen, he came to his senses and saw himself as he really was—foolish, rebellious, hardheaded. He saw his father through different eyes too, and sensed that he would accept him back, if not as a son, at least as hired help. All the lessons his father had tried to teach him made sense now. Out of love and inner anguish his father had released him to the world for discipline and training. Realizing at last what it meant to be controlled by love, not law, the boy headed home.

Have you ever been angry at God because things work out so well for your non-Christian friends, but not for you? Have you wondered why God deals more harshly with you in certain situations than He does with others? My dear friend, God deals with each of us on an individual basis. He knows what sort of discipline works best for you.

> "My son, do not regard lightly the discipline of the Lord, nor faint when you are reproved by Him; for those whom the Lord loves He disciplines, and He scourges every son whom He receives."
>
> It is for discipline that you endure; God deals with you as with sons; for what son is there whom his father does not discipline? But if you are without discipline, of which all have become partakers, then you are illegitimate children and not sons. Furthermore, we had earthly fathers to discipline us, and we respected them; shall we not much rather be subject to the Father of spirits, and live? For they disciplined us for a short time as seemed best to them, but He disciplines us for our good, that we may share His holiness.
>
> All discipline for the moment seems not to be joyful, but

sorrowful; yet to those who have been trained by it, afterward it yields the peaceful fruit of righteousness (Hebrews 12:5-11).

The purpose of discipline is to produce righteousness, not pain or suffering for its own sake. Discipline without love may yield an outward, fear-based obedience but with inward rebellion. Once the fear is broken, the inner child goes wild. The most effective control of the inner child is love. Love enables us to refrain from wrong, hurtful behavior toward ourselves and others, yet at the same time allows the healthy part of the inner child to grow and develop. It was the father's love that drew the prodigal son home to clean up his act.

The more you understand your inner child, the less surprised you'll be by the thoughts and ideas that pass through your mind. What stops you from acting impulsively from the inner child—fear or love? If you understand God's love for you, it will be love.

Why don't I sleep with every attractive woman I meet? Why don't I steal when I know I won't get caught? Why not cheat on that exam? After all, I know I can get away with it. You say Christians shouldn't have these thoughts and impulses? I've got news for you. They do. I do. What stops me from acting on my impulses? My love for God and my wife and family. Because I love them and they love me, I don't want to hurt them. Reverence for all that God is and for what He requires keeps me from behavior that displeases Him. Thus, loving discipline controls the inner child without killing its spirit.

PERSONAL
REFLECTION

■ What type of discipline did your parents use with you when you were a child? What would you say was the *goal* of their discipline?

_____

_____

_____

_____

■ In what ways do you relate to Dr. Dickinson's statement, "Discipline without love may yield an outward, fear-based obedience but with inward rebellion"?

_____

_____

_____

■ Can you think of a time when you experienced God's loving hand of discipline in your life? What happened, and what was the end result?

_____

_____

_____

_____

❑ *The Father's Compassion.* Have you noticed how angry you become when someone you love disappoints you? I have. Of course, what we really feel is hurt, but we do a masterful job of covering our hurt with a good dose of anger. Put yourself in the place of the prodigal's father. Suppose your child came and asked for the money you were saving for his inheritance after your death. You decide to give it to him, and he announces that he's quitting school and his job to travel around the country. You ask him how he's going to support himself and he answers, "Oh, I'm going to live off the money you gave me."

Think of it. You've spent years scrimping and saving and denying yourself extras to provide this inheritance, and now your son is taking off to see the world without a second thought or even a word of gratitude. Six months pass and you never hear a word from the boy. You feel a terrible weight on your heart, knowing he's probably in trouble or up to no good. If you were going to express your feelings aloud, what would you say? Something like, "How could that ungrateful kid do this to me?" Or, "After all I've done for him, this is the thanks I get!" Or, "Just wait till he comes home. I'll tell him a thing or two!"

Then one day you gaze out the windows as you have every day for the past six months, and there trudging up the sidewalk is your son. His clothes are tattered, he has a straggly beard, he's too thin, and looks like he hasn't showered in a week. You rush to the door and throw it open, and then . . . what do you do? What do you say?

"Well, son, I hope you're proud of yourself. You've had your mother and me sick with worry!"

Or: "Just look at yourself, young man. You're a mess! What on earth have you been doing?"

Or: "Well, smart guy, what did you do with the money I gave you? No, don't bother to tell me. I bet you've blown every penny."

All of these responses are typical inner critical parent reactions to help cover our wounded feelings. The prodigal's father gave none of these responses. At first sight of his son, he ran to embrace him with deep compassion.

You might ask, "But what about the boy's foolish lifestyle and the way he squandered his father's inheritance? Are parents just supposed to ignore such behavior?"

In our story of the prodigal, the father's joy over his lost son's return far outweighed his loss of material possessions. And his focus was not on punishment but restoration. Besides, the son had learned his lesson the old-fashioned way: He earned it.

Dear friend, as the prodigal's father responded to his wayward son, so your Heavenly Father responds to you. His caring, compassionate arms long to embrace you as you turn your heart toward home. There is no harsh, "I told you so." Your Heavenly Father does not delight in making you feel guilty or ashamed; rather, He desires to bestow on you His fullest blessing as His beloved child. Remember, God the Father is not your inner critical parent. He is a loving, nurturing Parent within you who draws your inner child to Himself and encourages you to be all He has designed you to be.

PERSONAL REFLECTION

■ What comes to your mind when you think of the word *compassion*?

_____

_____

_____

_____

■ Think of a person you know who exemplifies the meaning of the word *compassion*. How does he or she treat people—you in particular?

_____

_____

_____

_____

■ Are *you* able to be compassionate with yourself? Why or why not? What are some compassionate messages your inner child needs to hear?

_____

❏ *The Father's Guidance.* Several years ago I drove to Bishop, California, a little town at the base of the Sierra Nevada Mountains, to pick up Jeff who was returning from a backpacking trip with his Boy Scout troop. We stopped at a restaurant for lunch, and I chatted briefly with the man behind the counter. He told me about a lake in the High Sierras that contained two- to three-pound native eastern brook trout. "But it's a real hard place to find," he warned. I assured him if he gave me directions, I'd have no trouble finding the lake.

I thought about that lake all year. The next summer Jeff and I set out to find the lake and see if the fish were really as big as the man said. One thing he was right about—the lake was hard to find. There were no signs, no marked trails, just a big granite mountain. The man had told me to look for a dead tree at the top of the mountain; that was the only way to gain access to the lake. But not being one to follow instructions, I decided to find the lake on my own. The fact is, I wore myself out trying to find the lake my own way. Finally, in exasperation, Jeff and I returned to the base of the mountain and followed the man's instructions, to the letter. This time we found the lake right away. Would you believe?—the fish were every bit as big as the man said and we caught seven or eight of those beauties! But if I'd listened to the instructions of the man who had been there before, I would have saved myself a lot of time and energy.

The prodigal son had failed to listen to the guidance and instruction of his father. As a result, he had experienced needless pain, sorrow, and humiliation at the hands of so-called friends in a strange and distant land. He had suffered near-starvation and the degradation of slopping the hogs when he wasn't even allowed to eat the husks. What a blow to his self-esteem—that his employer considered him too lowly even to eat the garbage! Surely he lamented, "If only I'd listened to my father!"

We too need to listen to our Heavenly Father as He guides us on a path tailored to our individual talents and needs. And we need to allow Him to use our God-given abilities in service that strengthens the body of Christ.

Jesus invites those who are tired of trying on their own:
Come to Me, all who are weary and heavy-laden, and I will give you rest. Take My yoke upon you, and learn from Me, for I am

gentle and humble in heart; and you shall find rest for your souls. For My yoke is easy, and My load is light (Matthew 11:28-30).

Notice the great comfort offered to those who were worn out trying to work with yokes that didn't fit. For you, this could represent your inner critical parent that constantly places a load of unreasonable demands on your inner child. The inner critical parent doesn't know how to make well-fitting yokes, but the Lord does. The life God calls you to is one that is custom-tailored for you and your talents. As you learn of Him, you will discover that He never gives you more than you can handle. When life gets tough, He is there to empathize with you, love and encourage you, and strengthen you as no one else can.

PERSONAL REFLECTION

■ Describe a time when you failed to listen to the guidance and instruction of an "authority" of some kind. What happened?

_____

_____

_____

_____

_____

■ Do you think of yourself as a "teachable" person—that is, someone who remains open to direction and guidance from other people? Describe a time when an attitude of teachability paid off.

_____

_____

_____

_____

■ Have you found Christ's "yoke easy and His load light"? (Matthew 11:30) If not, what makes it seem to feel so heavy and over-whelming to you?

_____

_____

_____

_____

_____

You might conclude from what I've said so far that all you need is the Lord. Only Christ can effect our salvation; but for Christian growth, we need one another. We who are in the body of Christ—who place our faith in Jesus Christ as personal Lord and Savior—have the privilege of modeling the attributes of God illustrated in the story of the prodigal son. We are the hands and feet of God to minister to others who are in need. We can provide love, encouragement, compassion, loving discipline, and guidance, first to our own families, and then to our larger family—the body of Christ. Others will come to know a loving, caring God through His loving, caring people.

Our spiritual resources come through the vertical relationship we have with our Heavenly Father, who has taken up residence within our personalities through His Holy Spirit. As our inner nurturing parent, God nourishes our needy inner child. Then we can provide nourishment on a horizontal level to the people in our world.

PERSONAL REFLECTION

■ Which quality of a healthy, nurturing parent would you most like to see developed in your life right now? Check one.

❑ Love

❑ Encouragement

❑ Compassion

❑ Loving discipline

❑ Guidance

■ Try to think of some practical ways you can begin developing the nurturing quality you checked above in your own life.

_____

_____

_____

_____

_____

PRAYERFUL REFLECTION

■ Reflect back on the nurturing qualities demonstrated by the father of the prodigal son—his *love, encouragement, compassion, loving discipline, guidance*. Has God demonstrated to you at a personal level that He is like the prodigal's father? In what ways? Write a prayer thanking God for all the nurturing ways He has revealed Himself to you.

Heavenly Father,

_____

_____

_____

_____

_____

PERSONAL RENEWAL

■ Renew your thoughts and feelings this week by meditating on Psalm 103:8-18 (NIV). Let the words of this song nurture your inner child as you read and reread it.

The Lord is compassionate and gracious, slow to anger, abounding in love. He will not always accuse, nor will He harbor His anger forever; He does not treat us as our sins deserve or repay us according to our iniquities. For as high as the heavens are above the earth, so great is His love for those who fear Him; as far as the east is from the west, so far has He removed our transgressions from us. As a father has compassion on his children, so the Lord has compassion on those who fear Him; for He knows how we are formed, He remembers that we are dust. As for man, his days are like grass, he flourishes like a flower of the field; the wind blows over it and it is gone, and its place remembers it no more. But from everlasting to everlasting the Lord's love is with those who fear Him, and His righteousness with their children's children—with those who keep His covenant and remember to obey His precepts.

Chapter 10
Suggestions for People-Helpers

It may be that you desire not only to understand yourself and others, but also to help people in a counseling capacity. Most counseling is of an informal nature, done by people with no formal education in psychology.

I want this chapter to be helpful to those who do informal counseling as well as to those who are in the counseling profession. From my 23 years of experience as a marriage counselor and clinical psychologist, I am interested in principles that work. I do not intend to develop some new psychological-theological theory. Rather, I want to talk to you about principles that will increase your effectiveness as a lay counselor, a good friend, or a psychotherapist. First, let's begin with you and your talents.

Do you have a *helping talent?** What a silly question, you say. Doesn't everybody have the ability to help others? The key to answering that question is found in identifying the ways we help people. In previous chapters we talked about your natural talent as a part of your inner child. I also mentioned the IDAK Group that has identified 54 natural talents or inherent aptitudes for excellence. At IDAK we identify four specific talents that we call helping talents; two are especially important if you plan to enter the counseling profession. These four helping talents are:

√ *Tutoring.** This person has natural talent for assisting others on a one-to-one basis in overcoming educational deficiencies, learning disabilities, or other incapacities. This instruction may occur over a long period of time. The focus is on a specific deficiency which is tangible and concrete, such as problems in math, reading, writing, attention deficits, learning to overcome paralysis, loss of certain muscle usage, and retraining.

√ *Being of service.** This talent relates to those who enjoy helping others meet their needs or obtain their goals. In churches you find those who are always available to set up tables, lick envelopes, prepare food, wait on tables, and a host of often unnoticed tasks that help others get their jobs done. These people enjoy their work and find deep satisfaction in helping others. This service talent is also reflected in those who are always receiving phone calls to help others move, wallpaper, paint, fix the car, run an errand, watch the kids, do some shopping, and the list goes on. It's as if these people send out vibes that they are able and willing to be called on for help.

√ *Counseling.** This person enjoys the one-on-one counseling that focuses on personal problems, needs, and conflicts. Included in this category are marriage problems, self-image problems, spiritual and psychological concerns, and various abnormal behaviors. Individuals with this talent have great patience and are able to draw people out in order to uncover the underlying problems. They may work with counselees for long periods of time, even years. It's important to add here that the counseling talent by itself does not include finding solutions to problems. That aspect of counseling is more a function of proper training and education.

√ *Reassuring and supporting others.** The last of the helping talents stresses the ability to empathize with another's hurts, frustrations, or anxieties and convey a feeling of comfort and support. People with this talent know how to comfort those who have experienced a deep loss, a major disappointment, or other painful circumstances. They are able to put themselves in the other person's shoes and feel what he or she is going through. It's important to add that the talent of reassurance and support does not necessarily include the ability to provide solutions to people's problems; this again depends on education and training.

If you have a helping talent, you have *one* of the four, not all four. You may be involved in other areas as well, but these areas may be considered skills, not necessarily talents. A skill is learned through training and education; a natural talent is the result of your God-given aptitude; you just have it. The key question for you to determine if you are interested in the counseling field, either as a professional or as a layperson, is, *Do I have the natural aptitude of counseling? Or of reassuring and supporting?* You need one or the other.

PERSONAL REFLECTION

■ Do you have a natural *helping talent?** If you think you do, check the sentence below that best describes how you see yourself. Check only one.

❑ I am able to assist others on a one-to-one basis in overcoming educational deficiencies, learning disabilities, or other incapacities (*tutoring**).

❑ I enjoy helping others meet their needs or obtain their goals. I am always getting phone calls to help others move, wallpaper, paint, fix their car, run an errand, watch the kids, do some shopping, etc. (*service**).

❑ I often find myself involved counseling others one-on-one concerning their personal problems, needs, and conflicts. I seem to be able to draw people out in order to uncover the underlying problems (*counseling**).

❑ I have the ability to empathize with other people's hurts, frustrations, or anxieties and convey a feeling of comfort and support (*reassuring and supporting others**).

■ If you have the natural aptitude of *counseling** or *reassuring and supporting*,* what steps are you willing to take to develop and use your talent in a more significant way?

_____

_____

_____

_____

I have several friends with doctoral degrees in clinical psychology who found that, once they began to counsel people in private practice, they did not like what they were doing. That's a tough way to find out that you're in the wrong profession. What usually happens to these people is that they grin and bear it because they have too much time and money invested in education and training to change careers. But why do these things happen in the first place?

To my knowledge no graduate school requires prospective candidates to be assessed for the natural aptitudes needed for successful counseling and therapy. On the lay level, many people who attempt counseling, in church or with friends, discover that they do not have the counseling talent; the people they try to help do not improve or appreciate the assistance given. If this has been your experience when you counseled people, you may have rationalized that the people didn't want to be helped, or were out of fellowship, or living in sin. These factors may have been true, but that doesn't mean an individual couldn't be helped by the right person.

It's important to recognize the difference between a helping *talent* and a helping *value*. You may be a person who values people and deeply desires to help them emotionally, spiritually, or physically. However, there are many ways you can help others; counseling is only one way. I frequently encounter people who have high helping values but low helping talents.

There are two groups of talents that run contrary to the helping talents, especially the counseling talent. These are the *persuasive talents** and the *supervisory talents.** The persuasive talents include resolving differences among groups or individuals, closing deals and collecting commissions, and motivating people to get excited about an idea, a product, or just about anything. The reason individuals with the persuasive talents do not make good counselors is that they initiate action; they want action now. Therefore, they lose patience when people do not get moving.

The other group that runs contrary to the helping talents is the supervisory talents. These involve getting people excited about new ideas or programs, planning out how the programs will be accomplished, and working with people on a day-to-day basis to accomplish these plans and ideas. Again, the focus is on moving people to action. When there is some foot-dragging by the person being counseled, the supervisory person loses patience and feels frustrated with the lack of progress. The end result is discouragement on the part of the counselor as well as the counselee.

Once you have carefully decided that you have the natural talent to counsel, you should pursue education and training. Talent alone does not provide an understanding of the process of change necessary to bring about the resolution of various problems. There are a number of fine graduate schools that specialize in the integration of psychology and theology leading to either a Ph.D. or a Psy.D. degree in clinical psychology.

Or perhaps you are not interested in formal training but would like to be involved in a lay ministry of counseling. Many churches are now training their congregants so that they can participate in a counseling ministry within the church body. The main question is whether you have counseling talent, not just helping values. If you have the talent, you will achieve excellence as a counselor.

PERSONAL
REFLECTION

■ Do any of the traits Dr. Dickinson just described sound like you? Describe how you see yourself as a people-helper. Are you a person with a counseling *talent* or just helping *values*? Why not ask a friend?

_____

_____

_____

_____

There are those who take a strong position that a Christian counselor should use Scripture as a major tool in counseling other Christians. Some have tried rather diligently to apply a verse of Scripture to every problem. The more I study the Bible, the more I discover that God gives us principles to guide our behavior. But there are many issues in life that are not directly answered by a verse of Scripture.

A case in point is the Apostle Paul's discussion in Romans 14 about Christian liberty. The principle involves a heart attitude of being willing to give up something I may feel comfortable doing if it causes a Christian brother or sister to stumble in their faith or walk with God. But if you begin to apply this principle as a rule of conduct, then you turn it into a legal issue and must judge people's actions as either right or wrong, thereby missing the point.

Let me mention some cautions about using Scripture in a counseling setting.

√ *Scripture can obscure the real problem.* Put yourself in the place of someone who is seeking help with alcohol abuse. You are a Christian in good standing in your church and have managed to conceal your drinking problem from most of your Christian friends. You walk into your counselor's office for the first time and begin your conversation by asking whether the Bible condones the drinking of alcoholic beverages. The counselor opens the Bible and shows you passages that deal with the sin of overindulgence. How much more would you tell this counselor about your drinking problem?

The same situation could apply if you turned to a friend for counseling and he began to quote Scriptures. What would be the effect on you? I wouldn't want to reveal my lack of control over drinking to either of these individuals because I would feel guilty and ashamed. It's not that what the Bible has to say isn't important; it's the timing that presents the problem. Most of us need time in a trusting environment before we feel safe enough to talk about what's really on our hearts. A premature use of Scripture can turn people off from sharing the real nature of their problems.

PERSONAL
REFLECTION

■ Have you ever sought the help of a pastor because of a personal or marital problem you were facing only to have that person quote a Scripture to you as the magic "fix-all" to the problem? Give an example. How did the person's response to your problem make you feel?

√ *Scripture can be used as an inner critical parent.* Some people use Scripture in counseling in a confrontational way to punitively spank the inner child in others. This approach creates fear rather than a true brokenness leading to repentance and behavior change. A professional colleague related this story of one of his clients. An adolescent boy struggling with his sexual desires went to his youth pastor for counseling. The boy knew what the Bible taught about fornication, but he was having trouble with the in-between stuff, like petting. The well-meaning youth pastor seized the opportunity to scare the boy out of his sexual struggle by showing him Scripture passages on God's judgment of sin and lust, especially those verses that say no fornicator will enter the kingdom of heaven. The poor kid was scared to death of his sexual urges, which were actually quite normal for a boy his age. A friend of his recommended that he talk to a Christian psychologist about his fears and anxieties and, after some encouragement, he decided to seek help.

Now I'm not suggesting that all youth pastors counsel as this one did; but this pastor did not have counseling talent and used the Bible as a way of covering up his lack of skill, at the expense of the teenager. What the boy needed was to be able to talk out his struggles with someone who could understand how difficult sexual urges can be at this age (or any age). He needed help in distinguishing between sexual urges and the need to be close to another person, in this case, his girlfriend. It would have been helpful to explain to the young man how his emotions work, focusing on what he could control versus what he could not control. Finally, the young man needed help in understanding the emotional and spiritual basis for God's plan to reserve intercourse for marriage. With that principle in mind, the counselor could establish some controls to guide the youth in his dating relationships.

When the Bible is used primarily to generate fear as a way of controlling unwanted behavior, it creates a situation of war. The inner child begins to push to do that which is forbidden while the inner parent uses fear-induced intimidation to keep the rebellion in check. God's principal method for controlling the behavior of His children is not by being the critical inner parent. It's by becoming the nurturing, loving inner parent who desires that we walk in His ways out of a heart of love leading to obedience. The path to this kind of walk often starts with a talented counselor—whether a professional or a layman—who takes time to understand the problems and does not use the Bible as a means to scare people into a Christian walk.

PERSONAL REFLECTION

■ Can you think of a time when a "counselor" (be it a Sunday School teacher, pastor, family member, or friend) used the Bible to instill fear in you in order to control some unwanted behavior in your life? How did you respond?

_____

_____

_____

_____

■ Would you describe yourself as a strong-willed adult? In what ways do you struggle with personal obedience in your life? Tell why you think you struggle at times.

_____

_____

_____

_____

Up to this point we have focused on how *not to use* the Bible in counseling those who are in distress. Now let's look at some ways to use Scripture constructively.

√ *Scripture can be used to comfort and encourage.* Have you ever noticed how Jesus counseled those who came to Him? He always started right where they were and zeroed in on the most basic needs they had at the moment. He took time to listen to people and understand what their needs were.

Take the example in John 8 of the woman caught in adultery. Jesus was teaching in the temple when, right in the middle of His discourse, a commotion broke out. Several Pharisees entered the temple dragging a young woman, shouting to all around that she had been taken in the act of adultery. The men shoved her into the center of the room where she stood embarrassed, humiliated, and exposed.

Put yourself in her place. How would you feel? Terrified? Angry? Ashamed? Hopeless?

Actually, the religious leaders were using this poor woman to trap Jesus into contradicting the Mosaic Law so that they would have grounds to kill Him. The woman wasn't important to them at all; she was simply a pawn to be used. So often in counseling others we focus on being biblically correct and forget the importance of the person we are trying to help.

Jesus saw in this woman a valuable human being created in the image of God. She was deeply fallen, but she was also dearly loved. That morning Jesus taught a powerful lesson to all who were present about the value of one human being. He stooped to the ground and wrote something with His finger. What it was we do not know, but then Jesus straightened up and looked the Pharisees straight in the eye and said, "He who is without sin among you, let him be the first to throw a stone at her." He stooped again and wrote on the ground. The net effect is that the religious heavies left one by one until they were all gone. Jesus gazed tenderly at her and asked, " 'Woman, where are they? Where are your accusers? Did no one condemn you?' 'No one, Lord,' she replied. And Jesus said, 'Neither do I condemn you; go your way; from now on sin no more' " (John 8:10-11).

Could it be that the words Jesus wrote on the ground were a personal message to the woman about who He was? Could it be that as the woman read the message she believed in Jesus? Because of her faith, He did not condemn her but forgave her. You see, dear friend, you need to consider what communication occurred between Jesus and the woman before He commanded her to sin no more. It was His love and compassion that changed this woman.

Then Jesus quoted the Scripture regarding sin. When people we counsel believe that we are genuinely interested in them as persons, and when we take time to listen to their needs, then our use of Scripture can be a comfort and a help. On occasion, after I understand my client's problems, I use illustrations from the Bible similar to the issues the patient is experiencing. I've found this to be a real encouragement. I want the individual to realize that God is vitally interested in their pain and conflicts.

PERSONAL
REFLECTION

■ Have you ever had an experience similar to the one described in John 8, of the woman caught in adultery? What happened? How did you feel?

_____

_____

_____

_____

■ Reread Jesus' words in John 8:10-11. In what areas of your life do you need to hear Jesus' words, "Neither do I condemn you; go your way; from now on sin no more"?

_____

_____

_____

■ Is there anyone in your life at present who you feel is genuinely interested in you as a person—who takes time to listen to your needs? Who is it? Describe a time when this person showed you the kind of love and compassion Jesus showed the woman taken in adultery.

_____

_____

_____

_____

√ *Scripture is useful for giving instruction.* Another application of Scripture is to encourage the counselee to do some independent Bible study in the area he's struggling with, such as divorce, fear, anxiety, trust, security, and so forth. Counseling prevents a person from simply spiritualizing what he reads and enables him to bring Scripture into the arena of real life. He begins to see the practical application of scriptural principles to the events of daily life. Timing is important. If Scripture is used prematurely, you may miss the counselee's real feelings about touchy issues. And you need to guard against using the Bible and yourself as an extension of a person's inner critical parent. If this happens, he will perform for you and never talk about his real feelings and behavior. I also often encourage a patient to get into a good Bible study group of mature people who pray and support one another and are not afraid to share themselves openly.

PERSONAL REFLECTION

■ Scripture can bring comfort and help in your time of need. Think of an area in your life where you are currently struggling. EXAMPLE: *I continue to struggle with worry.* Look up your chosen word (e.g., WORRY), or a closely related word, in an exhaustive Bible concordance. Note all the places in Scripture where this word is used. Look up in your Bible all the Scripture references you find for that word in your Bible concordance. These Scriptures will show you what God says about the particular issue with which you are struggling. Jot down what you learn as you look up each Scripture reference.

_____

_____

_____

_____

_____

_____

■ Describe how you feel about the Bible. How do you see it? How comfortable are you reading or studying it? How well do you understand what it says?

_____

_____

_____

_____

One of the more frequent questions I am asked by both clients and those interested in counseling is, "Do you pray with your clients during the session?" My answer is generally no. I might add here that some Christian counselors I know do pray with their clients during the counseling session. It depends largely upon one's style and personal and professional convictions.

Prayer in the counseling room can act as a block to the expression of true feelings or the disclosure of conflicting behavior or thoughts. It's very difficult to share some non-Christian behaviors or thoughts with a counselor or friend when you begin the session with prayer. Generally, in that situation, the adapted child shows up and says something "acceptable" rather than revealing the conflicts the inner child is experiencing.

Another problem in the use of prayer is that some people use prayer to "magically" avoid painful experiences and feelings that need to be worked through. They consider God a personal genie to be used for escape. The Bible does not promise us a problem-free life. In fact, many Scripture verses inform us that our life will be challenging and at times painful because our values conflict with a non-Christian world; as a result we may be scorned or belittled for our convictions, and that hurts. But the Bible also tells us that God is with us in our pain and sorrow; while He may not always remove our difficulties, He will give us comfort and strength to endure them.

Those of us who counsel know that only when we confront pain and discomfort is there any hope for effective relief. In counseling, you must be certain that the ones you are helping are able to confront the real problems in their lives. That takes time to accomplish. Only when they feel safe and cared for will patients dare reveal what is really bothering them. *Premature use of prayer in counseling sessions can short-circuit that process.*

At this point, you may be asking, "Well, then, are there any effective times in counseling for prayer?" The answer is yes. Let's look at some.

√ *First, take time to listen to the problem of the person you are counseling so that you can determine his or her needs and concerns. Then if you feel led of God to pray, I would strongly suggest that you follow your inner prompting.* Some counselors feel they must pray with the counselee either before or at the close of each session. This rather mechanical approach may be ineffective because it is prompted by a procedure rather than the Spirit of God. If your prayer is that God would give you wisdom to know when to pray with your counselee He promises to give you that wisdom. This will make your prayerful intervention meaningful and appropriate.

√ *Although as a rule I do not use prayer in therapy, there have been times when patients have been so distressed that I have asked if I could pray for them.* I try to intercede by putting into words the nature of their conflict at a time when they are too upset to think clearly. This helps patients to formulate more accurately the major conflict they are experiencing and it models a caring concern for them that imitates God's loving care. Even though I pray infrequently *with* my patients, I often pray *for* them. This, I feel, is fundamental for Christian counselors. We need God's wisdom, discernment, strength, and patience to minister both spiritually and emotionally. Prayer is one means of making God an integral part of the healing process.

PERSONAL REFLECTION

■ Describe a time when prayer was used with you in a counseling session in a way that felt appropriate to you.

_____

_____

_____

■ Have you ever felt that a situation or problem you faced was being minimized by a counselor or friend who wanted to pray your problem away? How did you respond in that situation?

_____

_____

_____

One of the most effective ways of communicating love and value to others is through your ability to listen actively. This sounds simple enough, doesn't it? But it's more difficult than you think. When was the last time you gave someone your undivided attention for five minutes, during which time you were actively trying to understand what was being said? Generally, our minds wander to other topics, we jump ahead to our own ideas or intended responses, or we just space out. We may be looking right at the person, but mentally we are not there. It takes real concentration to pay attention to what others say to us.

How do you check yourself to see whether you have clearly understood what someone is saying? Try putting into your own words what you think the other person was trying to express; have them validate your accuracy. It might sound something like this: "Bill, have I got this straight? What you're telling me is that you feel . . . or the issue here is . . ." By asking such questions, you send the underlying message that the speaker is worthy of attention and that you are willing to take time to understand.

Active listening is of immense importance in all relationships, not just in counseling. One helpful guideline for active listening is to focus on the needs of the person speaking. While this sounds basic, it's easier said than done. One reason we don't hear the needs of those speaking is because of our own needs, or own hidden agenda. In the first years of my training as a psychologist, I was so focused on trying to understand the dynamics of my counselees that I often did not hear what they were saying to me. My agenda was to figure them out, not to really listen to what they were saying about their immediate needs.

I'm reminded of a story about a pastor who received a phone call from a man known to be both an intellect and a skeptic. The man said he needed to talk, so the pastor set up an appointment for that evening. On his way to the church, the pastor reflected that perhaps here was his opportunity to present a grand intellectual defense of the faith. But when he met his appointment, he found that the man simply wanted to know how to become a Christian. The pastor, already mentally rehearsing his arguments, didn't hear the man's request and, instead, launched into a great apologetic discourse on the evidence for Christianity. Still, the man kept asking, "How do I become a Christian?" Finally, after waxing eloquent for an hour, the pastor heard what the man was saying. Feeling sheepish and almost disappointed at the simplicity of the question, he led the man to Christ.

This story is an extreme illustration of our tendency to speak from a hidden agenda representing our own needs rather than the needs of others. What impresses me about the ministry of Jesus is His ability to listen for and truly hear the needs of the people He encountered. His impact on those around Him was due, in part, to His validation of their worth by listening and identifying their needs. Because they felt important to Him as persons, they were receptive to His message regarding their spiritual needs.

Another important benefit of listening actively is that you stand a better chance of understanding the real issues. One of my main objections to a more confrontational approach in counseling people is that it's very easy to give solutions before clearly understanding the real problems. It has been my experience that people will rarely tell the painful facts of their situation within the first several meetings. Usually, they talk about safer issues to protect their inner child from ridicule. It's only after a person feels safe and valued—something they feel when we as counselors actively listen—that the real issues surface. To be helpful to others, we need to understand these issues. In other words, we need to see the big picture. Are you aware that the Bible speaks about listening?

> But let every one be quick to hear, slow to speak and slow to anger; for the anger of man does not achieve the righteousness of God (James 1:19-20).

Permit a Dick Dickinson paraphrase, if you will. You who are beloved family members of God, take lots of time to actively listen to one another so that you fully understand what others are really trying to say. Then when you speak, you will be better able to meet the other person's needs because you understand the issues. This is also an effective way of reducing your anger, which often results from misunderstanding because you put your mouth in gear before engaging your ears. Remember, God gave you one mouth and two ears. The majority rules. I rest my case!

PERSONAL REFLECTION

■ How do you know when someone is really listening to you? When was the last time someone gave you their undivided attention?

_____

_____

_____

_____

■ What kind of listener are you? Ask two or three close friends to answer this question about you. Jot down what they tell you.

_____

_____

_____

_____

■ What might you do to become a more focused listener? Write down three or four specific ideas.

_____

_____

_____

_____

Once a week for two years during my graduate studies, I lay on the couch sharing my thoughts and feelings with my therapist. Much of the time he remained silent, especially when I deliberately used my intellect to avoid painful emotional issues. Many of his interpretations of my urges and wishes were correct, and I found myself understanding better some of my behavior.

But there was something fundamentally absent in my relationship with my therapist, and it was something I needed very much. It was my need of a friend as well as a therapist.

I can hear some of you therapists having a field day with that. Be my guest. What I'm saying is that I needed to feel and see the person behind the therapist role. I wasn't asking for disclosures about his personal life, nor did I want to be his buddy. But I did want to feel his personal caring behind his correct interpretations. I needed to know that he cared about me personally, that in some way I was important to him, especially after I would disclose some rather uncomfortable feelings and thoughts.

A therapist can be well trained and technically correct in his interventions but be so cut off personally that the counselee never feels the warmth and caring of his human personality. This underscores the importance of establishing a caring relationship with people you work with in a counseling capacity. Are they merely interesting cases, challenging dynamics, diagnostic labels? Or are they valuable human beings created in the image of God, but with a very hurting inner child needing your love and care?

You may argue, "You don't know some of the people I work with; they're impossible to love!" Some people do make it very difficult to love them, but that doesn't change the importance of a caring relationship in the healing process.

PERSONAL REFLECTION

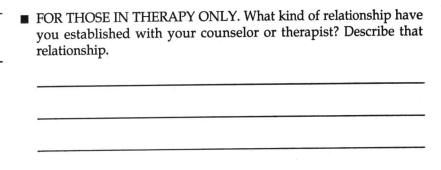

■ FOR THOSE IN THERAPY ONLY. What kind of relationship have you established with your counselor or therapist? Describe that relationship.

_____

_____

_____

_____

There are some common barriers in building a personal relationship with those we counsel. *Countertransference* is a common one. Countertransference takes place when the counselor/therapist's own personal needs, feelings, issues, or conflicts prevent him from seeing the client's needs clearly. This often prevents the client from making progress in some areas of conflict, especially if the therapist's reaction is adversative (expressing opposition) or, in some cases, amorous.

Here's an example. Sometimes I have difficulty liking a male client who conveys an aggressive, authoritative attitude. I can feel my inner child heading for the closet to hide. My behavior toward him is placation rather than an attempt to look behind my client's aggressive behavior to find the frightened inner child who uses intimidation for protection. My intellect tells me what is going on, but my emotional tendency is to retreat; this is not helpful to the client. This is an example of my countertransference. In the session, I am acting out my own conflicts with authoritative males, thus interfering with my ability to help the client understand himself.

Often the countertransference can take on a sexual flavor, which is equally unhelpful and potentially harmful. In an earlier chapter I mentioned a situation involving a female client. I found myself enjoying her presence, but I felt very uncomfortable with what I feared might be sexual feelings for her. I discovered that I wasn't trying very hard to work with her in understanding the deeper aspects of her problem. She had been sexually abused as a child; as an adult, sex was the only way she knew to satisfy her inner needs, and that always proved disappointing to her. What I didn't realize at the time was that I was responding to the subtle sexual cues she was unconsciously sending me, rather than trying to understand her deeper needs.

When I realized that therapy had ceased to be effective, I brought up my guilty feelings in a staff meeting, and the feedback was very helpful. My colleagues pointed out that what was actually happening in the patient/therapist relationship was that I was responding to my patient's inner-child need to be comforted, loved, and held. What I discovered about myself was that I was also covering my deeper inner-child needs to be held, loved, and cared for by sexualizing them. My reluctance to admit my deeper needs kept me focused on the sexual feelings. After talking with my colleagues, I understood my feelings and as a result was able to address those deeper inner-child needs within myself and my client.

For me to have acted in any way on the sexual feelings I was experiencing would have been not only sinful and unethical, but also damaging to my client, for it would have reinforced her feelings of being bad and worthless. She never would have felt safe enough to face the deeper unmet needs of her inner child. When therapists, counselors, and even pastors become sexually involved with their clients, they are generally not responding to real adult sexual needs but to unmet early needs of the inner child for love, closeness, oneness, and comfort—needs that have been mistakenly sexualized.

Another reason we find it hard to care for some of the people we counsel is that they are unattractive in their behavior or appearance. We see increasing numbers of patients with personality disorders that have at their core extreme narcissism, unstable relational abilities, impulsive behaviors, abuse of alcohol and drugs, sexual promiscuity, poor self-identity, and failure to understand or care about the consequences of their behavior. Such people present significant challenges to the counselor and therapist, not only because of their extreme behaviors that need to be controlled or changed, but also because of their unpleasant personalities. Often they take and take until we feel absolutely drained. It is as if we are pouring our efforts into a bottomless, thankless pit, and we resent them for it. If we confront them on their impulsive or destructive behavior, or if we deprive them of what they want from us, we know we're in for an emotional explosion, including suicidal threats or other distasteful behaviors aimed at hurting us for depriving them. In such cases, we as counselors will get very little appreciation for our efforts, especially in the early days of the therapeutic relationship.

When I can work through my own countertransference feelings as well as my normal frustrations, I am able to truly care for and appreciate people who present such a counseling challenge. Although I have been a Christian for many years, I am not immune to disliking people I work with; but I have also discovered that when I look at myself from God's perspective and think about His love, patience, and forgiveness for me, I see difficult people in a different light. Then, with God's help, I am able to form an effective working relationship with them. In the few cases where I cannot, I refer the clients to someone else.

PERSONAL REFLECTION

■ Can you think of a time when someone you were talking with brought out strong subconscious feelings in you (either bad or good) that got in the way of your relating to that person? Describe that encounter.

_____

_____

_____

_____

■ What can you do to guard against countertransference when meeting and spending time with people?

_____

_____

_____

_____

By now you are aware of the three basic ingredients of your own inner child: your thoughts and feelings, your God-given natural aptitudes, and your unique identity as one created in the image of God. It is only when we touch the inner child of another that we can make contact with the real person inside. Yet we all erect obstacles to protect ourselves from the hurt and shame felt so deeply by our inner child.

Unless we as counselors find that inner child, we generally succeed in affecting a change only in a person's intellect or outer protective behavior. This serves to strengthen the defensive barriers that keep the inner child hidden in the closet of one's mind. How do we contact that inner child? Let me give you some suggestions from my experience.

√ _Establishing the purpose of counseling._ It's so easy to become sidetracked by the unconsciously evasive tactics people use to protect themselves. They talk about the week's events, other people, old hurts, or they say that everything is going great when it's not. While these other topics may be important, counselees often use them to avoid their true feelings. Afterward, when I cannot put my finger on what really transpired during the session, I sense that I have been led on a bird walk.

During the actual therapy, it is important to be aware of the counselee's inner child. Do I feel it? Am I alert to this person's real feelings at this very moment? Or have I allowed him to divert me from that protective hiding place that contains his inner child? For me to be effective, it's fundamental that I know what my purpose and objectives are when I am counseling.

√ *Arresting counselee diversion.* When my mind wanders, it usually means that my client's words do not match what he really feels. In other words, he is using words to divert me from the true feelings of his inner child. When I feel myself not paying attention or at times fighting sleep during the session, I usually say to my client, "Bob, I noticed that my mind is wandering. I'm having a difficult time paying attention to what you're saying. When this happens, it usually means you're not telling me what you're really feeling right now."

I always couch these remarks in such a way that it leaves room for error on my part, but most of the time I'm right on. I use my own reactions as a barometer for gauging what is going on in my client, because a great deal of communication that occurs between us·is nonverbal and is experienced emotionally, not intellectually.

√ *Being in touch with my own inner child.* How can I find the hidden child within others if I am not in touch with my own inner child? I can't! Counseling is like looking into a mirror. In working with others, I am constantly being faced with myself.

The process of discovering the inner child is not static, nor is it a once-for-all matter; it goes on for as long as we are alive. If this growth and learning process stops, we will experience emotional isolation, a sense of deadness, and a painful awareness of being alone.

When small children play, they are rarely bored. They run and jump and shout and sing and laugh. There is always something to explore, something new to see, taste, touch, and hear. So it can be in adult life if we allow that creative, spontaneous child within to become fully alive.

So much of counseling involves resuscitating someone's smothered inner child. Think again about the story of Jesus with the children, when He gathered them into His arms and held them close and blessed them. His inner child was free to connect with their inner child in genuine empathy, and the youngsters responded joyously to His love and compassion.

I spent much of my early life alone, very much inside myself. Seldom did I share my real feelings with others. I never realized until later in life that my inner child was locked up in a dark room of my mind. As I have grown older, that child within has been released and has become an important part of my life.

Now I often sense intuitively in others their loneliness and inner child isolation, sometimes without their saying a word. Sharing my observation with a client usually brings a strong emotional response, often tears. Such moments are rare and special. I feel their inner child and that child responds to mine. There is an immediate emotional connection between us. Usually the connection is short-lived but, with time, there are longer periods in which a client allows his inner feelings to remain on the surface because he knows I feel with him and understand him with my inner child.

You can learn to use your own inner child as a way of sensing and relating to the inner child in others. You will be able to encourage those you care about to share more of their feelings, and to discover their natural aptitudes for excellence. Most important, you can help them experience their unique identity as a person in the image of God.

PERSONAL REFLECTION

■ How in touch are you with the "child" in you? Describe your inner child as you know him or her today.

_____

_____

_____

_____

■ Have you ever had the experience of connecting with the "inner child" in another person? Describe that experience.

_____

_____

_____

PRAYERFUL REFLECTION

■ Do you sense that perhaps God has given you a special talent for helping other people find emotional healing in their lives? If so, commit yourself to finding out more about what God's will is for you in this regard.

■ Finally, write a closing prayer. Thank God for at least one thing He has shown you about yourself or Him as you've worked the material in this book.

_____

_____

_____

_____

_____

PERSONAL RENEWAL

■ Let Paul's words to his friends in Philippi (Philippians 1:6, PH) serve as a source of encouragement to you as you get to know and love that wonderful child within YOU!

I am confident of this: that the One who has begun His good work in you will go on developing it until the day of Jesus Christ.

* The talent name and corresponding definition have been developed and copyrighted by the IDAK Group, Inc, Portland, Oregon and are used by permission. Other talents named in this chapter and their corresponding definitions have also been developed and copyrighted by IDAK and used by permission. Reproduction of these talent category names and respective categories and definitions is prohibited unless permission is granted in writing from the IDAK Group, Inc.

PART TWO

APPENDIX ONE

ENDNOTES

Chapter 1

1. *Hospitalism: Genesis of Psychiatric Conditions in Early Childhood,* R. Spitz Psychoanalytic Study of the Child, 1945, 1:53-74.

2. Film, *Second Chance,* Hoffman-LaRoche Laboratory, Hutley, New Jersey 07110. Summarization appeared in *Born to Win,* Transactional Analysis with Gestalt Experiments, Muriel James, Dorothy Jongeward, Addison-Wesley Publishing Company, pp. 42-43.

Chapter 2

1. Excerpt of *The Accommodation Syndrome,* Roland Summit, M.D., a paper presented at the California State Psychological Association's Child Abuse Seminar.

2. Two churches in the Southern California area offering support groups include: (1) The Evangelical Free Church of Fullerton, 2801 N. Brea Blvd., Fullerton, CA 92635, (714) 529-5544. Their program, *Vista,* for small groups, offers victims of incest support through awareness. A 9-week commitment is requested. (2) Eastside Christian Church, 2505 Yorba Linda, P.O. Box 4178, Fullerton, CA 92634, (714) 871-6844. *Virtues* offers small group sessions for those working with a therapist.

Chapter 3

1. M. Scott Peck, M.D., *The Road Less Traveled,* New York: Simon and Schuster, 1983.

Chapter 4

1. "The Age of Indifference," Philip Zimbardo, *Psychology Today,* August 1980, pp. 71–76.

2. Adapted from the Johari Window, presented in Joseph Luft, *Group Process: An Introduction to Group Dynamics,* Palo Alto, California: National Press Books, 1970, p. 11.

Chapter 7

1. M. Scott Peck, M.D., *The Road Less Traveled,* New York: Simon and Schuster, 1983, p. 15.

GROUP STUDY FORMAT

This workbook is designed for use both by individuals or in various group settings—such as support groups, Bible studies, or Sunday School classes.

Allow a minimum of eleven weeks for group study, focusing on one chapter of the book a week. Limit the length of each meeting to two hours.

How to Get a Group Started

Probably the best place to begin is by contacting the pastor of your church and letting him know of your interest in starting a support group using *The Child in Each of Us* as the basis of your study. Tell him why you feel a study of this nature would be valuable to the members of the church and also how it can serve as an outreach to the community. Once you have acquired the necessary approval, find a meeting location and establish a date and time to begin the group.

A word about your meeting place. It should be a neutral setting rather than someone's home, if possible. Homes are often full of distractions (e.g., children, telephone calls). It is difficult to maintain an environment of strict confidentiality when family members are home. A room in the church can actually provide one of the safest places for your group to meet.

The next step is to get the word out about your group. You should be able to fill a group quickly by running an ad in your church bulletin and in the church activities section of your local newspaper. Ideally, your group should have six to twelve members, but start with fewer if necessary. In time, a support group that is working right will promote itself and you will not lack for group participants.

Meeting Format for Week 1 ONLY

1. Start on time. Welcome people as they arrive and make sure each person has a copy of *The Child in Each of Us Workbook*. Provide beverages if you wish. Ask everyone to complete and wear a name tag during your first meeting.

SPECIAL NOTE: Group participants should be asked to purchase their own copy of *The Child in Each of Us Workbook* from a local Christian bookstore. Or, for the convenience of those who attend, you (the sponsoring church/organization) may choose to purchase a quantity of the books ahead of time and let group members buy them back from you at your first meeting.

2. Introduce yourself as the person who ran the ad. Explain that you would like the group to be a source of support for yourself and everyone present. Also let everyone know that the group is designed as an eleven-week program, including this first meeting.

3. Explain that leadership will rotate within the group so that each week a different member will lead the group. It is the responsibility of the person leading to start the meeting on time, remind group members of the writing assignment for the following week, and to find another leader for the following week, prior to closing the meeting.

4. Emphasize that everything that is said during the meeting is to remain in the meeting, that none of what is shared should be discussed outside the group. This is *crucial* to the effectiveness of the program.

5. Explain that it would be helpful for everyone to hear one another's reasons for coming to the group and invite each person to take up to five minutes to talk about what made him or her decide to attend. Let group participants know that no one has to talk for that long, but that this amount of time is available for anyone who wants it. Volunteer to begin by giving your name and briefly telling your own story.

6. Ask group members to turn to the Personal Journey Summary Sheet for Week 1 on page 248. Explain that the basic format for each meeting will be that of a writing workshop. Group members will be asked to write down their response to each of the questions listed on the page for that week. They will normally be given fifteen minutes to do their writing. A three-minute warning prior to the end of the writing time will be given to let group members know they should be writing their answer for the final question on the page.

7. Ask group members to take ten minutes at this point to complete their writing for the Personal Journey Summary Sheet, Week 1. Give a three-minute warning prior to the end of the writing time.

8. Go around the group and have each person read what he or she has written for *only* the last question on the sheet. Anyone may "pass" if they do *not* wish to answer the question, but encourage as many as possible to participate.

9. Discuss the Guidelines for Group Sharing which are spelled out on page 247.

10. Ask if anyone has a prayer request regarding themselves or others. Note those requests, then close in prayer for the group.

11. Ask if someone would be willing to lead the group the following week.

12. Remind group members to read and work the journaling

exercises in Chapter 1 for the following week.

Meeting Format for Weeks 2–11

1. Welcome everyone. Have first-time visitors introduce themselves by name.

2. Ask group members to join you for a moment of silent prayer. Encourage everyone to focus their thoughts and open their hearts and minds to what the Holy Spirit wants to say to them during this week's discussion.

3. Have group members turn to the Personal Journey Summary Sheet for the week and spend fifteen minutes writing down their response to each of the questions listed on the page. Give a three-minute warning prior to the end of the writing time.

4. If there are more than ten of you present at your meeting, split into smaller groups of five or six each for Family Group Sharing (described in the next step).

5. Family Group Sharing: Designate one person in each group as the lead reader. This means that that person begins the time of sharing by reading his or her answer to the first question on the page. Then proceeding around the circle, everyone in the group may take a turn reading what he or she has written for that question. IMPORTANT NOTE: Anyone in a family group may "pass" if he or she does *not* wish to read his or her answer to the question. Repeat this same process for each of the questions on the page. Before breaking into family groups, review these simple rules for sharing (see the next step).

6. Rules for Family Group Sharing: ❑ Allow equal time for each family member to share; ❑ Please limit individual sharing to explanations of the written material; ❑ Feedback from family members may be offered only after every person in the family group has had an opportunity to share what he or she has written for the question being answered.

7. Reassemble the whole group after approximately 60 minutes. Ask if anyone would like to share anything from their reading and writing experience during the week, or something they learned during this week's Family Group Sharing time.

8. Spend the last fifteen minutes of your meeting in prayer. Ask if anyone wants to share a prayer request regarding themselves or others. Then pray for one another.

9. Let group members know what the reading and writing assignment is for the following week. Encourage everyone to complete that work prior to coming to the next week's meeting.

10. Ask if someone would be willing to lead the group the following week.

GUIDELINES FOR GROUP SHARING

Each person experiences healing at a different pace. But everyone's healing process is enhanced by the mutual support and encouragement that is found in a group setting. The following guidelines will help keep the group process healthy. Take time to read these guidelines aloud at each session, if necessary, as a reminder of the way the group process should work.

Group Guidelines

1. Remember that trust grows over time. Share only as much as what feels safe for you. Risk sharing more when you feel safe doing so.

2. Be a focused listener. You can learn much from other people's insights if you will take time to really hear what they are saying.

3. Maintain confidences. Remember that anything that is said in the group is considered confidential and must **not** be shared outside the group unless specific permission is given to do so. Memorize this rule: WHO YOU SEE HERE, WHAT IS SAID HERE, WHEN YOU LEAVE HERE, LET IT STAY HERE. This is *crucial* to the effectiveness of this program.

4. Limit your sharing to what is written on your summary sheet. This will allow everyone in the group who wishes to share, the opportunity to do so.

5. Talk only about yourself and your own situation. Avoid getting into conversations that focus on other people (including your spouse, children, friends, etc.).

6. Avoid giving advice. Everyone is welcome to share their personal experience and what has worked for them in the healing process, but no one is to advise another person about what he or she should do.

7. No cross-talk. Cross-talk is when two people engage in a conversation that excludes the other members of the group. Speak only when it is your turn.

8. Be as honest with yourself and others as you possibly can be. Pray for the other members of the group. Remember what James tells us: "Confess your sins to one another and pray for each other so God can heal you" (James 5:16, NCV).

PERSONAL JOURNEY SUMMARY SHEET
"Telling My Story"

MEETING FOCUS: The best way to begin is to share your story, because doing so will forge an immediate bond and foster a sense of belonging.

■ What made you decide to come to this group? Briefly describe what has been happening in your life that makes a study dealing with "inner child" issues relevant to your life.

_____

_____

_____

_____

_____

■ Refer to the Preface on page 7 of this workbook. Of the three experiences described there by the author, which one do you most closely relate to? Why?

_____

_____

_____

_____

_____

■ How much do you know about your unique personality, your God-given talents, and your feelings? Write a brief description of yourself as you know YOU.

_____

_____

_____

_____

■ What would you like to see God do in your life as the result of going through this workbook, *The Child in Each of Us*?

_____

_____

_____

_____

PERSONAL JOURNEY SUMMARY SHEET
Chapter 1—Discovering the Inner Child

MEETING FOCUS: Discovering and learning to nurture your inner child will give you the means by which you can deepen your relationship with God and those you love.

■ Name some *childlike* qualities and also several *childish* characteristics. In what ways are YOU childlike? Have you noticed any childish behaviors in yourself lately? What are they?

_____

_____

_____

_____

_____

_____

■ How easy is it for you to express your feelings to other people? As a child were you encouraged to express your feelings in your family? Why or why not?

_____

_____

_____

_____

_____

■ What are your natural talents—those things that are as natural for you as breathing, require little to no effort, and give you great pleasure in doing them? How are you using your natural talents in your home, on the job, or in your church?

_____

_____

_____

_____

_____

_____

■ Ephesians 2:10 (NIV) says, "For we are God's *workmanship* created in Christ Jesus to do good works, which God prepared in advance for us to do." The Greek word for *workmanship* sometimes carries with it the meaning of a "work of art." There's no mistake—God made you just exactly who you are. Describe yourself as God's unique "work of art." Have you ever questioned or doubted how God made you? Why?

_____

_____

_____

_____

_____

_____

PERSONAL JOURNEY SUMMARY SHEET
Chapter 2—Abuses of the Inner Child

MEETING FOCUS: Abuse of any kind dramatically affects the way you relate to God, to your own inner child, and to other people.

■ What childhood abuse in your own life are you aware of from your reading of this chapter? List specific ways in which your significant caregivers abused you.

_____

_____

_____

_____

_____

■ Abuse of any kind in childhood sets in motion some self-despising messages. Many of these messages stay hidden in our subconscious and are carried with us into adulthood. What self-despising messages do you continue to tell yourself? How do these messages affect the way you live and relate to the people in your life?

_____

_____

_____

_____

_____

_____

_____

■ Write down several caring, nurturing messages your inner child needs to hear.

_____

_____

_____

_____

_____

_____

■ In what ways, if any, has religious shame impacted your ability to feel and experience the love of God in your life?

_____

_____

_____

_____

_____

_____

■ If God could speak aloud a word to your inner child right now, what would you like to hear Him say?

_____

_____

_____

_____

PERSONAL JOURNEY SUMMARY SHEET
Chapter 3—The Many Masks We Wear

MEETING FOCUS: God wants you to surrender all your protective masks to Him and become the unique person He created you to be.

■ A *mask* is "any type of behavior that hides the inner child who contains our true feelings, natural abilities, and unique personality." What masks have you worn in the past? What masks, if any, are you still wearing today?

_____

_____

_____

_____

_____

■ Remember the story of Jesus and the Samaritan woman at the well? (John 4:1-29) If you had been at the well that day, what do you think Jesus would have said to you? Are you able to let Jesus minister tenderly to your *needy* inner child? Why?

_____

_____

_____

_____

_____

_____

_____

■ In what ways do you identify with this statement: "True obedience comes from the heart—a heart that feels loved and valued for who he/she is"? Are you convinced at a heartfelt level that God loves and values you for who you are? Why or why not?

_____

_____

_____

_____

_____

■ What was the most important insight you gained this week as the result of working the material in this chapter?

_____

_____

_____

_____

_____

_____

PERSONAL JOURNEY SUMMARY SHEET
Chapter 4—Why We Feel So Alone with Others

MEETING FOCUS: A lack of intimate self-disclosure affects your relationship with other people and with God.

■ How easy is it for you to form close relationships with other people? Describe the most intimate relationship you have at present.

_____

_____

_____

_____

_____

_____

■ Do you believe that your inner child is worth knowing and loving? Affirm your own value by writing a brief paragraph expressing to your inner child why he or she is worth knowing and loving. Be honest and open with your inner child.

_____

_____

_____

_____

_____

■ How comfortable are you telling another person *directly* what you think and feel? Cite one or two examples of your disclosing to another person in this way. Can you be direct with God? Why?

_____

_____

_____

_____

_____

_____

■ To have an intimate relationship with God you must disclose your true self to Him and He to you. What specific things did you share with God in prayer this week? What did He reveal to you about Himself as you read His Word? Did He reveal to you anything about *yourself* this week? What was it? Do you feel like you grew in your feelings of intimacy with God this week through prayer and Bible reading?

_____

_____

_____

_____

_____

_____

PERSONAL JOURNEY SUMMARY SHEET
Chapter 5—Why Marriages Often Fail

MEETING FOCUS: If you are married or involved in a close relationship, be careful not to neglect the feelings of your own inner child.

■ Are you aware of any thought and behavior patterns in yourself that may be keeping you from experiencing an intimate connection with your spouse or someone with whom you are in a close relationship? What are they? What problems have those patterns created in your relationship?

_____

_____

_____

_____

_____

■ Admitting our fears, weaknesses, and limitations to the person we feel closest to is often difficult. It leaves us in a very vulnerable place. Sometimes we cannot even admit these things to ourselves. What personal fears, weaknesses, and limitations in yourself are you in touch with at this point? What keeps you from sharing them with the people you are most intimate with?

_____

_____

_____

_____

_____

■ What did you learn this week about your own natural, God-given talents as you worked the material in this chapter? What did you learn about your spouse's or significant other's talents? What tension points are created because of the differences in your natural talent areas?

_____

_____

_____

_____

_____

_____

■ From what you learned this week, what one thing—if applied in your life—could change the way you relate to your spouse, your best friend, or your children? How do you intend to apply what you have learned?

_____

_____

_____

_____

_____

_____

PERSONAL JOURNEY SUMMARY SHEET
Chapter 6—Creating Children in Our Own Image

MEETING FOCUS: As a parent, you must be careful not to mold your children into what you want them to be rather than what they were designed by God to be.

■ Can you think of any feelings you are carrying around today that really belong to your parents? What are they? How long have you been carrying them? If you are a parent yourself, can you think of any ways in which you have tried to put those feelings on *your* children?

_____

_____

_____

_____

_____

_____

■ No parent is all bad or all good. In what ways did your parents *positively* "create you in their own image"? What virtues and values did they instill in you? What, if any, godly attributes do you possess today because of your parents?

_____

_____

_____

_____

■ In his book, *Love: No Strings Attached*, Rich Buhler states that we often confuse *love* and *approval*. Approval must be earned and is granted because of what we do. Approval can be lost. Love is unconditional. It is given freely just because of who the person is. Describe a time when you lost the approval of someone who is important to you. How did you feel in relation to that person afterward? Then give an example from your life of being *unconditionally* loved.

_____

_____

_____

_____

■ What has been the result of critical treatment in your life? Do you struggle with being critical of yourself? Are you critical of other people? What steps might you take to become a less critical person?

_____

_____

_____

_____

■ The goal of parenting is not to be a *perfect* parent, but simply, a *good-enough* parent. All parents make mistakes. What part of parenting do you need God's help with most? Tell Him in a short written prayer what you need from Him just now.

_____

_____

_____

_____

PERSONAL JOURNEY SUMMARY SHEET
Chapter 7—Creating Our Own Stress

MEETING FOCUS: When you exceed your stress limits, you abuse your inner child.

■ Name five things that cause you the greatest amount of stress. How many of these stress points are you experiencing in your life at present?

_____

_____

_____

_____

_____

■ Change is one thing that causes stress in our lives. How do you react to change? Think about a change you've made in your life and/or behavior in the last year. Which of the three reasons for change mentioned in this chapter—boredom, new understanding or fresh insight, emotional or physical pain—prompted you to make that change?

_____

_____

_____

_____

■ There are many factors in our hectic, fast-paced world that can cause us to reach and often exceed our stress limits, even though our inner child is screaming for relief. Which of the following causes of excessive stress are creating problems in your life at present?

    ❑ Unrealistic expectations (*Do you expect too much of yourself or other people?*)

    ❑ Out-of-balance work habits (*Are you a workaholic?*)

    ❑ Unbridled ambition (*Are you caught up in the rat race of life in an attempt to acquire things*)

    ❑ An unstable economy (*Has the high cost of living got you down?*)

    ❑ Unsuitable work environment (*Are you in the wrong occupation or wrong work situation?*)

■ Jot down specific ways you are abusing your inner child by exceeding your stress limits. Let your inner child talk back to the adult you about the abuse he or she is feeling. Write down what you hear your inner child saying to you. *EXAMPLE: I never have time to play anymore because you are always working.*

_____

_____

_____

_____

_____

■ Write a short prayer asking God to show you what steps you need to take to better manage the stress in your life right now. Trust Him to show you how He can use that stress for good in your life.

_____

_____

_____

_____

_____

PERSONAL JOURNEY SUMMARY SHEET
Chapter 8—Releasing the Inner Child

MEETING FOCUS: The only sure way for you to release your inner child and find healthy self-esteem is by having a personal relationship with God through His Son Jesus Christ.

■ What is it that makes you feel loved and valued as a person? Who is the person that most often makes you feel that way? What does he or she do to make you feel loved and valued?

_____

_____

_____

_____

_____

■ In Jesus' day the Pharisees conformed to the letter of the law—they *did* all the right things. But in their hearts they were like "whitewashed tombs" (Luke 23:27-28, NIV). Their sense of value was based on what they did, not on who they were. What kind of "doing" have you gotten caught up in to find your sense of value? Has your "doing" brought you the sense of value you've sought? Explain.

_____

_____

_____

_____

_____

_____

■ As a Christian, there is nothing you have ever done, or ever *will do* that can separate you from the love of Christ (Romans 8:38-39). You are free to be completely transparent before God because you stand *guiltless* before Him on the basis of what Christ has accomplished on the cross. Is there anything in your life you feel so ashamed of that you have never been able to admit it to anyone? Write down anything that comes to mind. *NOTE: When it is your turn to share in the group, disclose only as much as you feel comfortable sharing at this point.*

_____

_____

_____

_____

_____

■ In your mind's eye try to picture the scene in Scripture of Jesus with the children. Can you imagine your inner child being held in Jesus' arms, or sitting on His lap, or having Him gently place His hand on your head and speak words of kindness and love to you? In what ways does *your* inner child long to be touched and blessed like the children in that story? Tell Jesus what you need.

Loving Jesus,

_____

_____

_____

_____

_____

PERSONAL JOURNEY SUMMARY SHEET
Chapter 9—Developing a Caring Inner Parent

MEETING FOCUS: To release your inner child and experience growth, you must develop a caring inner parent and get rid of the critical, punishing, devaluing one within your personality.

■ Write a description of your inner parent as you know him or her. How does your inner parent compare with your real parents?

_____

_____

_____

_____

_____

■ Write a description of God as you understand and know Him today. In what ways is He like your real parents? In what ways is He different?

_____

_____

_____

_____

_____

_____

_____

■ Dr. Dickinson uses the story of the Prodigal Son's father to illustrate five qualities of a healthy, nurturing parent. Were you ever a prodigal? How did your parents treat you? What caring messages does your inner child need to hear when he or she "messes up"?

_____

_____

_____

_____

_____

■ God the Father is not your inner critical parent. He is a compassionate, nurturing Parent within you who draws your inner child to Himself and encourages you to be all He has designed you to be. Think of a person you know who exemplifies the meaning of the word *compassion*. How does he or she treat people—you in particular? Are you able to be compassionate with yourself? Why or why not?

_____

_____

_____

_____

■ Which quality of a healthy, nurturing parent would you most like to see developed in your life right now—love, encouragement, compassion, loving discipline, guidance? Choose one. Then try to think of some practical ways you can begin developing in your life the nurturing quality you chose.

_____

_____

_____

_____

PERSONAL JOURNEY SUMMARY SHEET
Chapter 10—Suggestions for People-Helpers

MEETING FOCUS: You can learn to use your own inner child as a way of sensing and relating to the inner child in others.

■ Describe how you see yourself as a people-helper. Are you a person with a counseling *talent* or helping *values*?

_____

_____

_____

_____

_____

■ Have you ever had an experience similar to the one described in John 8, of the woman caught in adultery? What happened? How did you feel? In what areas of your life do you need to hear Jesus' words to that woman, "Neither do I condemn you; go your way; from now on sin no more"?

_____

_____

_____

_____

_____

_____

■ Is there anyone in your life at present who you feel is genuinely interested in you as a person—who takes time to listen to your needs? Who is it? Describe a time when that person showed you the kind of love and compassion Jesus showed the woman taken in adultery.

_____

_____

_____

_____

_____

■ Before you can connect with the inner child in other people, you must first be in touch with your own inner child. How in touch are you with the "child" in you? Can you think of a time when you connected with the "inner child" in another person? Describe that experience.

_____

_____

_____

_____

■ What is the most important thing you have learned about yourself or God as the result of working the material in this book?

_____

_____

_____

_____

APPENDIX TWO

SUPPORT GROUP RESOURCES

CHRISTIAN RESOURCES

Alcoholics for Christ, Inc.
1316 North Campbell Road
Royal Oak, MI 48067
(313) 399-9955

Alcoholics Victorious
International Service Office
1700 Eighth Street
Lewiston, ID 83501

Christian Alcoholics
Rehabilitation Association
FOA Road
Pocahontas, MS 39072

Exodus International
P.O. Box 2121
San Rafael, CA 94912
(415) 454-1017

Institute for Christian Living
Riverside Medical Center
Minneapolis, MN 55427
(612) 593-1791

Liontamers
2801 North Brea Blvd.
Fullerton, CA 92635-2799

Minirth-Meier Clinic West
260 Newport Center Drive #430
Newport Beach, CA 92660
(800) 877-HOPE

National Association for Christian Recovery
P.O. Box 11095
Whittier, CA 90603
(213) 697-6201

New Life Treatment Centers
570 Glenneyre, Suite 107
Laguna Beach, CA 92651
(800) 227-LIFE

Overcomers Outreach, Inc.
2290 West Whittier Blvd., Suite A/D
La Habra, CA 90631
(213) 697-3994

Tools for Recovery
1201 Knoxville Street
San Diego, CA 92110-3718
(800) 873-8384

SECULAR RESOURCES

Adult Children of Alcoholics
Central Service Board
P.O. Box 35623
Los Angeles, CA 90035
(213) 464-4423

Alcoholics Anonymous
P.O. Box 459
Grand Central Station
New York, NY 10163
(212) 686-1100

Al-Anon/Alateen
Family Group Headquarters, Inc.
P.O. Box 182
Madison Square Station
New York, NY 10159
(800) 344-2666
(212) 302-7240

Codependents Anonymous
P.O. Box 33577
Phoenix, AZ 85067-3577
(602) 944-1141

Debtors Anonymous
314 West 53rd Street
New York, NY 10018
(212) 969-0710

Emotions Anonymous
P.O. Box 4245
St. Paul, MN 55104
(612) 647-9712

Gamblers Anonymous
P.O. Box 17173
Los Angeles, CA 90017
(213) 386-8769

Incest Survivors Anonymous
P.O. Box 5613
Long Beach, CA 90800

Narcotics Anonymous
World Service Office
16155 Wyandotte Street
Van Nuys, CA 91406
(818) 780-3951

Overeaters Anonymous
World Service Office
2190 190th Street
Torrance, CA 90504
(213) 320-7941

Sex Addicts Anonymous
P.O. Box 3038
Minneapolis, MN 55403
(612) 871-1520

Sex & Love Addicts Anonymous
P.O. Box 119
Boston, MA 02258

SPECIALIZED READING RESOURCES

BOOKS RELATED TO FAMILY SYSTEMS

- John Bradshaw, *Bradshaw On: The Family* (Deerfield Beach, Florida: Health Communications, Inc.), 1988.
- Rich Buhler, *Love: No Strings Attached* (Nashville: Thomas Nelson Publications), 1987.
- Dave Carder, Earl Henslin, John Townsend, Henry Cloud and Alice Brawand, *Secrets of Your Family Tree* (Chicago: Moody Press), 1991.
- David Stoop and James Masteller, *Forgiving Our Parents, Forgiving Ourselves* (Ann Arbor, Michigan: Servant Publications), 1992.

BOOKS RELATED TO ABUSE

- John Bradshaw, *Healing the Shame That Binds You* (Deerfield Beach, Florida: Health Communications, Inc.), 1988.
- David Johnson and Jeff Van Vonderen, *The Subtle Power of Spiritual Abuse* (Minneapolis: Bethany House), 1991.
- Grace H. Ketterman, *Verbal Abuse: Healing the Hidden Wound* (Ann Arbor, Michigan: Servant Publications).

OTHER BOOKS RELATED TO THE INNER CHILD

- John Bradley and Jay Carty, *Unlocking Your Sixth Suitcase* (Colorado Springs, Colorado: NavPress).
- Ron Ross, *When I Grow Up . . .* (San Diego: Recovery Publications, Inc.), 1990.
- David Seamands, *Putting Away Childish Things* (Wheaton, Illinois: Victor Books), 1982.
- Cathryn L. Taylor, *The Inner Child Workbook* (Los Angeles: Jeremy P. Tarcher, Inc.), 1991.
- Charles L. Whitfield, *Healing the Child Within* (Deerfield, Florida: Health Communications, Inc.), 1987.

BOOKS RELATED TO CODEPENDENCE

- Jim Conway, *Adult Children of Legal or Emotional Divorce* (Downers Grove, Illinois: InterVarsity Press), 1990.
- Alfred Ells, *One-Way Relationships* (Nashville: Thomas Nelson Publications), 1990.
- Nancy Groom, *From Bondage to Bonding* (Colorado Springs, Colorado: NavPress), 1991.
- Earl R. Henslin, *The Way Out of the Wilderness* (Nashville: Thomas Nelson Publications), 1991.
- Robert S. McGee, *The Search for Significance* (Houston: Rapha Publishing), 1990.
- Pia Mellody, *Facing Codependence* (San Francisco: Harper & Row), 1989.
- David Seamands, *Healing for Damaged Emotions* (Wheaton, Illinois: Victor Books), 1981.
- Charles Sell, *Unfinished Business* (Portland, Oregon: Multnomah Press), 1989.
- John Townsend, *Hiding from Love* (Colorado Springs, Colorado: NavPress), 1991.

BOOKS RELATED TO MEN'S ISSUES

- Stephen Arterburn and David Stoop, *The Angry Man* (Waco, Texas: Word Books), 1991.
- Gordon Dalbey, *Father and Son: The Wound, The Healing, The Call to Manhood* (Nashville: Thomas Nelson Publications).
- David B. Hawkins and Ross A. Tunnell, III, *Reclaiming Manhood* (Wheaton, Illinois: Victor Books), 1992.

BOOKS RELATED TO THE 12-STEP PROCESS

- Friends in Recovery, *The Twelve Steps—A Spiritual Journey* (San Diego: Recovery Publications, Inc.), 1988.
- Keith Miller, *A Hunger for Healing* (San Francisco: Harper & Row), 1991.
- Keith Miller, *Compelled to Control* (Deerfield, Florida: Health Communications, Inc.), 1992.

APPENDIX THREE

SUPPLEMENTAL JOURNALING PAGES

PERSONAL JOURNAL

The Lord is gracious and compassionate, slow to anger and rich in love.

PSALM 9:9

PERSONAL JOURNAL

All the days ordained for me were written in
Your book before one of them came to be. PSALM 139:16

Be kind and compassionate to one another, forgiving each other, just as in Christ God forgave you. EPHESIANS 4:32

The Lord is . . . a stronghold in times of trouble.
PSALM 9:9

I know the plans I have for you . . . plans to give you hope and a future. JEREMIAH 29:11